Camerton Parish
Somerset

A Step Back in Time

Volume 1

Densley View to Meadgate East

by Julieann Biggs

First Edition

Published by CJ

ISBN: 978-0-9935116-1-5

Printed by
Fosseway Press Ltd
7 Frome Road, Radstock, Somerset, Great Britain

Sketch from the Seat in Parsonage field

Front cover photograph of a bonfire by kind permission of John Arnold.

Inside cover – Watercolour of Tunley Hill by Reverend John Skinner. By kind permission of St Peter's Church, Camerton.

Back cover – Photograph of Jack Cavill and children going up Tunley Hill with horse and cart. By kind permission of Gay Fear.

Background map on cover by kind permission of Janet Holbrook.

Contents

Foreword

I was educated at Broadlands Comprehensive school in Keynsham and will always remember my English teacher Mr Alan Pridgeon, he was firm but fair; he installed an enduring love of the English language. He always thought I would make a good 'Maggie' in the play Hobsons Choice.

My family come from Keynsham, I have 3 brothers and we all grew up in Coronation Avenue. We played in fields near our home, sadly they are all housing estates now!

The Gallop family – 3 boys and a girl with a mop of curly hair. Andy stood at the back, Dave to the left and Mike in the middle and yours truly.

At the tender age of 19, I started my own business, at 21 years of age I opened the first Tool and Plant hire shop in Keynsham. It was called 'Dual Services'. It was a tool and plant hire with a repair service. Sadly due to the recession and cash flow problems, it folded a few years later.

I am a proud mother to 3 wonderful children and a very grateful grandmother to 4 gorgeous grandchildren. My best friend is my husband Nick, he is the backbone of our family. My passion for history started when Nick first introduced me to Camerton.

A sleepy village that you can drive through, blink and it's gone!

I have been collecting information on the whole village for about 14 years. It got a bit too much to put into one book so I decided to split it into 6 small volumes, hoping it would make for an easier read.

A special Thank You to my brother Dave; he is the artist who has sketched various drawings in this volume.

Dedication

Julieann dedicates this book to her family, Camerton people past and present. A special thank you to all her friends and neighbours who have provided information and photographs to help her compile this record of history on the parish of Camerton.

Heartfelt gratitude to my darling husband Nick for all his patience and understanding, my grateful thanks to my brother Dave and cousin Alison, for their support and for both encouraging me not to give up!

A special thank you to Mike Meloy (O.B.E) friend and neighbour who has helped to proof read and edit this volume.

Last but not least, a very special thank you to all my friends at Fosseway Press, especially Ian Comer. They have put up with me popping in and out of their premises over the years, with documents, maps, photos etc, for what must have seemed like a never ending book.

Introduction

Camelertone was a settled village before recorded history, traces of the early Neolithic period, the Bronze age and Iron age have been found locally; confirming people have roamed and settled in the parish of Camerton over 5,000 years ago.

The Roman Fosseway runs along the south side of Camerton, on the approximate line of the present A367 is believed to have been built from around 43 A.D. Various remains of Roman occupation have been found in several minor settlements. The varied collection of artefacts found helped to confirm 'British Roman Settlement' took place in Camerton throughout this period.

It is suspected that Camerton held a brigade of auxiliary troops belonging to a small mounted contingent of a legion. A vast collection of metalwork was found including a great collection of military origin and dates to the decades around the time of the Roman conquest of southern Britain. The pieces of military metalwork include items associated with both infantry and cavalry soldiers.

It is believed that Camelertone was named after the river 'Cam' that rises at Cameley, snakes through the valley towards Dunkerton, Combe Hay and Midford; eventually joining the river Avon. It is also a possibility that the word 'Cam' is connected with an ancient Celtic god 'Camulos'. It is understood that the word 'Cam' could have derived from an Anglo Saxon word meaning: windy or bendy.

The Saxons helped to define the present county of Somerset in around 700 A.D.

In 954 Alfred with the consent of Kind Edred; gave the manor of Camelertone (Camerton) to the monks of Glastonbury.

The manor of Camelertone continued in the possession of Glastonbury Abbey until William the Conqueror invaded England. He acquired the kingdom of England by right of conquest on the 14th October 1066. Unfortunately he had no regard for the owners of property who did not agree with his rule, these were seen as rebels and their land was confiscated.

William the Conqueror ordered a survey of all the land in England, this was recorded and known as the 'Domesday Book' it provides a detailed account of the effects of the conquest. Camelertone is first mentioned in the 'Domesday Book' under 'Summerset' now 'Somerset'; the book gives a detailed account of different areas of land all over the country.

William the Conqueror was crowned the King of England in January 1067 at Westminster Abbey (William I) Norman French became the language of nobility and the English court, most of the peasants would have only spoke old English, Anglo-Saxon.

The Saxon period between the battle of Hastings and the Domesday survey, was witness to the greatest change of landholding in English history.

WILLIAM the CONQUEROR.

William the Conqueror, seized Camelertone Manor from the Monks of Glastonbury and bestowed it upon his favourite Robert the Count of Mortain; his half brother. Robert wanted to consolidate his estates around the castle of Montacute. An unfair exchange between the Manor of Camelertone and the manor of Tutenelle was arranged by Robert with the Abbot in 1068.

(Domesday Book) Summersete

Summerſete. [Domeſday-Book.

ac. paſturæ. Silva 9 quarent. long. & una quarent. & dimid. lat. Tot. val. inter eos 14 lib. & 10 ſolid. Valuit 11 lib.

De eiſdem 30 hid. ten. de Rege Alfric & Eurardus 1 hid. Hanc tenuit unus tainus T. R. E. nec potuit ab Æccleſia ſeparari. Valet 20 ſolid.

De eiſdem 30 hid. ten. Comes Morit. de Rege 7 hid. Has tenebat unus tainus de Abbate T. R. E. nec poterat ab æccleſia ſeparari. Valet 100 ſol.

Ipſa Æccleſia ten. CAMELERTONE. Edmer tenuit T. R. E. & geldabat pro 10 hid. Terra eſt 10 car. De ea ſunt in dominio 7 hidæ & ibi 2 car. & 8 ſervi & 6 villani & 6 bord. cum 2 car. Ibi 2 molini redd. 5 ſolid. & 80 ac. prati & 20 ac. paſturæ & 40 ac. ſilvæ. Valet 7 lib.

De hac terra hujus M. ten. Rogerius de Abbate 1 hid. & ibi habet 1 car. cum 1 ſervo & 1 bord. Ibi 10 ac. prati & 6 ac. ſilvæ. Val. 10 ſol. Hoc M. ded. com. Moriton Abbati pro excambio TUTENELLE.

Translation of the previous page 2

The same church holds CAMERLERTONE [Camerton]. Edmer[3] held (it) T.R.E. and paid geld for 10 hides. There is land for 10 ploughs. Of this (land) 7 hides are in demesne where are 2 ploughs and 8 serfs and (there are) 6 villeins and 6 bordars with 2 ploughs 'and 2 hides.' 'There are 1 riding-horse and 13 swine and 154 sheep.' There are 2 mills paying 5 shillings, and 80 acres of meadow and 20 acres of pasture and 40 acres of wood(land). It is worth 7 pounds. 'And when Turstin the abbot received it, 6 pounds.'

Of the land of this manor Roger holds of the abbot 1 hide 'of thegn-land which Ailuin held T.R.E. and could not be separated from the manor (*mansione*),' and there he has 1 plough with 1 serf and 1 bordar. There are 10 acres of meadow and 6 acres of wood(land). It is worth 10 shillings. The Count of Mortain gave this manor to the abbot in exchange for TUTENELLE,' 'TITTENELLE' [Tintinhull].

Table below showing the unfair value of the exchange between The Count of Mortain and Glastonbury Abbey

	Camerton	**Tintinhull**
Land Hides	10	7 ¾
Land Ploughs	10	10
Demsne		
Hides	7	4
Ploughs	2	2
Slaves	8	5
Villages	6	19
Small holders	6 with 2 ploughs	9 with 8 ploughs
Mills	2 off at 5/-	1 at 30d
Meadow	80a	60a
Pasture	20a	200a
Woods	40a	57a
Total Area	140a	317a
Value	£7	£16

5 Hides was equivalent to about 600 acres of land

The original Bayeux Tapestry is believed to have been commissioned in the 1070's by Bishop Odo of Bayeux, half brother of William the Conqueror. It is 70 metres long, although it is called a tapestry it is in fact an embroidery, stitched not woven in woollen yarns on linen. The original is on display at Bayeux in Normandy, France.

Thanks to Elizabeth Wardle who had the idea of making a full sized replica of the tapestry, in order for England to have their own copy.

The Bayeux tapestry portrays the tale of William the Conqueror and Harold, Earl of Wessex, the men who led the Norman and Saxon armies in 1066. Williams defeat of Harold at the battle of Hastings ensured the success of the Norman invasion to England.

Pictured below is a section of the Bayeux tapestry illustrating William in council with his two half brothers (Odo to the left and Robert to the right). They were both key figures in the Norman administration of England.

Summersete was one of the largest counties in the survey ordered by William the Conqueror and believed to be above average in wealth as well as size. A manor was a piece land or a unit of land that was managed in the countryside usually by a lordship, known locally as the Lord of the manor.

Over a period of time, the spelling of Tutenelle changed to Tittenelle and then to Tintinhull and Camelertone changed to Camerton as it is known today.

Camerton's Old Manor House

The above oil painting shows the old residence that was home to early Lords, it was painted by an unknown artist, believed to be a traveller. For a bite to eat and a bed for the night, the traveller would have given the painting to the owner as a gift. Locals are believed to have said there was nothing interesting or distinctive about it!

Camelertone changed to (Camerton) and Tutenelle changed to (Tittenelle) and finally to (Tintinhull) both estates granted to Glastonbury Abbey during the 10th century formed a nucleus of the present parish of Tintinhull. Five hides, probably once part of the Saxon royal estate of Martock; were granted between 939 and 946 by King Edmund to Wilfric who left this property to Glastonbury for his soul scot. Between 959 and 975 Aelfswith granted another 5 hides of land to Glastonbury. The Abbey retained these two holdings until Robert the count of Mortain wanted to consolidate his estates around the castle at Montacute in exchange for his manor of Camelertone (Camerton). Around 1102 Robert's son William Count of Mortain gave the manor of Tutenelle (Tintinhull) as part of the endowment of Montacute priory. The priory retained the manor until the dissolution in 1539.

The complicated division of land between Camerton and Dunkerton is the result of a division of common land enclosure after the black death.

An old map showing Camerton's boundary lines dated around 1400 to 1883 pictured below:

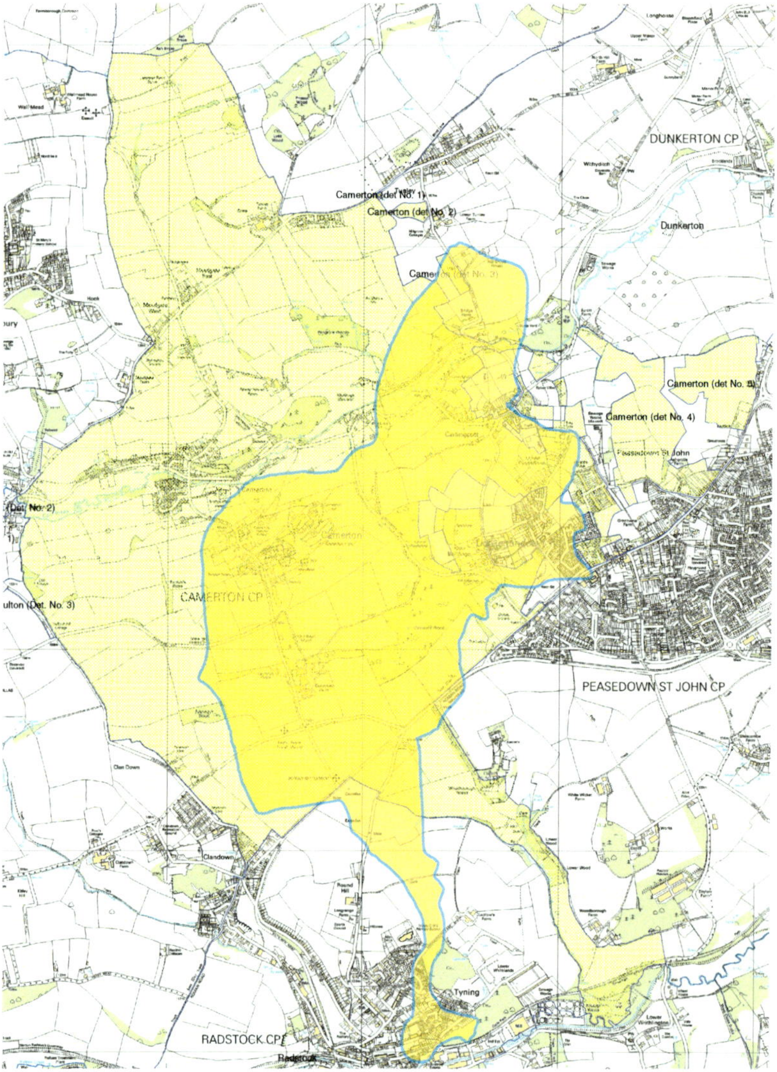

In 1483 the Camerton estate was owned by the Carew family, they were a highly distinguished family, Sir Rhys ap Thomas was the chief builder of Carew Castle, Pembrokeshire, he was the most renowned in history. He helped place Henry VII on to the throne and accompanied Henry VIII to the Field of Cloth of Gold.

The Carew family held Camerton manor until the mid 17th century when Thomas Carew sold the manor to Phillip Stephens who came from Radford.

Camerton was a village and parish in the Clutton Union, in the deanery of Frome, archdeaconry of Wells, diocese of Bath and Wells, hundred of Wellow (Wellow Hundred). Clutton Union appears on a lot of paperwork because it covered a large area, it was based on the old poor law district.

Pictured below is the current parish boundary line, outlined in blue showing the whole of Camerton parish.

Current Map of Boundary Line

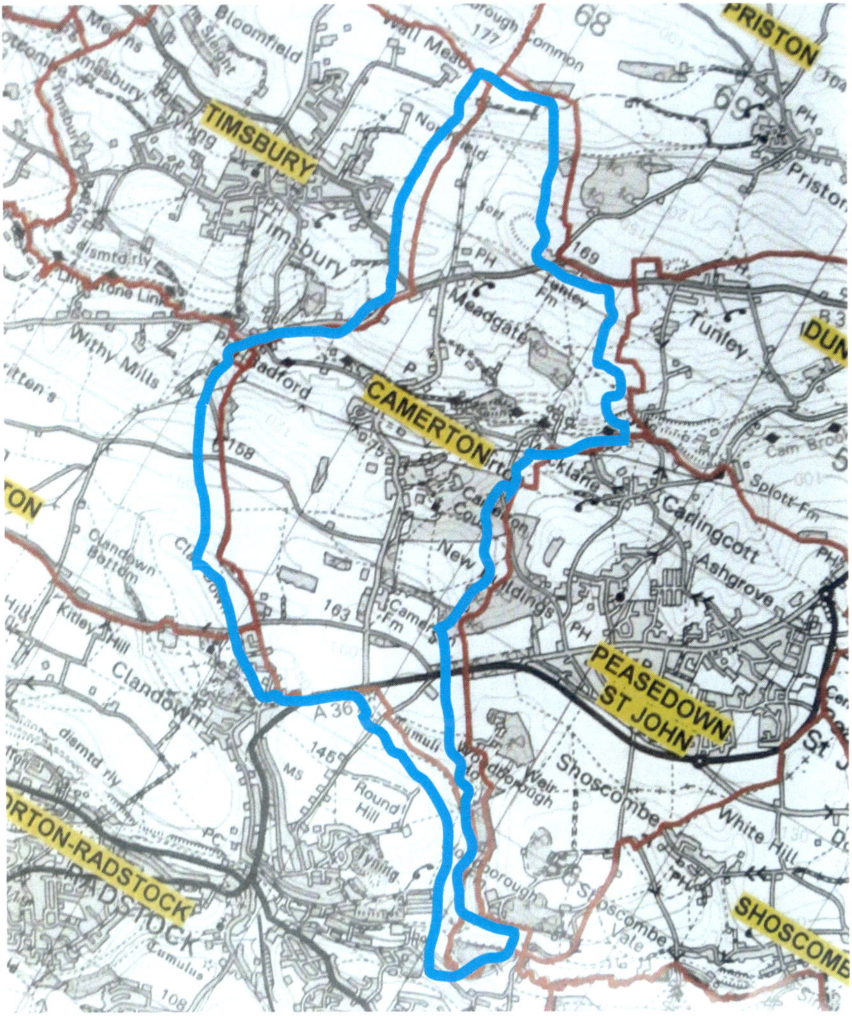

Entry from C & J Greenwood Directory dated 1822

CAMERTON—a parish in the hundred of Wellow, seven miles S. W. from Bath, containing 181 houses, and 188 families, 32 of whom are employed in agriculture. The brook Cam, which rises at Cameley, likewise gives name to this parish, through which it passes, and continuing its course by Dunkerton, Combe, Hay, and Midford, discharges itself into the river Avon. North of the church is *Camerton-House*, the residence of Mrs. Jarrett. The church is a handsome Gothic structure, dedicated to St. Peter, and consists of a nave, chancel, and a chapel on the north side, with a large tower at the west end. The living is a rectory, in the deanery of Frome; Rev. John Skinner, incumbent; instituted 1800. Population, 1801, 594—1811, 786—1821, 1004.

Entry from Morris's Directory dated 1872

CAMERTON is a village and parish in Clutton union, containing, by the census of 1861, 1368 inhabitants, and 1748 acres; in the deanery of Frome, archdeaconry of Wells, diocese of Bath and Wells, hundred of Wellow, East Somerset; 2 miles north from Radstock, and 7 south-west from Bath, on the Somersetshire Coal Canal. The rectory, in the incumbency of the Rev. Edward Holland, M.A., had the tithes commuted at £417 per annum, with residence and 50 acres of glebe land, and is in the patronage of Miss Jarrett. The church is an ancient edifice, dedicated to St. Peter, consisting of nave, south aisle, porch, and tower containing five bells; it was restored and enlarged in 1848, and contains several monuments of the Carew family. There are schools for children of both sexes and infants. The Wesleyans have a place of worship here. Miss Jarrett is lady of the manor, and chief owner of the soil, and also owner of the coal mines, two of which are in full work. On the south-west side of this parish are the remains of an ancient Roman Fosseway.

In 1874 the ecclesiastical parish of Peasedown St John was formed from the civil parishes of Camerton, Dunkerton and Wellow.

Under the Parishes Act of 1882 - Local government ordered land from Tunley, 1 mile north to be transferred from Dunkerton to Camerton and a detached part of the latter was added to Dunkerton:

Extract from Kelly's Directory

TUNLEY, 1 mile north, was by Local Government Board Order 18,115 transferred from Dunkerton to Camerton, and under the provisions of the Divided Parishes Act, 1882, a detached part of the latter added to Dunkerton.

Map/Plan of the rearrangement of Camerton and Dunkerton divided parish lands into the compacted districts as suggested by the inhabitants and officers of Camerton parish.

Pink is Camerton and Green is Dunkerton parish

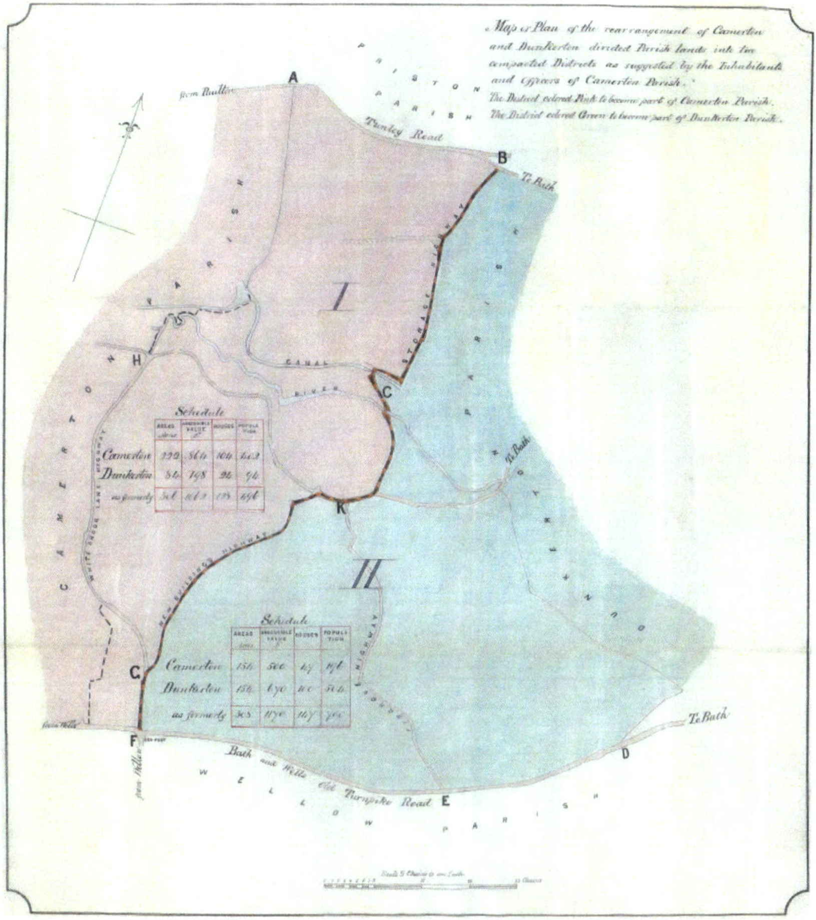

In 1891 the population in Camerton was 1,877 in the civil and 866 in the ecclesiastical parish. Durcot, Smallcombe 1 mile south, a portion of Radford, Redhill, Meadgate were hamlets of this parish. It also reveals the increase in the population due to boundary changes. At this time, the area including Peasedown St John was 1,730 acres, the rateable value was £5,363.00.

In 1911 records (2,386) the highest figure reached, this was due to the colliery development, many people travelled from afar to find work.

Extract from the Purnells' Almanac Directory dated 1914

PEASEDOWN.

PEASEDOWN St. JOHN ecclesiastical parish was formed in 1874 from the civil parishes of Camerton, Dunkerton, and Wellow. It is 2½ miles north-east of Radstock Stations on the Great Western and Somerset & Dorset Railways, 6½ miles south-west of Bath, 10 miles north-west of Frome, in the Frome Division of the County of Somerset, Wellow Hundred, Weston Petty Sessional Division, Bath Union (Camerton Portion in the Clutton Union), and County Court District, Rural Deanery of Midsomer Norton, Archdeaconry of Wells and Diocese of Bath and Wells. This is a fast growing district, many new houses and shops having been recently erected, especially since the opening of Dunkerton Colliery.

Illustrated below is a table showing the population from 1801 to 2011:

Camerton's population from 1801 to 2011

Year	Male	Female	Total
1801			594
1811			786
1821			1,004
1831			1,326
1841			1,647
1851			1.543
1861			1,368
1871			1,268
1881			1,361
1891	960	917	1,877
1901	914	858	1,772
1911	1,270	1,116	2,386
1921	1,175	1,062	2,237
1931	1,058	945	2.003
1941	No Census was carried out during this year!		
1951	1,058	1,015	2,073
1961	297	323	620
1971	321	317	638
1981			630
1991			575
2001	330	330	660
2011	325	330	655

In **1737** there were only **30** houses in Camerton.

In **1822** there were 181 houses, 188 families, 32 were employed in agriculture.

Camerton was part of the Wellow Hundred and once a strong mining community, full of lovely characters and wonderful buildings. It is surrounded by picturesque hills and valleys that extend into the surrounding countryside. If you venture off the beaten track, down a twist of a lane; it will lead you to a wealth of knowledge and a vast history that we can be proud of.

The Sketch below is of the replica miner statue that currently stands proud on the site of the old pit head in Camerton.

Statue of a Miner

Drawing by Dave Gallop

The original statue was cast from Bronze for the Festival of Britain in 1951. The replica was made from fibreglass and stood in the car park outside the Jolly Collier pub in Camerton for many years. When the pub ceased trading it was purchased and presented to the Camerton's heritage site by the Kendall brothers, in memory of their father C. H. Kendall (locally known as Harry) founder of Camerton building supplies.

Pictured below is a current map illustrating the red boundary line between the parishes of Camerton and Dunkerton.

Boundary line

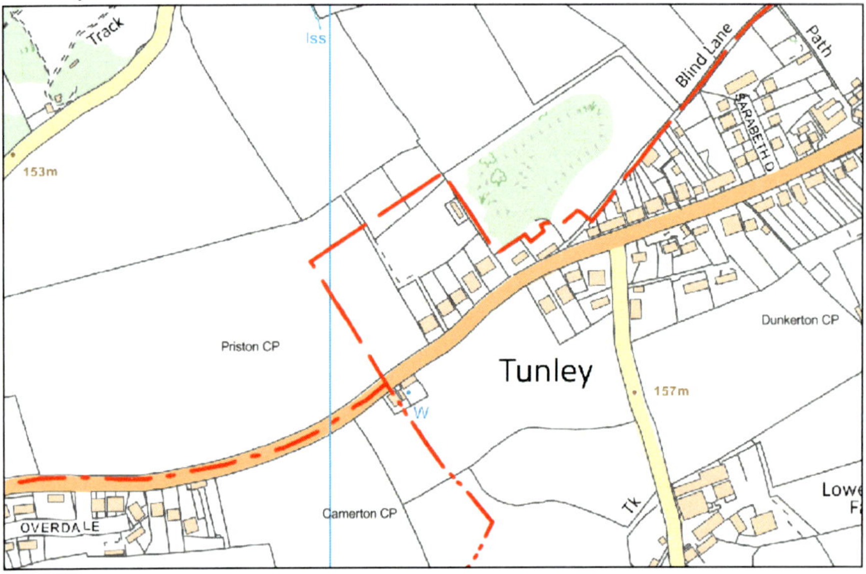

Pictured below is the boundary line, it would appear to be going straight through the middle of 'Densley View' house; but in real life that would not be the case.

Boundary Line starting from Densley View house

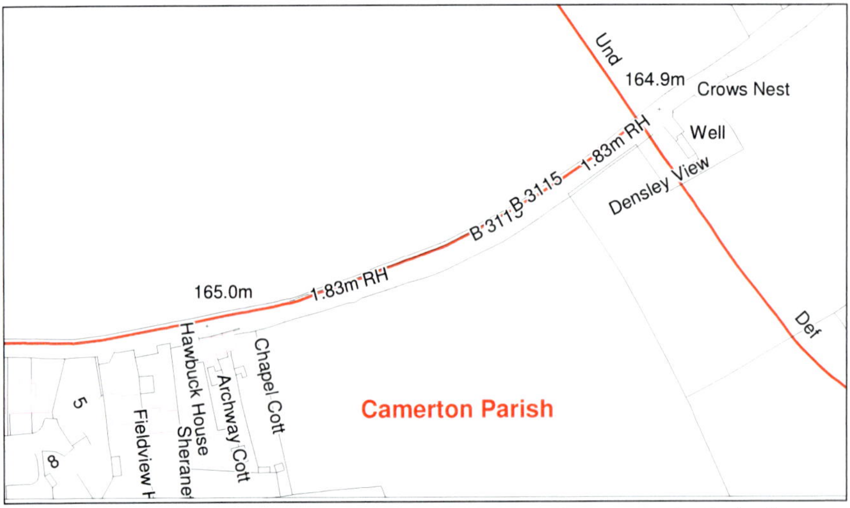

The boundary line was there, long before Densley View house was built, back in 1913.

Directions from the City of Bath

Travelling to Peasedown St John from Bath City on the A367 to Odd Down go straight over the roundabout and continue until you reach the next roundabout, go straight across the roundabout and continue along the A367 heading towards Radstock.

You will pass the Fosseway Environment Park, a recycling depot; which used to be the site of the 'Fuller's Earth Works'. The fine clay was used for ladies foundation.

Turn right at the Tunley/Timsbury sign post, on to the B3115; proceed along the bendy main road for about 2 miles, until you reach the village of Tunley; passing the site of the old 'Advanced Services' garage on your left. Unfortunately the land has been sold for housing.

Carry on past the King William public house, through the two traffic calming islands. Immediately to your right you will see a large square house with a double pitched roof, this used to be the colliery office for Tunley's pit.

Carry along the road passing bungalows on your right then over to your left you will see two semi-detached houses; the first house has a pretty little gable window and is called the 'Crows Nest'.

Crows Nest House

Chapter 1

Next door to the Crows Nest house is a house built of natural stone and was built in 1913. Densley View is the first house in the parish of Camerton, it was the home to John and Ann Smith for 47 years! In 2015 it changed hands and is the current home to Jay Symes, his wife Sarah and their son Thomas.

This is where our journey begins 'Densley View House'

In the early 1800s the land opposite Densley View house was referred to as (Densleys), this is clearly shown in a beautiful hand drawn map below:

A Map of Camerton parish by Reverend John Skinner

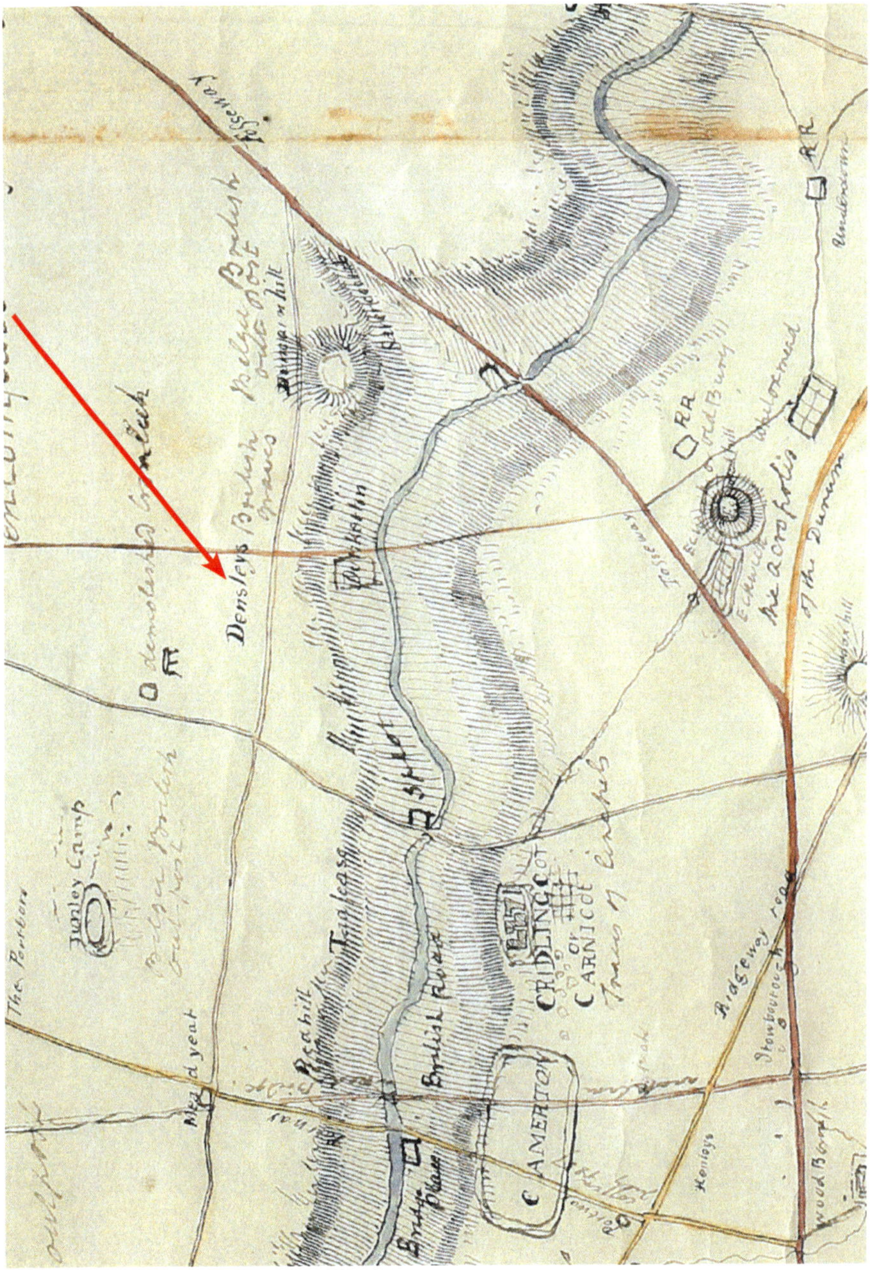

Drive past Densley View house and the adjoining field, you will see a rank of three cottages on the left on the road edge. The first semi-detached cottage is called Chapel cottage.

Chapel Cottage

This old cottage is built from Bath stone and has a new extension built in reconstructed stone to the side of it. It would have probably been the home to the minister or the caretaker of the Methodist chapel; that once stood a little further along the road.

Pictured below is the first Chapel Cottage, currently the home to Liz and Robert Buckley and their family.

Terraced No: 2 Chapel Cottage

This cottage was built in 1846 and is currently owned by Patricia Main.

Archway cottage is adjacent to the two Chapel cottages, an end terraced cottage that is full of period charm and has the words 'Archway Cottage' clearly written above the archway.

Archway Cottage

Local man and fellow historian Ken Taylor, kindly informed the author of his family connections to Archway cottage, Tunley.

Benjamin Taylor ran a Coal Haulier business, the horses would have been led through the archway and around the back of the cottage to where the yard and stables would have been. Benjamin and his wife Ann (nee Collins) had a son George who married Prescilla (nee Loxton) in 1860, they had a son James Frederick who was born in 1868. The expansion of the business led to new premises at 11 Lampards Building, Bath. The family business was ran by father and son, they operated two branches, Tunley and Bath; eventually Tunley closed.

The man stood by the trace horse is believed to be Benjamin Taylor, the cart is full of very large pieces of coal that would have probably been picked up direct from Dunkerton Mine. You can clearly see the Cross Ways Inn in the background.

Mr Taylor Esq, Local Coal Haulier

As you proceed up Dunkerton Hill (A367) you will see the old Bath stone building; the 'Cross Ways Inn' on your left. It stands on a triangle between the B3115 Tunley road and the A367 Bath road and Crossways lane, hence the name 'Cross Ways Inn'. Today, opposite Crossways house; you can still see the building pictured below; it used to be the stables; horses would have stopped here for a well earned rest and drink of water.

The Stables

Ken Taylor informed the author of a lovely story about his great, great grandfer, George Taylor. George was summoned by P S Coles and received a fine or imprisonment for 7 days. This was for undue care and attention and not being in control of his horse and cart on the Wells Road in 1862. Apparently before George set off up the steep Dunkerton Hill, he would call into the Swan Inn at the bottom of Dunkerton Hill for a pint or two. The lead horse knew the journey very well and often would go on up the hill with the trailing horse, both horses pulling the heavily laiden cart but often without George. The horses would wait patiently for George to catch them up outside the Cross Ways Inn.

.

1862 Newspaper Article

TUESDAY.

(Before the Mayor, T. Gill, Esq., Capts. Marsh and Ford.)

George Taylor, of Lampards Buildings, was summoned by P.S. Coles for being at such a distance from his cart in the Wells Road on the 24th ult, that he could not have due controul over the horse drawing the same.—Fined 2s. 6d. and costs, or 7 days' imprisonment.

Joseph Gumm, driver of No. 37 fly, was summoned by P.S. Payne for driving furiously in Southgate Street, on the 25th ult.—Discharged with a caution.

1867 Newspaper clipping (Sale of Auction) September 1867

Sales by Auction.

FREEHOLD COTTAGES AND GARDENS,

DUNKERTON and TUNLEY, near BATH.

Messrs. RAINEY

WILL SELL BY AUCTION,

At the SWAN INN, Dunkerton,

On MONDAY, SEPTEMBER the 9th, 1867, at Five for Six o'Clock in the Afternoon,

LOT 1.—ALL that Freehold COTTAGE RESIDENCE, with Garden well-stocked with choice fruit trees, situate in the parish of Dunkerton, for many years the residence and property of the late Mr. W. Keeling, Auctioneer.

LOT 2.—All that Freehold COTTAGE RESIDENCE, with Workshop, Stable, and Gighouse, adjoining Lot 1.

LOT 3.—A PIECE of Freehold PASTURE LAND, situate nearly opposite the "Swan Inn," Dunkerton, containing about 20 Perches (more or less).

LOT 4.—All those THREE Freehold COTTAGES, with Outbuildings and Gardens, situate at Tunley, in the parish of Camerton, two of which are let to James Parsons and Benjamin Taylor, at the annual rents of £6 and £4, and the third is now void. Also, a GROUND-RENT of Six Shillings per annum, issuing out of a Chapel in the rear.

In the summer of 1952 film producer Michael Truman wanted to portray a story showing the effects of the closure of a branch line upon a rural community and of the subsequent successful attempts of the villages to restore and run the railway service themselves.

The motive power – (0-4-2 Lion) was the 1838 vintage locomotive borrowed from the Liverpool engineering society. It was named the Titfield Thunderbolt for the film as you can see below, running through the beautiful countryside with full steam ahead.

Photograph courtesy of Ivo Peters

During the filming of the Titfield Thunderbolt it showed some beautiful scenes of the Cam Valley; shortly after the film was produced the Cross Ways Inn pub changed it's name to the (Titfield Thunderbolt).

When the pub closed, it was converted into business offices, the name changed from the Titfield Thunderbolt to Crossways House and is currently a private house.

Pictured below is the former post office and village store

Advert of 'The Post Office Stores' Tunley showing Mr V Amos as the proprietor in the Camerton Parish Magazine dated October 1940. .

BUY YOUR

GROCERIES, CONFECTIONERY

TOBACCO, Etc.

at

The Post Office Stores,

TUNLEY.

V. AMOS

We shall be sure to please you.

Cynthia Ashley was the postmistress from the late 1940s until the early 1950s. Wesley Cottle ran the Post Office from the early 1950s until the early 1960s, local man, Ray Hawkins whilst a young boy; used to stand on the running board of Wesley's car shouting "Cottles Express Delivery" and delivered the newspapers. Mr and Mrs Atkins ran the village store from the early 1960s until the early 1970s, when the store closed and the building became a private dwelling.

Pictured below is a painted iron ring that would have been used to tie and secure the horses to, whilst their owners called into the post office/stores.

Iron Ring

A previous owner's son Benjy Fox is holding the iron ring that is still attached to the stone wall inside the archway (2013).

This was the home to Dan Fox, his wife Rhian and their family, they sold it in 2015 and is the current home to Mark Donaldson and his partner Abby Coleman.

Next door to Archway cottage you will see a low levelled stone wall with a slate sign 'Hawbuck house'.

The pebbled driveway leads you down to Hawbuck House, the house is set a lot further back from the main road than the rank of 3 cottages, Chapel Cottages and Archway Cottage.

Hawbuck House used to be the site to the old Methodist Chapel built in 1832, it would have over looked the beautiful Cam Valley, looking very impressive, probably seen for miles around.

John Wesley

Reverend John Skinner

Illustrations by Dave Gallop

The little Chapel on the hill was well attended, it had successfully converted a lot of Reverend John Skinner's parishioners from his church, St Peter's. Reverend John Skinner loathed any form of irreligion and Methodism that did not conform to the rules and authority of the Church of England. He watched people in the village being converted to Methodism and in his diary he writes "If I were to commence a new system as an evangelical teacher, the Methodists would attend; but I cannot prevail upon myself to do evil to work attend; unless it be good to gratify one's vanity by procuring full benches at the expense of one's principles".

Reverend John Skinner was brought up in a different class of people to Camerton and they clashed, education against knowledge against ignorance. Unfortunately he was a judgmental man, often telling people of their faults, convicted them of evil when there was none. Most people in Camerton disliked him, his standards were so high, they were out of reach for most people, he expected people to respect him but they seldom did.

Pictured below is a 1902 map showing the Methodist Chapel

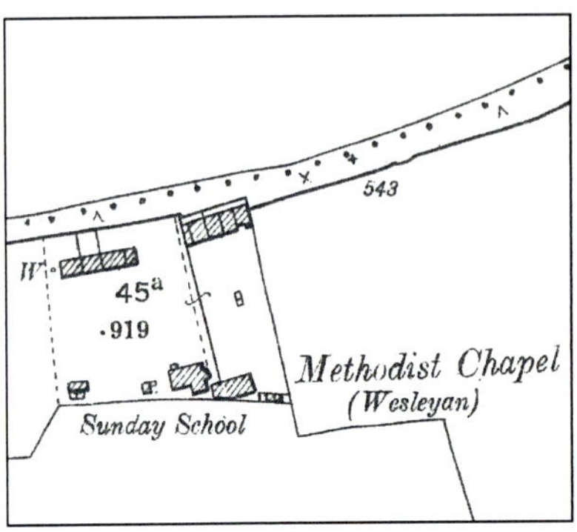

You can see on the above map how much the chapel is set back from the main road and another three cottages in-front and to the side of it.

The original Chapel was not big enough for the needs of the community, it was pulled down and a new Chapel was built to replace it on it's existing footings in 1885.

Pictured below The Methodist Chapel

Above you can just make out the intricate details of the beautiful arched windows, stone walls and pretty little porch. To the east side is an unusual cone shaped annex.

Entry No:47 from the 1865 Farm Lands of Camerton Manor record book. The trustees of the chapel responsible for paying 5 pennies rent.

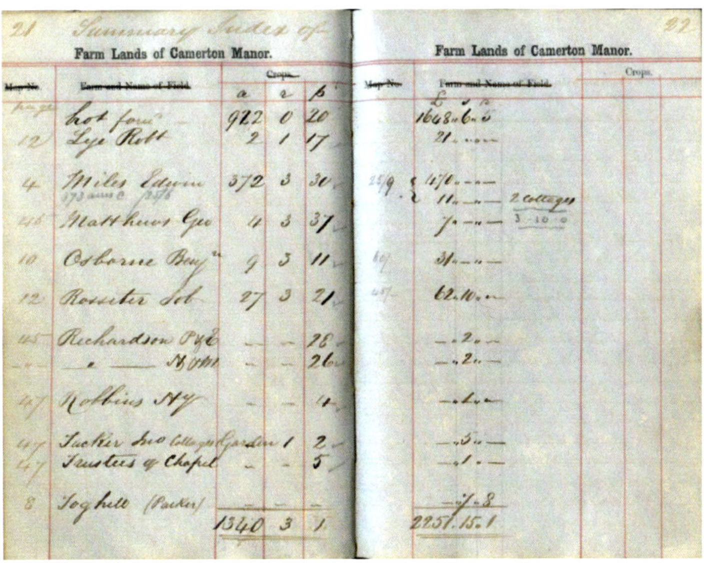

21 Summary Index of — 22

Farm Lands of Camerton Manor. | Farm Lands of Camerton Manor.

Map No.	Farm and Name of Field	a	r	p	Map No.	£ s d	
page	Lot farm	922	0	20		1648.6.5	
12	Lye Rott	2	1	17		21..	
4	Miles Edwin	372	3	30	25/9	470.. / 11..	2 cottages 3.10.0
26	Matthews Geo	4	3	37		7..	
10	Osborne Benjn	9	3	11		31..	
12	Rossiter Jol	27	3	21		62.10..	
45	Richardson P&E	–	–	28		.2.	
–	— N Wm	–	–	26		.2.	
47	Robbins Hy	–	–	4		.1.	
47	Tucker Jno Cottage & Garden		1	2		.5.	
47	Trustees of Chapel	–	–	5		.1.	
8	Fog hill (Parker)	–	–	–		.7.8	
		1340	3	1		2251.15.1	

Pictured below is the Methodist chapel showing how it would have been seen from the main Bath Road. It had a long driveway that led you to the church, you can see the notice board that advertised the times of the services to the left just behind the wall.

Methodist Chapel facing south

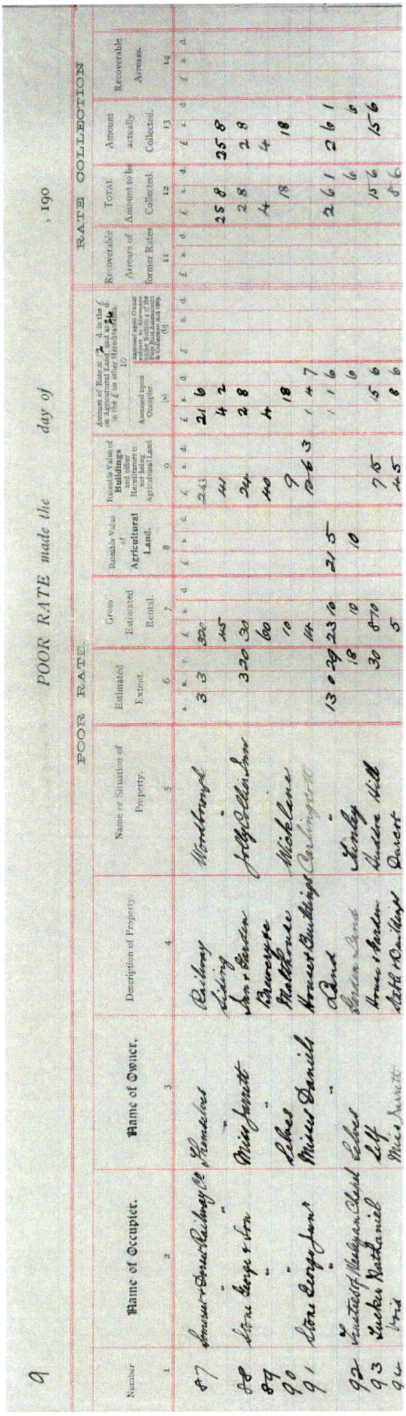

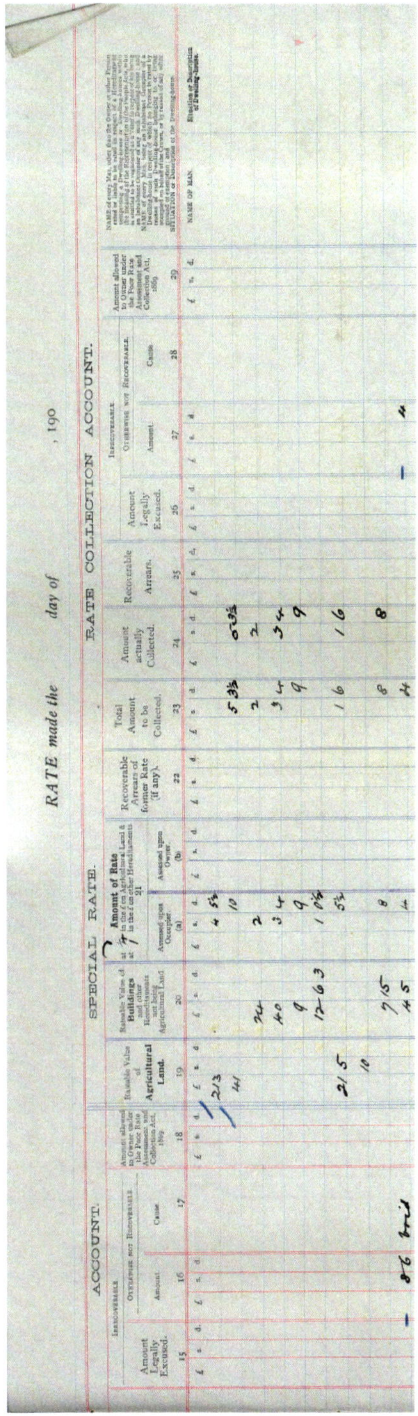

Entry 92 showing the rent value for the methodist chapel

The Methodist's Notice Board

You can see the lovely blue painted wooden notice board being held by Ann Meloy, it has been very well looked after although the Methodist chapel has always been known as The Chapel, you can see the sign has the wording Methodist Church.

On a Sunday there were two services a day. Children attended the Sunday school at 2.30 pm giving the parents time to drop the children off and get themselves into the church for their service.

As an interesting aside, the religious link is continued by Ann who is the lay-reader at Camerton's Parish Church, St Peter's.

Methodist Belief

John Wesley was born on 17th June 1703, he was educated at Charterhouse, Christchurch, Oxford. He took his holy orders in 1725 and returned to Oxford in 1729 as a tutor in Lincoln College. He was the founder of Methodism and travelled thousands of miles all over the countryside and with his brother Charles; preached in the open air. He engaged with ordinary people, the poor were welcomed and shown respect. He fought for prison reform, universal education, he helped to make people feel valued but most importantly gave them hope. Nonconformists supported Methodism as it did not conform to the rules and authority of the established Church of England. Methodism appealed to mining and farming communities, it was more easily understood and approachable, unlike the established church. It helped take a person away from the harsh reality of life and gave them something to believe in. No one was out of the reach of God's love and John Wesley succeeded in recruiting millions all across the world.

His brother Charles was born on 18th December 1707 and was educated at Westminster School and Christchurch in Oxford. He helped his brother to found the Methodist movement. He took part in Evangelistic work, but is known today as one of the greatest hymn writers in the 18th Century.

His best known hymn is:

Jesus, Lover of my Soul
Plenteous grace with Thee is found,
grace to cover all my sin,
Let the healing streams abound,
Make and keep me pure within
Thou of life the fountain art;
Freely let me take of Thee

A front page of a typical period 'Wesleyan Methodist' magazine pictured below:

McVITIE & PRICE'S OATCAKES.

JUNE, 1898. Commenced 1778.

The Wesleyan Methodist Magazine

EDITED BY THE REV. W. L. WATKINSON

Contents.

Frontispiece—MORNING ON THE NILE.

		PAGE
The Law of Spiritual Enrichment	*William A. Gray*	403
Memory	*Isela*	407
Moorish Religious Duties	*Budgett Meakin*	408
In Depression	*Minimus*	416
"Through the Gold Fields of Alaska"	*R. Corlett Cowell*	417
"Tiny Feet"	*Frances Lockwood Green*	425
The Charterhouse. II.	*John Telford, B.A.*	431
A Man on the Highway	*William A. L. Taylor, B.A.*	438
Popular Notes on Science	*W. H. Dallinger, D.Sc., F.R.S.*	441
Breaking the Tables	*William Griffith*	446
C. H. Spurgeon in his own Writings	*Arthur J. Johnson*	447
The Many Deaths we Die	*C. H. Williamson*	452
The Rose of Dawn. Chapters XI., XII.	*Dora M. Jones*	454
The Class-Room	*Alfred G. Haughton*	463
The Home Circle:		
"Captain, Crew, and Pilot too"	*J. Macdonald Oxley*	467
The Queen's Donkey	*William Harrison*	472
"Always Ready"	*James Learmount*	473
George Colbeck	*Anthony Stones*	475
James Shipstone	*George S. Tyler*	476
Chastened	*Mary E. Kendrew*	477
The Library		478

Missionary Notices for June.

6d 6d

Vol. CXXI

LONDON: WESLEYAN METHODIST BOOK ROOM,
2, CASTLE ST. CITY ROAD; AND 26, PATERNOSTER ROW E.C.

Cone shaped Annex

To the east side of the Methodist Chapel, the right hand side of the photograph, is an unusual beautifully octagonal shaped bay that housed the communion table. Opposite you can see the purpose built Sunday school building, local children would have spent many a happy hour in there.

Locals residents fondly remember the chapel being used for various functions in the village as there was no village hall back then.

Pictured below is the Cone shaped Annex and Sunday school

The chapel was closed in 1971 renovated and changed into a private house when it was renamed Hawbuck House. It is currently the home of Mike and Ann Meloy.

Pictured below is Hawbuck House

Archway lines on the front of the house

Look closely above the bottom window, in the stone work you can just make out an archway line which would have been the old archway window to the chapel.

Old Oak Vestry Door from inside the house, it is still well used and beautifully preserved.

Vestry Door on the outside of the house, this would have led into the Vestry. You can see the intricate stone work above.

Chapter 2

Next door to Hawbuck House you can see two houses, Sharonet and the other Field View House. Before these houses were built, stood 3 stone cottages as you can see on the map below:

Ordnance Survey Map 1902

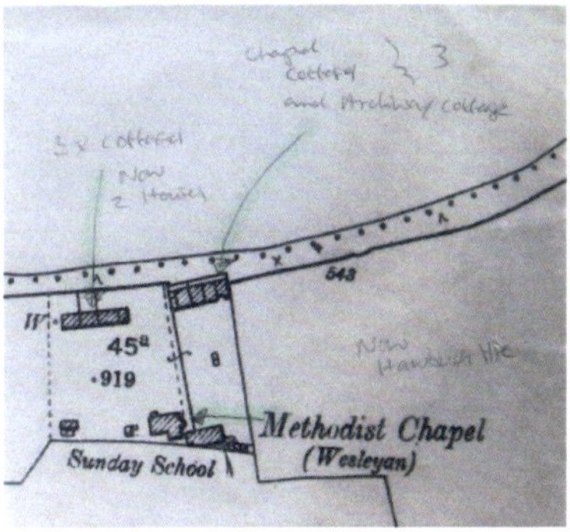

The back gardens to the Overdale estate houses run along side the main road to your left, along this stretch is where some of the old cottages used to stand before they were condemned and demolished. (Cross reference pages 41 and 42, old cottages).

Continue along the road until you see the entrance to Overdale housing estate on your left; you can see the Overdale road sign engulfed inside a fir tree.

Overdale Sign

Overdale Housing Estate

In the late 1940's several cottages and the local pub was condemned, these old buildings were demolished, the land was sold to Clutton Rural District Council. The council built the housing estate called 'Overdale'.

In 1875 a land owner by the name of James Daniels, left a will, there is also a local map dated 1951 that clearly shows a large piece of land belonging to the old post office, Tunley. This is now known as Kelston View.

Extract of James Daniel's Will dated 1875

ABSTRACT of TITLE

to a piece of land containing 2 roods 32 perch or thereabouts and Nod. 43 on the Ordnance Survey Map with the dwellinghouse erected thereon known as the Old Post Office situate at Tunley in the County of Somerset.

1875. BY his Will of this date James Daniels the elder of Tunley in the Parish of Dunkerton in the County of Somerset, Farmer, appointed his sons James Daniels, Charles Daniels and William Kelson Daniels joint executors and trustees of that his Will.

AND after directing payment of his debts funeral and testamentary expenses he devised unto the said James Daniels Charles Daniels and William Kelson Daniels certain specifically described messuages and parcels of land upon trust that they or the survivor of them or the heirs executors or administrators of such survivor or other the Trustees or Trustee for the time being of his said Will (thereinafter called his said Trustees or Trustee) should pay the rents and income of the said heredits and premises unto the said James

A local family by the name of Lippiatts lived in Kelston View house for many years, they set up an covenant for the piece of land well known as 'The Green' to be preserved and protected. This piece of land over looks the picturesque view of the Cam valley.

A O/S Map dated 1951 showing Kelston View and it's garden, the road and the adjoining land 'The Green'.

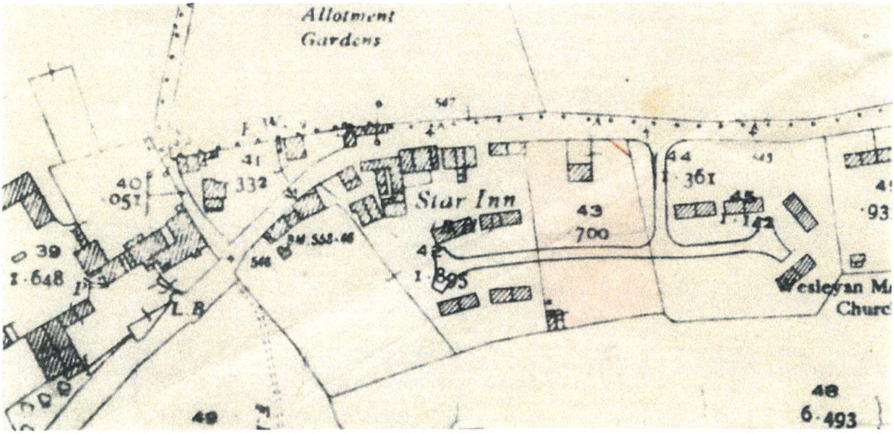

The Green over looking the Cam valley

Thankfully, local children can play safely and local residents can enjoy the beautiful view.

From 'The Green' locals would have been able to see the plumes of smoke in the distance as the steam engines chugged along the bottom of the valley. The railway played such a vital part in everyone's daily lives.

Camerton enjoyed a few moments of fame, the train station was used for staging the famous 1931 'Ghost Train' film, the story was written by the much loved actor and Bath man, Arnold Ridley who played (Private Godfrey) in the Dad's Army series.

Private Godfrey (Arnold Ridley)

Arnold Ridley wrote the play (The Ghost Train) on Mangotsfield train station's platform whilst he was waiting for his train to go to work.

The film was made by Herbert Wilcox and produced by Gainsborough pictures in June 1931, Camerton was the location of many of the scenes in the film .

The Ghost Train – The Cornish Riviera Express train engulfed in plumes of smoke and screaming it's way in to Camerton's train station.

(please see volume No: 3)

Mr Lippiatt made a special stipulation in his will regarding Kelston View House and garden. He would not allow his wife to sell the house and left it in his will to Edith Violet Fear. Pete and Gay Fear married in 1958 and purchased the house from Pete's mum Edith.

The South West Electricity Board paid Mrs J Lippiatt the sum of sixpence to run a cable over her home, Kelston View.

Form of Consent dated 3rd April 1951

ORD MAP SOM No. XX·3

FIELD Nos. 43

C.

OWNER'S CONSENT LANDOWNERS COPY

Form of Consent

THE ELECTRICITY ACT, 1947

ELECTRICITY SUPPLY ACTS, 1882-1936

I, MRS. J LIPPIATT

KELSTON VIEW

TUNLEY (hereinafter called "The Grantor")

being the Owner of property at TUNLEY

in the County of SOMERSET

HEREBY CONSENT to The South Western Electricity Board, whose Principal Office is at Electricity House, Colston Avenue, Bristol 1 (hereinafter called "the Board") placing in the position indicated approximately on the annexed plan the works specified in the Schedule hereto and maintaining, repairing, inspecting and removing the same subject to the following conditions:—

(1) The Board shall make good to the reasonable satisfaction of the Grantor any damage to the property of the Grantor caused by the placing, repairing, inspecting and removing of the said works and the Board shall be answerable in accordance with the Electricity (Supply) Acts 1882 to 1936 and the Electricity Act 1947 for all accidents, damages or injuries happening through the act or default of the Board in connection therewith

(2) The Board shall pay to the Grantor on the first day of JANUARY in each year, the sum of SIXPENCE the first payment being proportioned from the date of commencement of the work

(3) This Consent shall be terminable by either party giving to the other of them not less than six calendar months' previous notice in writing, but without prejudice to their respective rights under the Electricity Acts aforesaid.

SCHEDULE

OVERSAIL

DATED this 3rd day of April 1951

Signed by the said

in the presence of:—

Signature of Witness

R. Windebank PP J. Lippiatt

(Signature of Grantor or Agent)

On the main road just past the Overdale sign, immediately to your left, is a lovely stone cottage with a narrow gable window on the end and a pretty wooden porch over the front door.

'Kelston View', home to Pete and Gay Fear and their family.

Fear & Co Builders was set up in 1966 with several partners and is still run by Peter as a family business with his sons.

The Fear family has a great sporting tradition. Bill Fear played football for Camerton in the 1900's and his five sons played for Tunley Athletic F.C. Pete, who trialed for West Ham, went on to play in Western League for several clubs. He is a life member of Tunley Athletic and is still actively involved with the club.

Pete Fear on the left wearing a shirt and Jacket.

Gay Fear (née Bourton) played Hockey until she was 70 years of age.

Gay is on the second row, the second lady from the end and as always giving a warm smile.

■ FAMILY AFFAIR: Camerton Ladies Hockey Club has developed into a real family club in recent times.

Sisters Kylie and Sam Upton, and Nikki Mason are members of the club which plays at the village recreation ground.

Also in the squad are sisters Carol Harris and Sharon Grimsby.

There are two mother and daughter combinations in Sharon and Charlotte Grimsby and Chris and Sally Ware and even a grandmother and granddaughter in Gay and Natasha Fear

PICTURE: Kerry Miller

Gay Fear is well known in the village for her beautiful handwriting:

Handwriting by Gay Fear

In 1821 the Reverend John Skinner wrote in his diary about a local man by the name of Fear 'e', the Bailiff of the Coal works. It also records George Fear being the manager of the coal works and the steward to Miss Jarrett, he was the manager from 1866 to 1883.

Very often records show the same family surname but over a period of time the name can be spelt slightly different. For example the spelling of the surname 'Feare' alternates from being spelt 'Feare' with an'e' to 'Fear' without an 'e' this was typical of a lot of surnames spelt differently. It was usually due to how the person read or interpreted the name, it often depended on how the name was written down. Handwriting could be scruffy and unreadable or so beautifully written with fancy scrolls it was illegible; therefore spelling mistakes often occurred.

In the Kelly's directory, it records Uriah Fear as being a Parish Clerk from 1861 to 1872. It also records another family member having the same name 'Uriah Gibbons Fear' in 1897 also being a Parish Clerk and a village Taylor for several years.

In 1910 ; Mrs Feare was a carrier and responsible for the post through to Meadgate; post daily except Fridays.

1902 Ordinance Survey Map

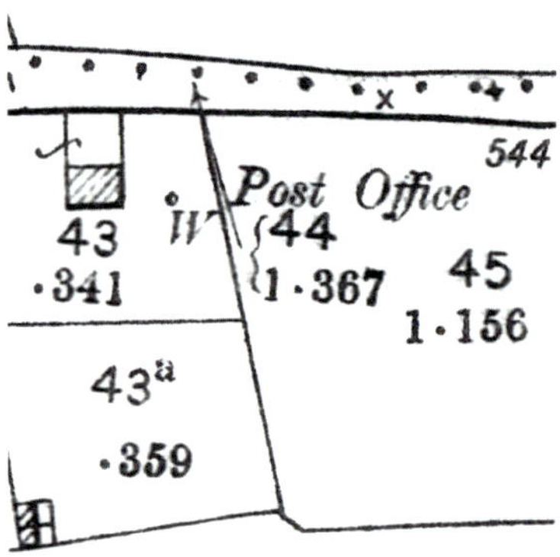

Post Box at Meadgate

Photographed overleaf is the Fear family sitting on a wall taking in the atmosphere at Weston Super Mare. On the wall in the back ground you can see a sign saying 'Roller Skating' over to the right another sign saying 2/s.

The Fear Family in the early 1900's

Stone Cottages on dirt road leading to Bath

To your left on the road edge, once stood these lovely old stone cottages, the dirt road is running back towards Bath. You can see the end of Archway cottage in the distance. There is a group of 8 women, one holding a toddler, all women are wearing long skirts. One wearing a bonnet, another holding a bicycle and on the end, one wearing a long apron.

Left to right: Nancy Brimble, Granny Fry, ??, Child believed to be Louie Kelly, Granny Cavill, ??, Gran Brimble.

Stone Cottages leading towards Camerton

The same rank of stone cottages but heading towards the old Star Inn public house. You can see local people, men, women and children, the sign for the Star Inn in the distance and a pony and trap to the right.

Taking Care of the 'Poor'

Tradition of the village supporting the 'Poor' was established in Saxon times. Before Henry VIII dissolved the monasteries in 1536, the monasteries took care of the poor in England and Wales. Once the monasteries were gone, a Poor Law Act 1597 required each parish to appoint overseers of the poor to give relief in kind. 'Provisions of the Elizabethan Poor Law 1601' was introduced and the responsibility was moved to each parish; a compulsory poor rate was levied on them.

The term 'Lady Day' was established in the middle ages, the 'Lady' of 'Lady Day' referred to the 'Virgin Mary'. As legend will lead us to believe the angel Gabriel announced to Mary that she would conceive a child who would be the son of God. 25th March is exactly 9 months before Christmas day (25th December) which is when Jesus Christ was born. Midsummer Day falls on the 24th June and Michaelmas Day falls on the 29th September. Each fall close to a solstice or equinox therefore marking the changing of the seasons.

Lady Day is just after the vernal equinox and the first of the four English quarter days, Lady Day takes place at the beginning of spring when nature is wakening up, starting new.

Tenant farm leases always ran for a year and the only time a farmer would consider moving would be in the spring time and the only time he or she could sign a lease for their new farm. The lease always began and ended on 'Lady Day'.

An order of the guardian of 'Clutton Union' was given to the parish of Camerton in the county of Somerset, to carry out a Poor Rate Survey each year. The Overseers held the responsibility to manage the parish monies while trying to show mercy to those in need. The appointed Overseers would collect rates to cover the cost of the relief, in turn would give out (dole out) to those in need.

The Overseer was usually a man who owned property, lived in the parish and was of a prominent position or stature. Parish Overseers, Churchwardens and other officials were elected at a meeting held in the vestry room church. The Overseer's accounts were also a good record of where people lived within the parish for that particular year. Records held before 1841 act like a modern day census.

In the parish of Camerton 1846 the Poor Rate book records Mr James Daniel as being the owner of Tunley Paddock.

Entry reference no: 409

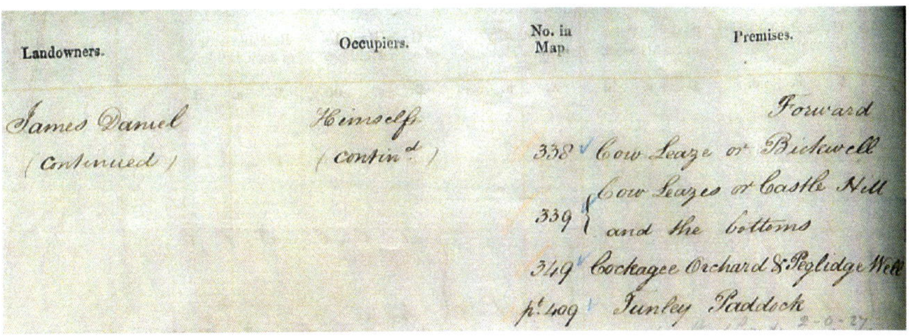

Landowners.	Occupiers.	No. in Map.	Premises.
James Daniel (Continued)	Himself (contind)		Forward
		338	Cow Leaze or Bickwell
		339	Cow Leazes or Castle Hill and the bottoms
		349	Cockagee Orchard & Peglidge Well
		pt 409	Tunley Paddock

1844 Tithe Map showing reference no: 409

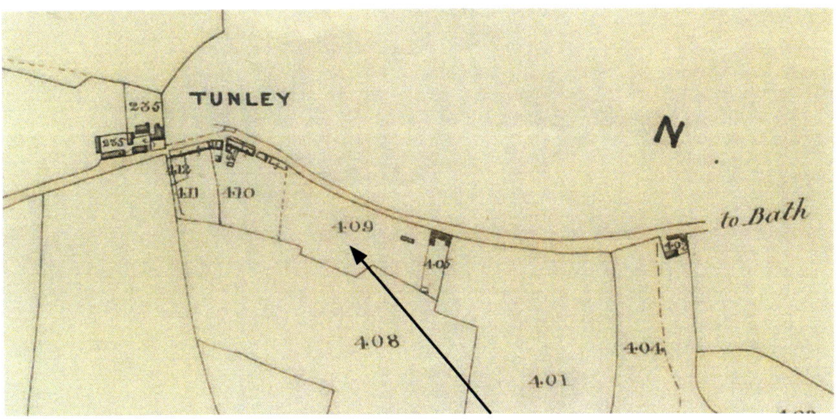

In the parish of Camerton 1846 the poor rate book states Mr Anstey was the owner of the Beer House and Baker's House in Tunley, reference no: 410 and John Strickland was the occupier.

1846 Poor Rate Book reference No: 410

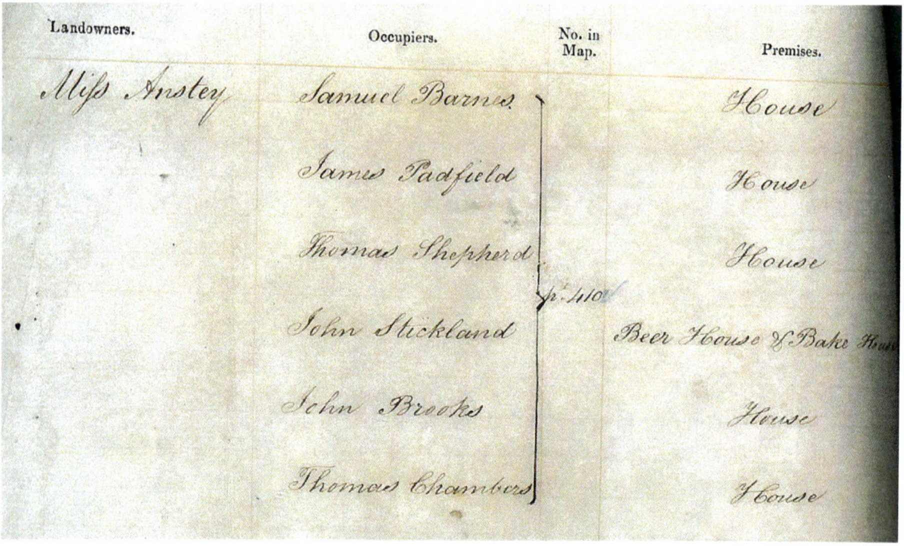

Landowners.	Occupiers.	No. in Map.	Premises.
Miss Anstey	Samuel Barnes		House
	James Padfield		House
	Thomas Shepherd		House
	John Stickland	No. 410	Beer House & Bake House
	John Brookes		House
	Thomas Chambers		House

1844 Tithe Map

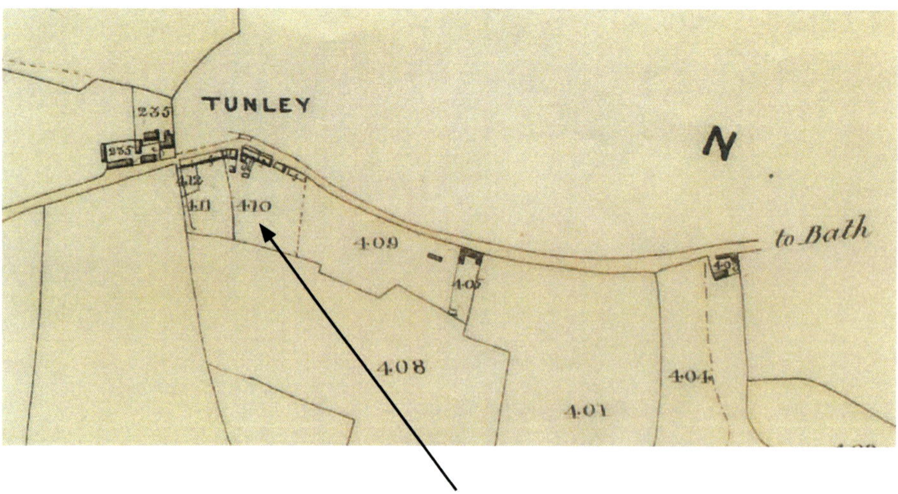

Beer House

Camerton's Poor Rate Book dated October 21st 1882

Front Cover

Declaration and Signatures of the Overseers

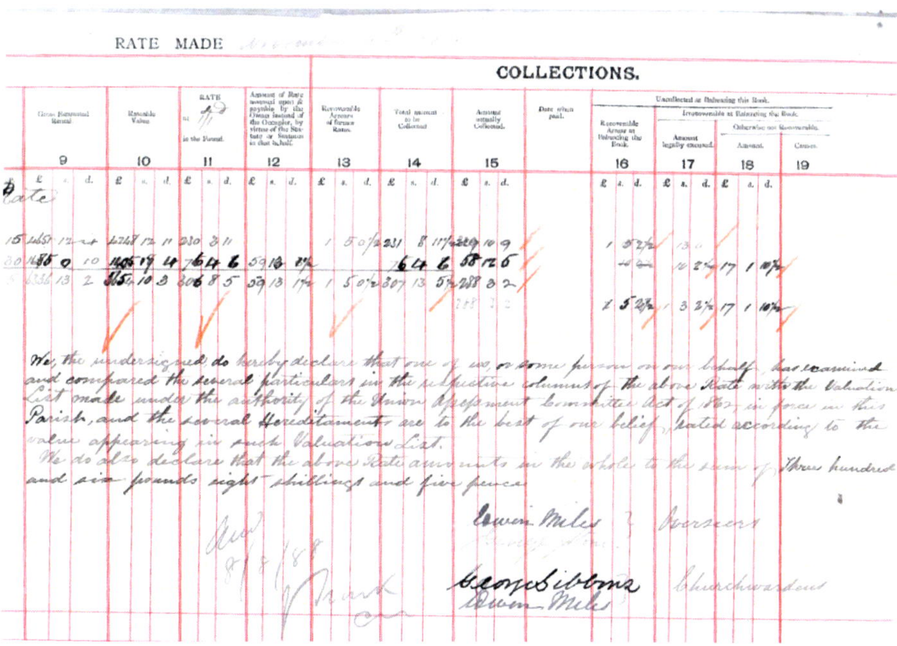

RATE MADE

COLLECTIONS.

We, the undersigned, do hereby declare that one of us, or some person on our behalf, has examined and compared the several particulars in the respective columns of the above Rate with the Valuation List made under the authority of the Union Assessment Committee Act of 1862, in force in this Parish, and the several Hereditaments are to the best of our belief, rated according to the value appearing in such Valuation List.

We do also declare that the above Rate amounts in the whole to the sum of Three hundred and six pounds eight shillings and five pence

Edwin Miles } Overseers

George Gibbons

Edwin Miles } Churchwardens

Camerton's Poor Rate Book dated November 19th 1887

Front Cover

Declaration and Signatures of the Overseers

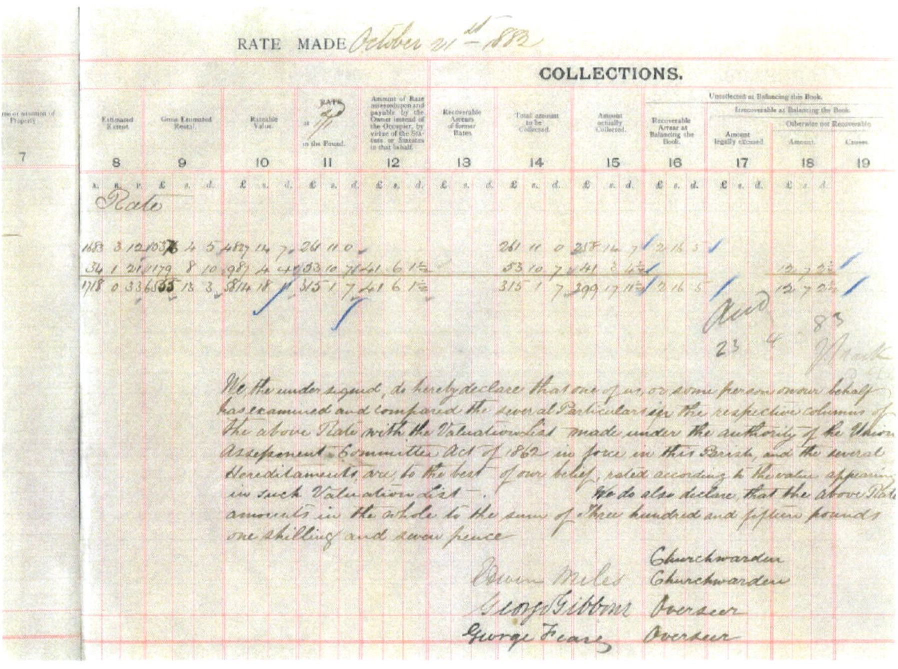

RATE MADE October 21st 1882

COLLECTIONS.

We the under signed, do hereby declare that one of us, or some person on our behalf has examined and compared the several Particulars in the respective columns of the above Rate with the Valuation List made under the authority of the Union Assessment Committee Act of 1862 in force in this Parish, and the several Hereditaments are, to the best of our belief, rated according to the value appearing in such Valuation List. We do also declare, that the above Rate amounts in the whole to the sum of Three hundred and fifteen pounds one shilling and seven pence

Churchwarden
Edwin Miles Churchwarden
George Gibbons Overseer
George Feare Overseer

1881 Census

According to the 1881 Census, the owner of the Beer House, Tunley; locally known as the 'Star Inn' was George Coombs. Martha Strickland was the head of her family and the landlady (publican) she was about 67 years of age. Her son John was recorded as being a servant barman and would have been about 26 years of age.

Examples of a few entries:

The Poor Rate Book 1881 (reference No: 64)

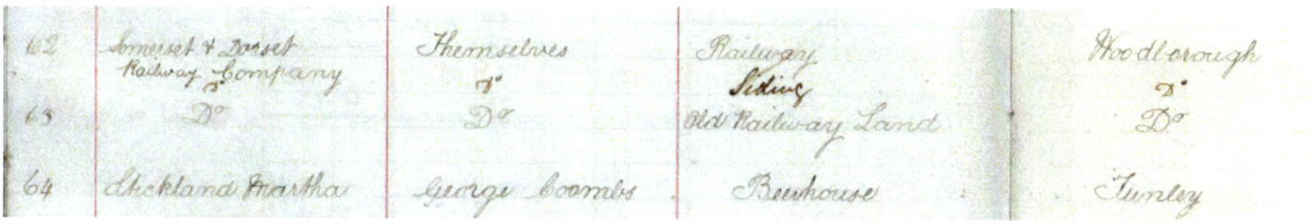

62	Somerset & Dorset Railway Company	Themselves	Railway Siding	Woodborough
63	Do	Do	Old Railway Land	Do
64	Stickland Martha	George Coombs	Beerhouse	Tunley

The Poor Rate Book 1882 (reference No: 42)

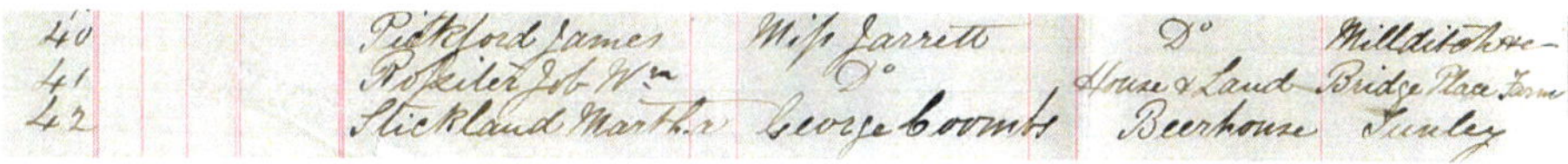

40	Pickford James	Miss Jarrett	Do	Millditch
41	Rossiter Job Wm	Do	House & Land	Bridge Place Farm
42	Stickland Martha	George Coombs	Beerhouse	Tunley

The Poor Rate Book 1887 (reference: 60)

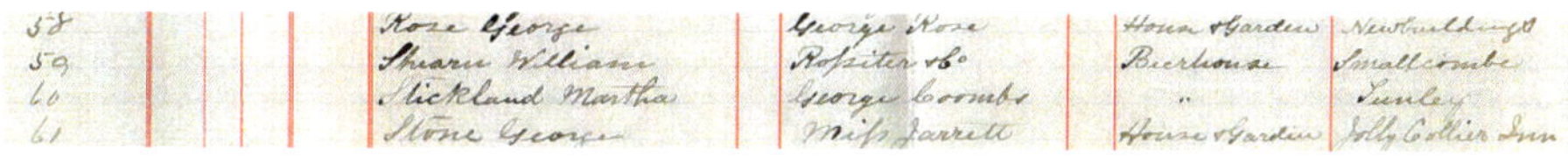

58	Rose George	George Rose	House & Garden	Newbuildings
59	Shearn William	Rossiter & Co	Beerhouse	Smallcombe
60	Stickland Martha	George Coombs	"	Tunley
61	Stone George	Miss Jarrett	House & Garden	Jolly Collier Inn

Some names of local people who received parochial relief in 1910

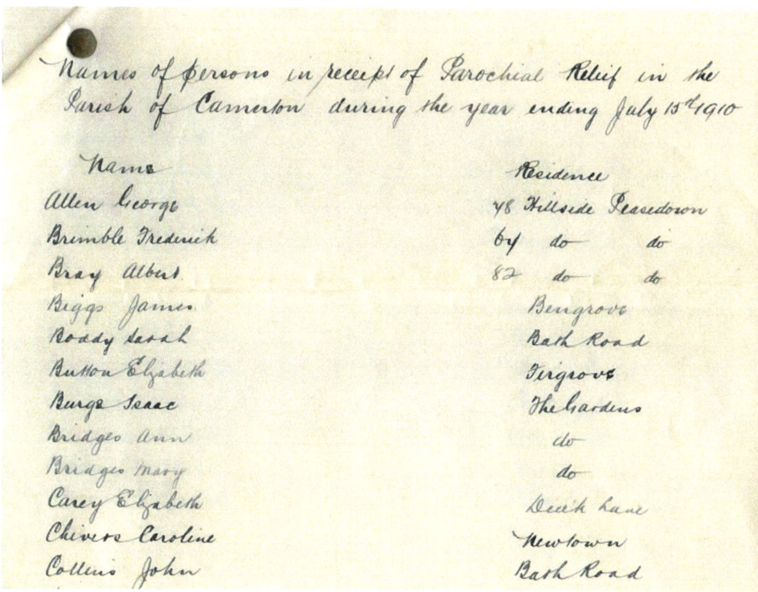

Names of persons in receipt of Parochial Relief in the Parish of Camerton during the year ending July 15th 1910

Names	Residence
Allen George	48 Hillside Peasedown
Brimble Frederick	64 do do
Bray Albert	82 do do
Biggs James	Bengrove
Roddy Sarah	Bath Road
Button Elizabeth	Fergrove
Burge Isaac	The Gardens
Bridges Ann	do
Bridges Mary	do
Carey Elizabeth	Duck Lane
Chivers Caroline	Newtown
Collins John	Bath Road

Life used to be grim and work was hard. The main work available was either working on the farm or down the pit; if you were fit and able you could join the Armed Forces.

Pictured below is a group of local men outside the Star Inn enjoying a drink: (Messrs) Blacker, Emery, Parfitt, Combes, Padfield, Dowling and boy Blacker. The pet dog stood by the door in-front of the man wearing a waistcoat with a watch chain, is believed to belong to Blacker. The two men sitting on the floor with the jug of ale in front of them are Sperring and Cavill.

A group of local men outside the beer house (The Star Inn)

From 1846 to the early 1900's the beer house was occupied and ran by the Strickland's family for over 50 years!

Folk used a public house as a way of release, a pint of ale, an ounce of backy and a good old natter with their mates. The brewers sold mainly to public houses and to private establishments but the public house sector was the back bone of the brewer's trade.

The owner 'George Coombs' changed his own name to a business name 'Coombs & co' according to the 1900 Poor Rate book.

Poor Rate Book 1900 (reference No: 68)

No. 1.—KNIGHT & Co., La Belle Sauvage, E.C.—(S 689-99) PARISH OF Camerton

No.	NAME of OCCUPIER.	NAME of OWNER.	DESCRIPTION of PROPERTY RATED.	NAME OR SITUATION of PROPERTY.
1	2	3	4	5
68	Strickland Martha	Coombs & Co	Beerhouse	Tunley
69	Stone George	Miss Jarrett	Inn & Garden	Jolly Collier Inn

Changes - In 1903 the owner is the same Coombs & Co but the occupier changed to a Mr George Lippiatt.

The Poor Rate Book 1903 (reference No: 59)

No.	Occupier	Owner	Description	Situation
57	Tuff Rev Edgar	Miss Jarrett	House & Garden	The Firs
58	Lippiatt George	Self	Land	Tunley
59	"	Coombs & Company	Beerhouse	"
60	Maggs Frank	Exors of J. Daniels	House	"

The Poor Rate Book 1907 (reference No: 60)

No.	Occupier	Owner	Description	Situation
58	Langley Elizabeth	"	Cottage & Garden	"
59	Long Francis	B. Hill	Land	Cleeves
60	Lippiatt John George	Coombs' Company	Beerhouse	Tunley
61	"	Self	Land	"
62	Masters Robert	F. B. Beauchamp	"	Woodborough Farm

The Poor Rate Book 1913 (reference No: 82)

No.	Occupier	Owner	Description	Situation
79	Langley Emma	Self	House & Shop	Peasedown
80	Langley Elizabeth	"	House & Garden	"
81	Langley James	"	"	Carlingcott
82	Lippiatt J. G.	Coombs & Company	Beerhouse	Tunley
83	"	J.G. Lippiatt	Land	"

Going back before modern public houses, most places to drink were ordinary households where the owner served home-brewed ale and beer. These were referred to as Ale Houses, Taverns, or Beer Houses, where a room for the night was available to a traveller, this might have been bedding on a floor or in a barn; it would have been classed as an Inn. By the mid 1800s there used to be a pub on almost every street corner.

Pictured below 'The Star Inn' on the road edge

The sign attached to the outside stone wall reads: 'The Star Inn, Coombs Brewery', the rest is illegible.

In the late 18th century 'Pale Ale' was popular with the gentry. A great innovation was the introduction of Porter brewing. Porter was thicker, blacker and more bitter than other beers. It was brewed from malt that had spent a longer time in the kiln so it was slightly scorched. Cheaper malt could be used than was needed for the finer pale ales.

Pictured below is a ordinance survey map dated 1902, it shows the location of the Star Inn, the sharp bend was notorious for accidents.

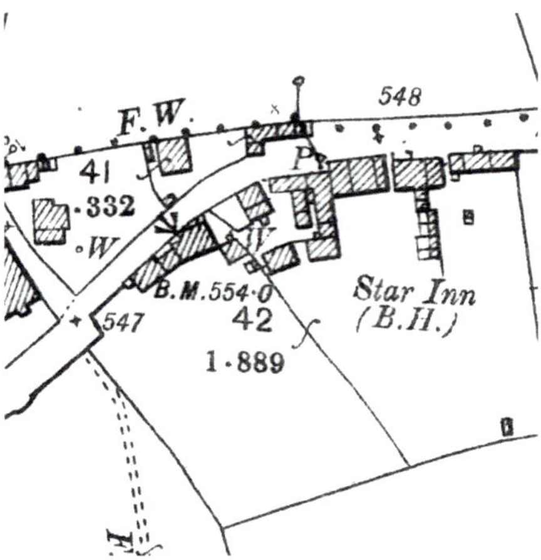

The Star Inn around 1928

Above you can see the landlady holding her baby son, Ron Fear who was born at the Star Inn, she was about 21 years of age. Her name is Edith Violet Fear, born in 1907, wife to William Fear the proprietor of the Star Inn. Edith was mother to 3 more sons; Brian, Lesley and Peter.

Oakhill Brewery was the owner of the Star Inn. 'Oakhill Beer' was advertised on a large sign on the front of the building, another small sign advertising 'Invalid Stout' can also be seen. Oakhill brewery was founded in 1767, the local brewery to Camerton and it's surrounding area for many years; it was based in the village of Oakhill about 8 miles approximately south of Camerton.

Oakhill Brewery

Pictured below is a Beerhouse renewal licence document dated 1st February 1930 authorising William Fear to sell Beer, Cider and Perry by retail, in the parish of Camerton.

Beerhouse Renewal

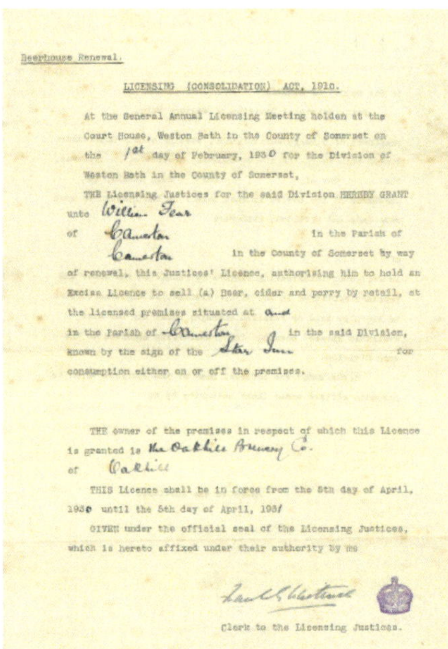

Beerhouse Renewal.

LICENSING (CONSOLIDATION) ACT, 1910.

At the General Annual Licensing Meeting holden at the Court House, Weston Bath in the County of Somerset on the 1st day of February, 1930 for the Division of Weston Bath in the County of Somerset,

THE Licensing Justices for the said Division HEREBY GRANT unto William Fear of Camerton in the Parish of Camerton in the County of Somerset by way of renewal, this Justices' Licence, authorising him to hold an Excise Licence to sell (a) Beer, cider and perry by retail, at the licensed premises situated at and in the Parish of Camerton in the said Division, known by the sign of the Star Inn for consumption either on or off the premises.

THE owner of the premises in respect of which this Licence is granted is the Oakhill Brewery Co. of Oakhill

THIS Licence shall be in force from the 5th day of April, 1930 until the 5th day of April, 1931

GIVEN under the official seal of the Licensing Justices, which is hereto affixed under their authority by me

Clerk to the Licensing Justices.

The landlords were usually highly respected and well known locally. They usually handed the public house licence to their son or daughter. Women were not allowed in the public house unless they went to the children's room.

In March of 1930 Harry and Nora Arnold became the landlord and landlady of the 'Star Inn'.

Landlord Harry Arnold

Landlady Nora Arnold

Reference 1, letter from W.A Candy (Tunley Farm)

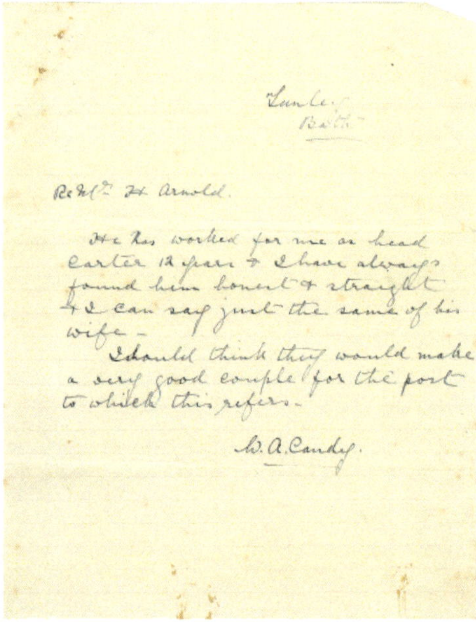

Tunley
Bath

Re Mr H Arnold.

He has worked for me as head carter 12 years & I have always found him honest & straight & I can say just the same of his wife –

I should think they would make a very good couple for the post to which this refers.

W. A. Candy.

Reference 2 – Letter from Holbrook's Stores

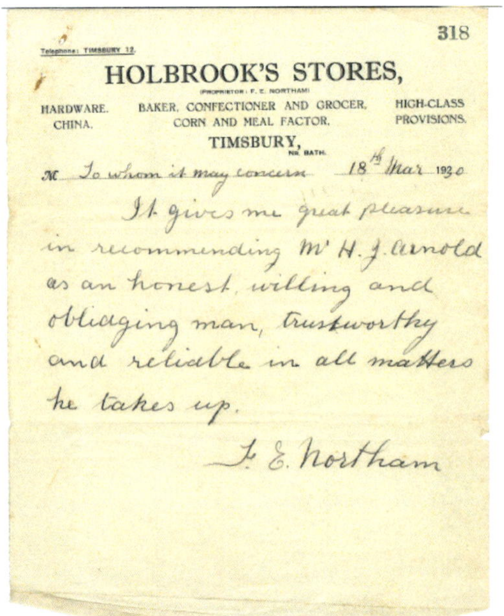

318

Telephone: TIMSBURY 12.

HOLBROOK'S STORES,

(PROPRIETOR: F. E. NORTHAM)

HARDWARE. CHINA. | BAKER, CONFECTIONER AND GROCER, CORN AND MEAL FACTOR, | HIGH-CLASS PROVISIONS.

TIMSBURY,
NR. BATH.

M To whom it may concern 18th Mar 1930

It gives me great pleasure in recommending Mr H. J. Arnold as an honest, willing and obliging man, trustworthy and reliable in all matters he takes up.

F. E. Northam

Tenancy Agreement 'Oakhill Brewery' 24th March 1930

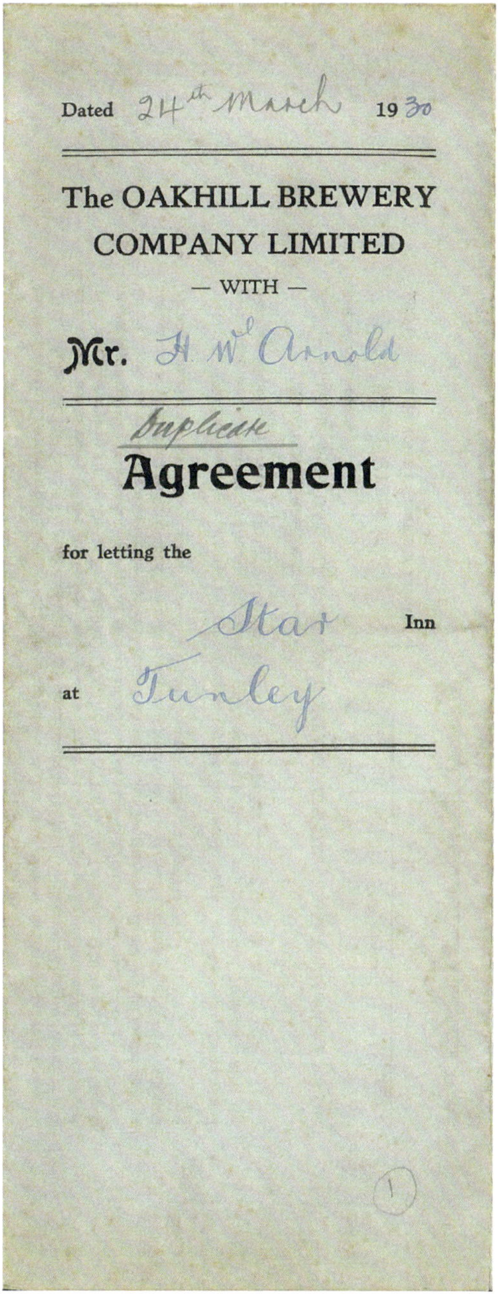

Dated 24th March 1930

The OAKHILL BREWERY
COMPANY LIMITED

— WITH —

Mr. H. Wd Arnold

Duplicate

Agreement

for letting the

Star Inn

at Tunley

(1)

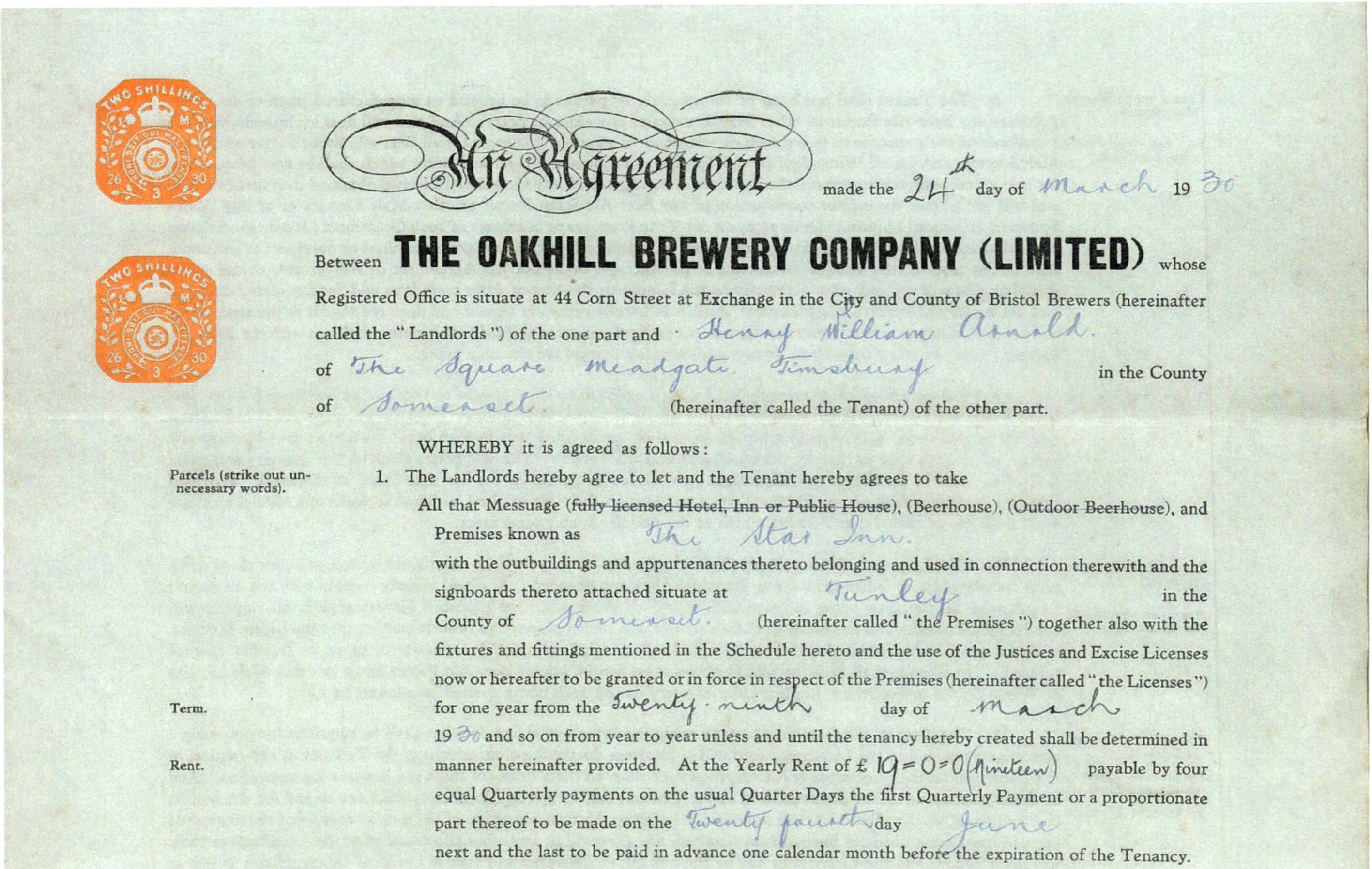

An Agreement made the 24th day of March 1930

Between THE OAKHILL BREWERY COMPANY (LIMITED) whose Registered Office is situate at 44 Corn Street at Exchange in the City and County of Bristol Brewers (hereinafter called the " Landlords ") of the one part and Henry William Arnold. of The Square. Meadgate. Timsbury in the County of Somerset. (hereinafter called the Tenant) of the other part.

WHEREBY it is agreed as follows:

Parcels (strike out unnecessary words).

1. The Landlords hereby agree to let and the Tenant hereby agrees to take All that Messuage (~~fully licensed Hotel, Inn or Public House~~), (Beerhouse), (Outdoor Beerhouse), and Premises known as The Star Inn. with the outbuildings and appurtenances thereto belonging and used in connection therewith and the signboards thereto attached situate at Tunley in the County of Somerset. (hereinafter called " the Premises ") together also with the fixtures and fittings mentioned in the Schedule hereto and the use of the Justices and Excise Licenses now or hereafter to be granted or in force in respect of the Premises (hereinafter called "the Licenses")

Term. for one year from the Twenty-ninth day of March 1930 and so on from year to year unless and until the tenancy hereby created shall be determined in

Rent. manner hereinafter provided. At the Yearly Rent of £ 19=0=0 (Nineteen) payable by four equal Quarterly payments on the usual Quarter Days the first Quarterly Payment or a proportionate part thereof to be made on the Twenty fourth day June next and the last to be paid in advance one calendar month before the expiration of the Tenancy.

Agreement showing Henry William Arnolds name and the amount of £19 yearly rent.

the amount to which the Landlords shall be entitled for such dilapidations as aforesaid and an account shall be rendered for any difference between the amount so deducted and the amount of such lowest tender.

19. The Landlords hereby agree with the Tenant that the Tenant paying the said Rent and observing and performing the stipulations and agreements herein contained shall quietly enjoy the said premises during the Tenancy without any lawful interruption by the Landlords or any person claiming through them.

AS WITNESS the hands of

(for and on behalf of the OAKHILL BREWERY COMPANY LIMITED) and the Tenant the day and year first above written.

For and on behalf of
THE OAKHILL BREWERY COMPANY LIMITED. } Reg. A. Hobhouse Director

Henry William Arnold Tenant.

WITNESS to the Signature of

R. A. Hobhouse

For and on behalf of
THE OAKHILL BREWERY COMPANY LIMITED.

Witness's Name S. Smith

Address Ashwick Oakhill.

Description Clerk.

WITNESS to the Signature of the Tenant

Witness's Name John. Durham

Address Meadgate Inn. Timsbury Bath

Description Publican.

SCHEDULE OF LANDLORDS' FIXTURES.

The Schedule to be signed by Landlords and Tenant.

Pictured below is of a presentation for either pigeon racing or darts around the late 1940s. It was held downstairs in the long room of the Star Inn.

The first row from front to back: Tom Parfitt, Jack Parfitt, Cecil Ruddick, Fred Parfitt, Albert Biggs (Talkie), Bill Biggs, not known and Roy Jones.

The back row from the dart board, from left to right: Jack Hookins, Harry Arnold (Landlord of the Star Inn), Tom Durham, Trevor Davis and Gwen Bryant.

The second row from front to back: Bill Jones, Hillman (Squeaker), Harry Parfitt, George Moore and not known.

The third row from front to back: George Arnold, Charlie Brimble, Jackie Wines, Albert Durham, Most Durham and Walt Biggs.

The Fourth row from front to back: Mrs Wines, Mrs Parfitt, Maud Hawkins, Ron Fear, Dot Fear, Phil Windybank and not known.

Behind the fourth row from front to back: Brian Biggs, Bill Fear, Jasper Pickford, Mrs Bryant and John Arnold.

Nicknames

Happy Days Angel
Shilling Millen
Nutty Colmer
Boozer Derrick
Punch Cottle
Moses Box
Woodbine Willie Barrett
Dumpty Durham
Mattin
Sony Combs
Sticker Ashman
Bacco Biggs
Budget Biggs
Talkie Biggs
Nudger Rogers
Sammy Webber
Pop Slade
Dinky Doel
Smudger Smith
Boots Goold
Emmet Gould
Hitchie Moon
Shilling Moon
Puffer Greening
Bucket Sage
Yummy Jeffrey
Lardy Parfitt
Taffy Venebles
Pussy Sperring
Nobby Clarke
Bronco Hawkins
Slippery Hawkins
Neddy Hawkins
Tappy Hawkins
Pansy Fear
Nunc lewis
Chico Fry
Nooker Lewis
Popper Gregory
Chiney Parfitt

Picture of the local skittle team about 1957

Back row from left to right:
Sam Collins (Landlord of the King William), Brian Biggs, Eddy Skuse, Johnny Willcox, Arthur Moore, Mrs Collins (Landlady of the King William) and Bryan Moore.

Front row from left to right:
Daniel Willcox, Norman Millen, Bill Millen and Michael Skuse.

Typical Pub Games

Bagatale	Pigeon Racing
Card Game – Cribbage (Trix)	Darts
Shove Ha'penny	Skittles

Children's Games: Hide 'n' seek, eye spy, skipping, knock out ginger, marbles, football, rounders, cricket, hopscotch, football etc.

Raffle Prize

Very often the landlord would hold a raffle and sometimes put a pig in for the first prize. Food was very scarce and to win a pig was a wonderful prize, it would feed a family for weeks! A local man won a pig but had no where to put it, when he got home he put it in his sitting room, apparently you could hear the pig squealing for miles. A young boy peered through the man's living room window to see what all the noise was about, he saw the pig running around in circles; causing chaos. He remembered it as one of the funniest things he had seen.

Going back to the poor rate book of Camerton parish in 1846, the field behind the Star Inn is recorded as being the property of Mr Anstey who also owned the Beer House and garden; the occupier was recorded in 1846 as a John Strickland. It is shown on the old Camerton Tithe map as reference No: 410.

The field adjacent to field No: 410 is No: 411 and according to the 1846 poor rate book, the owner is Mrs Fear and the occupier is William Anstey. It is shown on the old Camerton Tithe map as reference No: 411.

1846 Poor Rate Book

Reference No: 411

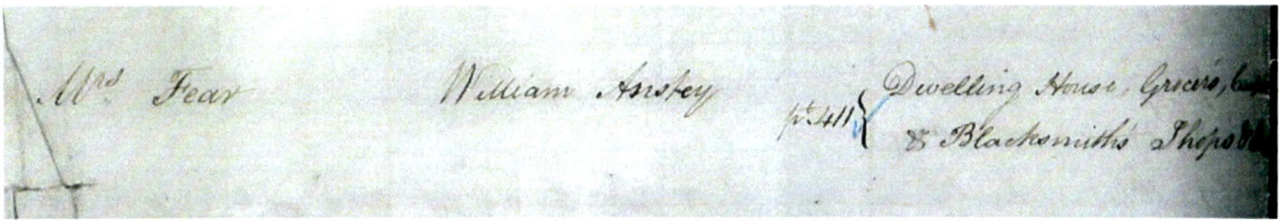

Mrs Fear owned a house, grocers shop, carpenter and blacksmith's workshop; also stables.

1846 Tithe Map – Field No's 410 & 411

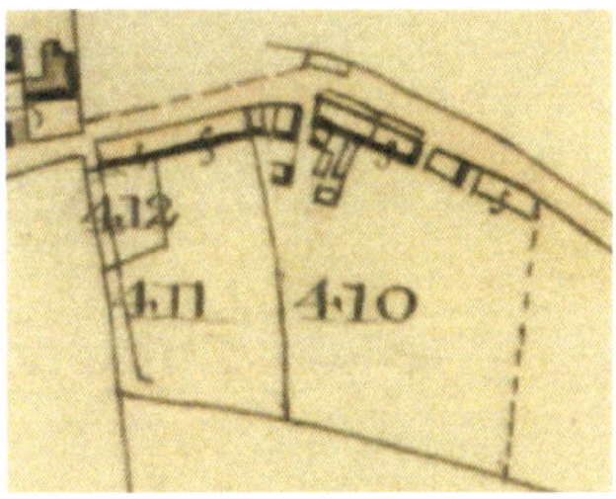

Below is a sketch showing how the Star Inn would have once looked, positioned on the road edge and how close it was to the sharp bend before the road was widened.

The Star Inn

by Dave Gallop

The Star Inn ceased trading in 1953 and was demolished some years later. The main road was widened and road improvements were carried out. Sadly since the 1950s many pubs have closed and more often than not have been turned into a private residence.

In the field Ref No: 411 a corner of it is sectioned off and referenced as No: 412, recorded as being a Timber yard.

Tithe Map dated 1846 showing reference No: 411 and 412

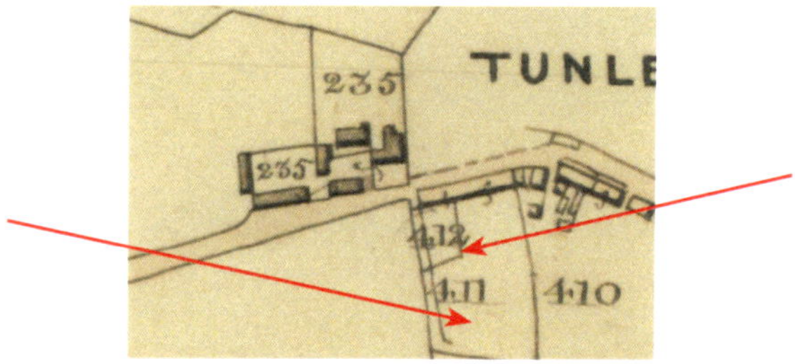

As you proceed along the road you will see a bus sign alongside a bus stop pull- in area on your left. Almost opposite a stone built bus shelter to your right.

Bus Stop Pull- in area and Bus Stop Shelter

To your right is a stone built bus shelter and opposite are two cottages.

Two Adjoining Cottages as seen from the main road (2014)

The first cottage below has a small square gable window (left on photograph below) It is believed to have been built early 1890s the land owner was Job Moon.

No: 1 Star Cottage

To the left of the cottage stands a double garage, if you can imagine it positioned and brought forwards to the edge of the yellow dotted line marking the bus stop on the main road and running back a lot further to the left of the garages and long in proportion, you will have a good indication of the location where the Star Inn once stood.

The lease below clearly shows how the property was handed down to various members of the same family.

Schedule showing previous tenants

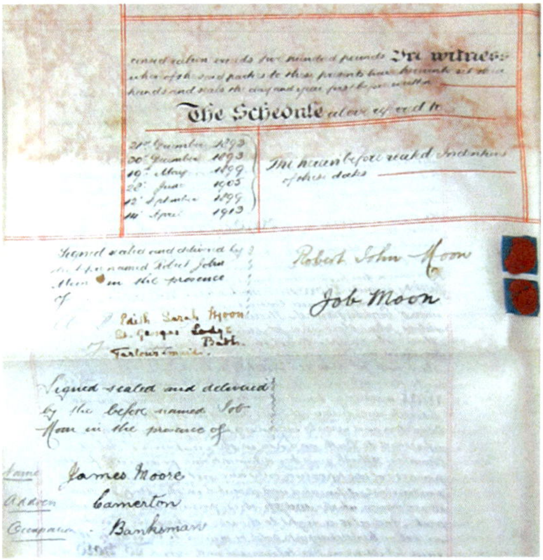
The Schedule above referred to

30th December 1893	The herein before recited Indentures of these dates
19th May 1899	
28th June 1905	
12th September 1899	
14th April 1913	

Signed sealed and delivered by the before named Robert John Moon in the presence of

Edith Sarah Moon
St. Georges Lodge Bath.
Tailoress.

Robert John Moon

Job Moon

Signed sealed and delivered by the before named Job Moon in the presence of

Name James Moore
Address Camerton
Occupation Bankman

1913 Plan of buildings and land

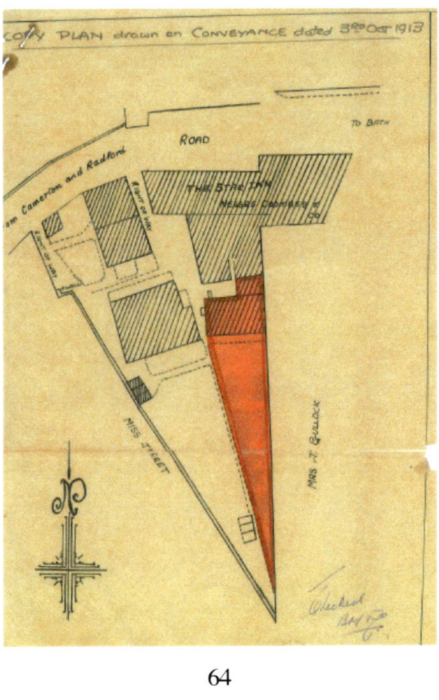

No: 1 Star cottage as seen today with the outside rendered

Clive and Marya Turner are the current owners of No. 1 Star Cottage, they moved in to the cottage that was then named Windridge; in July 2001. They decided to change the name from 'Windridge' to No. 1 Star Cottage. It was difficult for them to move into as it had restricted space. They decided to make alterations that took several years to achieve but succeeded in making it the beautiful cottage you can see today. Clive informed the author of some previous tenants names that were; Richard Cattle and Sally Duck. Clive is currently a local parish councillor and leading on community engagement.

The back of the two adjoining cottages in 1993

No: 2 Star cottage remained in the hands of the Moon family until 1944, Sarah Ann Moon sold the cottage to Oakhill Brewery Co. Ltd. In 1955 Oakhill brewery sold it Mr & Mrs W Jones.

Plan 1 (referred to No: 2 Star cottage)

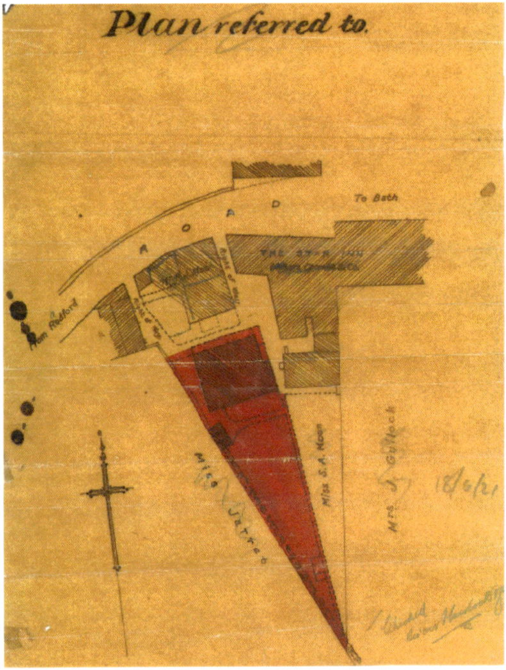

Schedule clearly showing previous tenants from 1893 to 1913

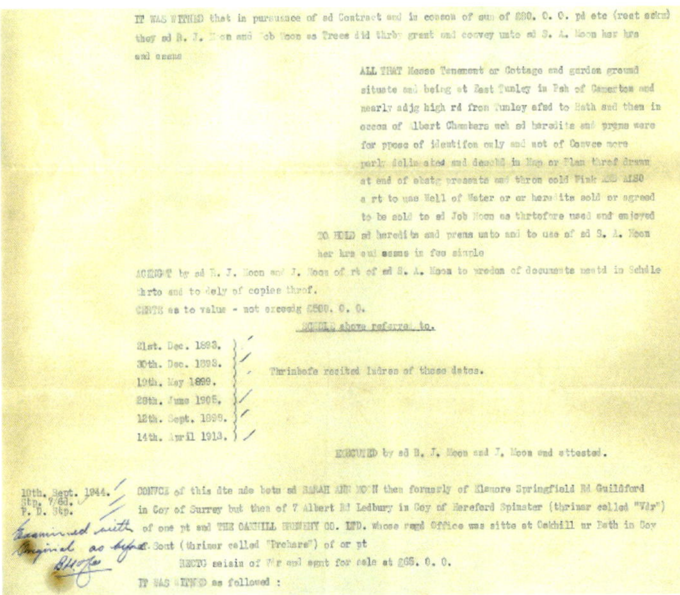

IT WAS WITHED that in pursuance of sd Contract and in consn of sum of £80. 0. 0. pd etc (rect ackd) they sd B. J. Moon and Job Moon as Trees did thrby grant and convey unto sd S. A. Moon her hrs and assns

ALL THAT Messe Tenement or Cottage and garden ground situate and being at East Tunley in Psh of Camerton and nearly adjg high rd from Tunley afsd to Bath and then in occon of Albert Chambers wch sd heredits and prems were for ppose of identifon only and not of Convce more parly delineated and descbd in Map or Plan thref drawn at end of abstg presents and thron cold Pink AND ALSO a rt to use Well of Water or or heredits sold or agreed to be sold to sd Job Moon as thrtofore used and enjoyed

TO HOLD sd heredits and prems unto and to use of sd S. A. Moon her hrs and assns in fee simple

ACKNGT by sd B. J. Moon and J. Moon of rt of sd S. A. Moon to prodon of documents mentd in Schdle thrto and to dely of copies throf.

CERTE as to value - not exceedg £500. 0. 0.

SCHDLE above referred to.

21st. Dec. 1893.
30th. Dec. 1893.
19th. May 1899.
28th. June 1905.
12th. Sept. 1909.
14th. April 1913.

Thrinbefe recited Indres of these dates.

EXECUTED by sd B. J. Moon and J. Moon and attested.

10th. Sept. 1944. Stp. 7/6d. P. D. Stp.

CONVCE of this dte mde betn sd SARAH ANN MOON then formerly of Elsmore Springfield Rd Guildford in Coy of Surrey but then of 7 Albert Rd Ledbury in Coy of Hereford Spinster (thrinar called "Vdr") of one pt and THE OAKHILL BREWERY CO. LTD. whose regd Office was sitte at Oakhill nr Bath in Coy of Somt (thrinar called "Prchsre") of or pt

RECTG seisin of Vdr and agmt for sale at £65. 0. 0.

IT WAS WITNESD as followed :

Examined with original as before

Schedule clearly showing previous tenants from 1913 to 1944

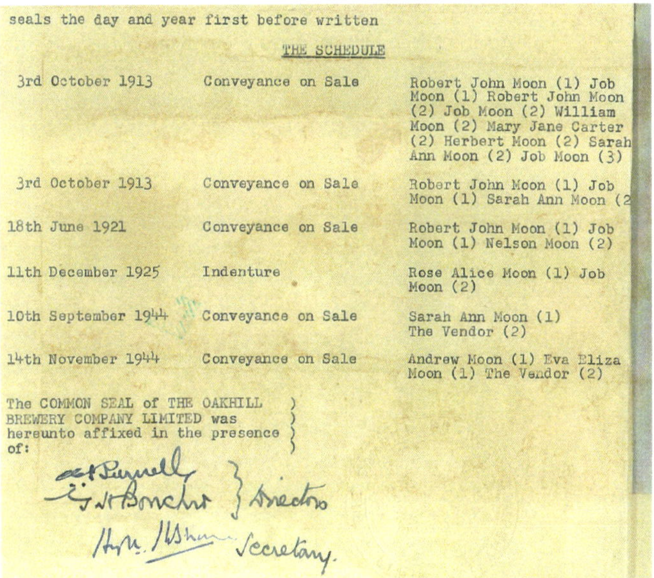

seals the day and year first before written

THE SCHEDULE

3rd October 1913	Conveyance on Sale	Robert John Moon (1) Job Moon (1) Robert John Moon (2) Job Moon (2) William Moon (2) Mary Jane Carter (2) Herbert Moon (2) Sarah Ann Moon (2) Job Moon (3)
3rd October 1913	Conveyance on Sale	Robert John Moon (1) Job Moon (1) Sarah Ann Moon (2
18th June 1921	Conveyance on Sale	Robert John Moon (1) Job Moon (1) Nelson Moon (2)
11th December 1925	Indenture	Rose Alice Moon (1) Job Moon (2)
10th September 1944	Conveyance on Sale	Sarah Ann Moon (1) The Vendor (2)
14th November 1944	Conveyance on Sale	Andrew Moon (1) Eva Eliza Moon (1) The Vendor (2)

The COMMON SEAL of THE OAKHILL BREWERY COMPANY LIMITED was hereunto affixed in the presence of:

Directors

Secretary.

Conveyance dated 1955 of 'Star Cottages' between Oakhill Brewery Co. Ltd and Mr & Mrs W Jones

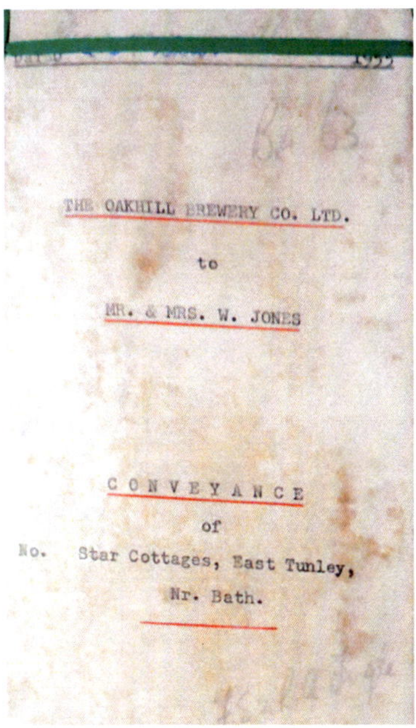

THE OAKHILL BREWERY CO. LTD.

to

MR. & MRS. W. JONES

CONVEYANCE

of

No. Star Cottages, East Tunley,

Nr. Bath.

Mr & Mrs Jones lived in the No: 2 cottage for over 50 years, William died and later his widow Mary passed away at home in 1991.

No: 2 Star cottage in 1992

No: 2 Star cottage was put up for sale, Nick and Steven Offer tried to purchase the cottage in 1993 but the cottage was in such a dilapidated state; even the bank would not give them a mortgage. There was no toilet, bathroom or kitchen and the cottage was in a grim state. Their father and mother helped them purchase the cottage by re-mortgaging their own home.

Father and son, Dave and Nick took on the challenge of renovating the old cottage and whilst working they discovered an old baking oven within the large fire place, unfortunately it was impossible to restore.

Baking Oven

The present owner is Nick Offer an electrician, he and his father Dave, took the cottage from a dilapidated state to the beautiful country cottage you can see today.

No: 2 Star Cottage today

No: 1 and No: 2 as seen today

It is believed the two cottages used to be one large cottage, possibly a bakery/store; it was once known as 'Star Cottage'; Dave Offer believes it is a lot older than we are able to trace.

The view from the back gardens of No: 1 and No: 2 Star Cottages is breathtaking, from the rear of both cottages over looks the beautiful Cam Valley. Apparently on a good clear day, facing south in the distance is Alfred's tower at Stourhead; to the west is Penn hill mast, Wells. The owners say from their bedroom windows they can see the White Horse, Wiltshire and the Suspension Bridge, Bristol.

Local residents also say, in the height of the summer, you can see shadow lines which show the outlines of the old medieval strips that formed part of the old three field systems on the south side of the valley.

In the mid 1950s the main road was widened and road improvements were carried out.

Plan showing the New road

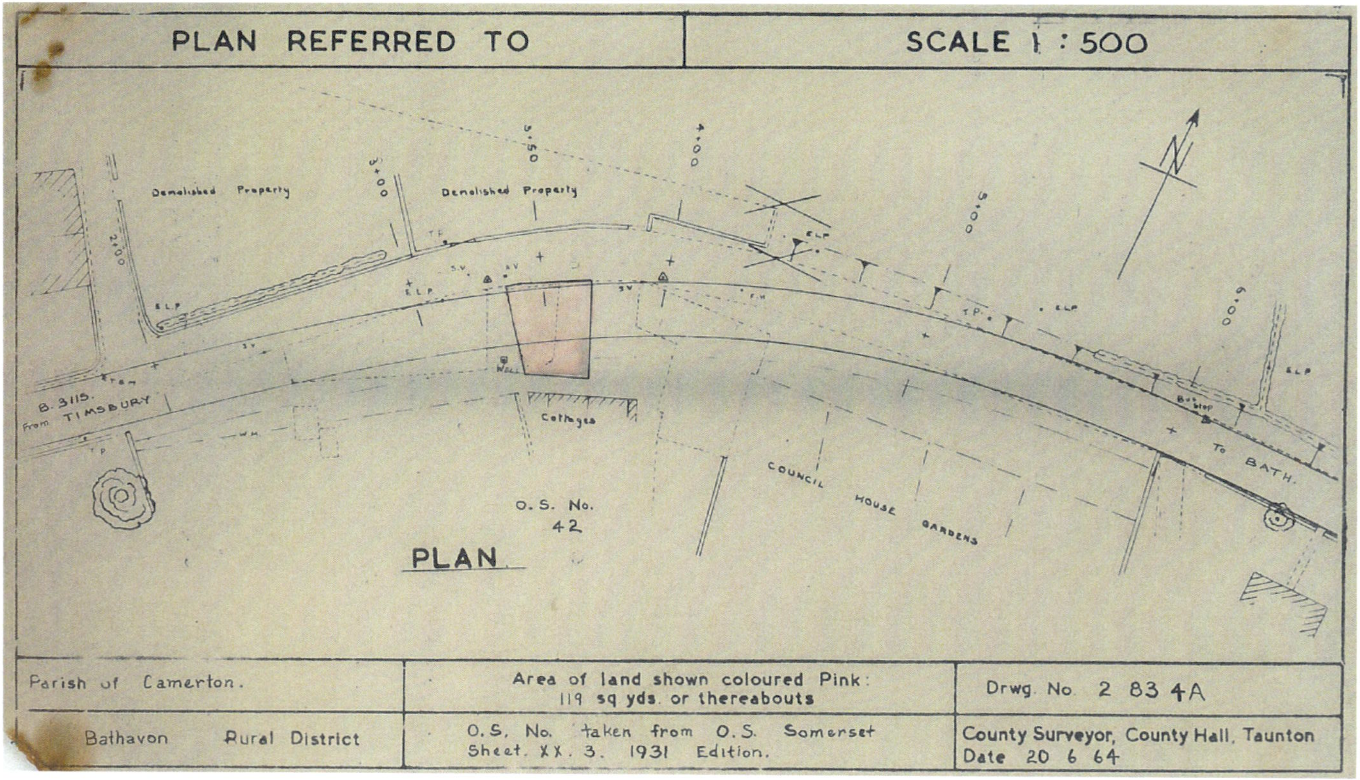

Mining Coal – can bc traced as far back as the Roman times, in places near Hadrian's Wall in Scotland traces of coal and coal dust have been found.

Mining was such a vital part of Somerset life, many people travelled from afar into Camerton village for work. The population of Camerton in 1801 was 594, by 1911 it had risen to 2,386. During the year 1910, Camerton pit employed 400 men, many walked 2 to 3 miles to get to work.

In the mid 1700's the Camerton estate, including the Old Manor House, was owned by the Stephens family, James Stephens was granted a lease to mine for coal in 1781. The pit only (higher coalfield) produced coal for a few years, by 1794 a new pit (lower coalfield) only about a half a mile away was opened.

Opposite the site of the old Star Inn is a field known as the 'Slate'. In this field used to stand several cottages; from the corner of Priston Lane running back towards the old Methodist Church.

The Great War (1914 to 1918)

Friends and neighbours very kindly loaned the author photographs, pieces of memorabilia and shared their stories about members of their loved ones who fought and lost their lives in WW1. The author was moved so much that she felt that all Camerton men who served and gave their lives in the 'Great War' should be part of her book (see chapters 2, 4 and 5 in this volume and chapters in future volumes).

John and Emily Fry (nee Parfitt) married in 1880, John was a farm labourer; they lived in Bath, Marksbury and Bristol. They had 11 children although 2 had unfortunately died in infancy. Whilst in Bristol, John worked as a haulier, he died in 1907 at the age of 53. Emily and the whole family moved to live with her eldest son William who lived at 22 Priston; and worked as a coal miner. Williams brothers and sisters were; Georgina, James, Henry, Beatrice, Charles, Ida, Annie and Bertie.

William's younger brother James found work as a farm labourer before deciding to enlist at the age of 18. James was born on the 21st October 1989; he had enlisted in the 1st Battalion Coldstream Guards and was known as 72667 Corporal James Fry.

Sergeant James Fry

By the time he was 22 years of age he was based at Victoria Barracks, Windsor. In 1912 he married Amelia Shephard, they briefly lived with Amelia's parents in London, at the end of his service; both moved to a cottage on the top of Tunley Hill.

The cottage amongst many others had been condemned and has been long since demolished. James was employed as a coal miner Amelia gave birth to their daughter Ida Edith on the 30th April 1913.

James was a reservist and was called back to the colours at the outbreak of war, his regiment the Coldstreams were sent to France and Flanders; just two days after his 25th birthday he was killed. James did not know his wife was 6 months pregnant when he left and in December 1914 she gave birth to a boy and named him 'James Arthur George Fry'. He has no known grave but is commemorated on panels 21 and 22 of the Menin Gate Memorial at Ypres, also his name is on the Camerton War Memorial in St Peter's Church yard and states Sergeant James Fry. James' brother William served as Pte 6462 in the 5th reserve Battalion of the Guards Machine Gun Regiment.

Old cottage with a slate tile roof

George & Annie Fry

Photo 1 - George Henry Fry with his wife Annie as a young couple standing outside their home with their pet dogs. Photo 2 - George Henry Fry with his wife a little older in years, stood in their back garden with the Methodist Church in the background.

George Pickford was born on the 29th December 1891, he lived in one of the condemned cottages since demolished near the old Star Inn. George worked as a miner down the local Camerton pit and in his early 20's decided to enlist with the Royal Marines at Bristol in April 1912.

After his training he was posted to Portsmouth Division and in July 1913 he was transferred to HMS Diadem an 11,000 ton cruiser for a few months and transferred back to Portsmouth.

On the 3rd September George was posted aboard the HMS Queen Mary, on the 28th August 1914 the HMS Queen Mary took part in Heligoland Bight naval engagement that witnessed the Royal Navy sink three German cruisers and a destroyer with the loss of over 700 sailors. In comparison the British lost 35 sailors but did not loose a vessel. Newspaper reported PO/16315 Pte George Pickford being just 24 years of age when he died 2 years later at the battle of Jutland. He is commemorated on the impressive Portsmouth Naval memorial as well as on the Camerton War Memorial in St Peter's churchyard.

The Sign Camerton and Peasedown St John Parochial Magazine dated July 1916

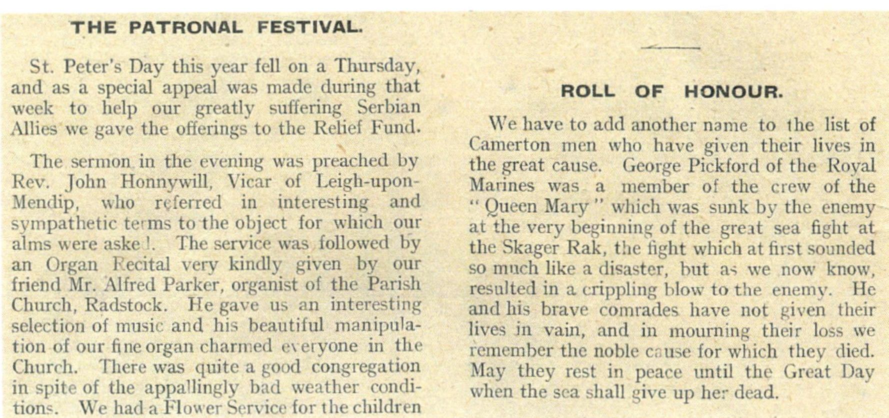

THE PATRONAL FESTIVAL.

St. Peter's Day this year fell on a Thursday, and as a special appeal was made during that week to help our greatly suffering Serbian Allies we gave the offerings to the Relief Fund.

The sermon in the evening was preached by Rev. John Honnywill, Vicar of Leigh-upon-Mendip, who referred in interesting and sympathetic terms to the object for which our alms were asked. The service was followed by an Organ Recital very kindly given by our friend Mr. Alfred Parker, organist of the Parish Church, Radstock. He gave us an interesting selection of music and his beautiful manipulation of our fine organ charmed everyone in the Church. There was quite a good congregation in spite of the appallingly bad weather conditions. We had a Flower Service for the children

ROLL OF HONOUR.

We have to add another name to the list of Camerton men who have given their lives in the great cause. George Pickford of the Royal Marines was a member of the crew of the "Queen Mary" which was sunk by the enemy at the very beginning of the great sea fight at the Skager Rak, the fight which at first sounded so much like a disaster, but as we now know, resulted in a crippling blow to the enemy. He and his brave comrades have not given their lives in vain, and in mourning their loss we remember the noble cause for which they died. May they rest in peace until the Great Day when the sea shall give up her dead.

Joe and Sarah Biggs stood outside one of the condemned houses

Old condemned houses/cottages of the working classes

The above cottages were referred to as "Up the Barton" by locals.

Housing of the Working Classes - Report of the Medical Officer of Health of the parish of Camerton in 1910.

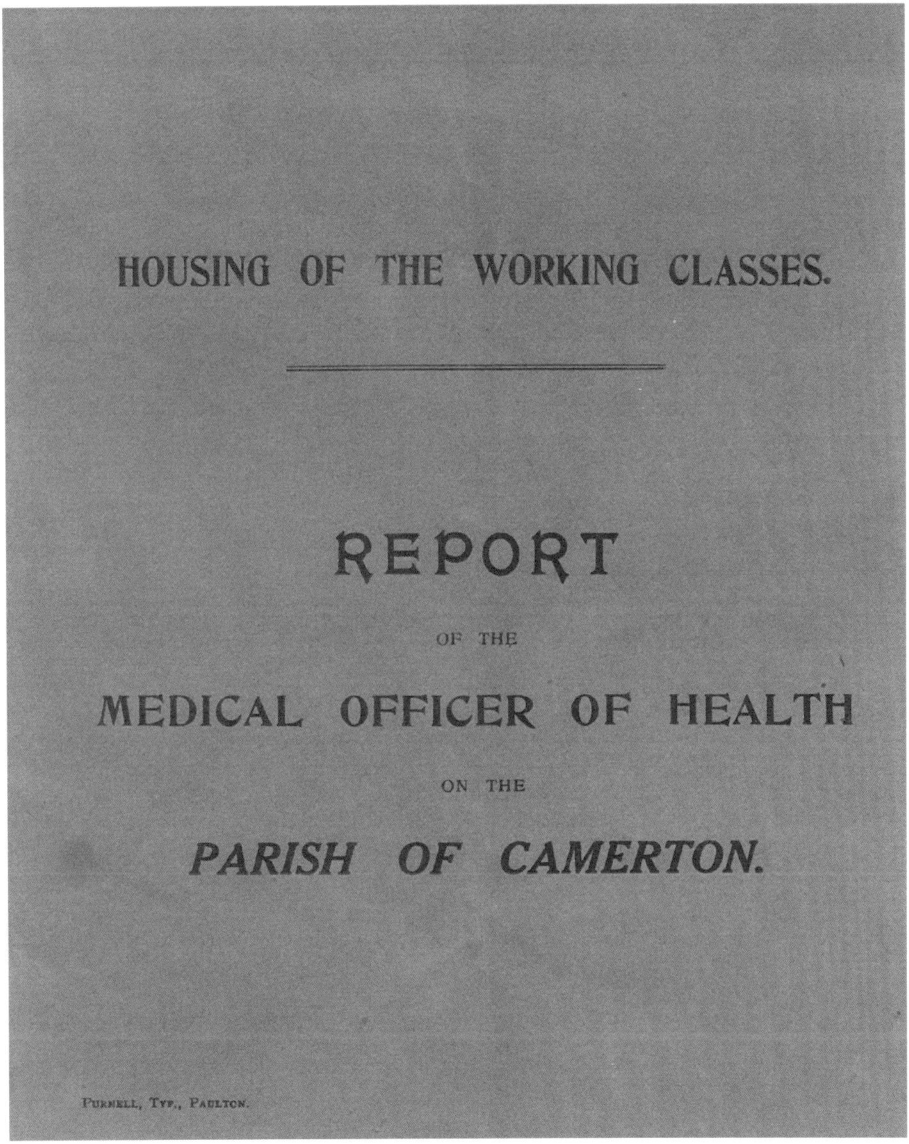

HOUSING OF THE WORKING CLASSES.

REPORT

OF THE

MEDICAL OFFICER OF HEALTH

ON THE

PARISH OF CAMERTON.

PURNELL, TYP., PAULTON.

Some houses were built back to back which never ought to have been allowed. Many houses were old and badly kept up, defects on property owned by Miss Jarrett and Mr J Moon.

REPORT BY THE MEDICAL OFFICER OF HEALTH

ON THE

PARISH OF CAMERTON.

(September 12th, 1910.)

GENTLEMEN,

Housing of the Working Classes.

At your request I have made careful inquiries into the alleged bad and insufficient accommodation. The acreage of the Parish is 1752 acres. The population is 2044; Census of 1901 it was 1772. The number of houses is 542; of these 519 may be classed as workmen's dwellings—8 have only one room up and one down—256 have two up and two down. 278 have three up and two down, or more.

At Peasedown and Carlingcott many new and good houses have been put up within the last few years. In the rest of the Parish, Camerton village, Radford, Durcot, Camerton Hill, Camerton Valley, Meadgate, Smallcombe, etc., I can only hear of about 5 houses having been erected within living memory. Here the houses are old, and badly kept up; the rooms are few in number, very low, badly lighted and badly ventilated, with rough stone floors; often damp from defective or absent rain-water shooting, and insufficient sill protection of doorways; they look neglected, and the tenants say it is almost impossible to get anything in the way of repairs done. Many of them have good gardens, and the rents are low. Quite a number that are called two bedroom houses are not really so, as the back room has a "lean-to" ceiling, and gives only a cubic capacity of about 350 feet. I noticed some houses built back to back, which never ought to have been allowed.

I found in two cottages at Meadgate a bedroom in each, without any window at all, the only ventilation and light available being from the door. The majority of these houses are owned by Miss Jarrett, who also owns most of the land. There is not a great deal of actual overcrowding, though it is dangerously near it in some cases. In one house at Tunley 2 adults and 6 children were sleeping in two small bedrooms. In a house in New Buildings a man and wife, 3 lads of working age, a daughter—shortly to be confined, and her husband were sleeping in a house with two small bedrooms. The same state of affairs had very recently existed in another house at Whitebrooks Lane. In quite a number of instances I found grown-up lads and their sisters occupying the same bedroom, and I was assured that it was entirely owing to the impossibility of getting houses in those parts.

The number of inmates is occasionally largely in excess of the accompanying figures, as when grown-up children return for their holidays, from service, etc., sometimes even bringing friends with them. In one house at Doglands there were 8 or 10 such on the occasion of my visit.

Dilapidations and faulty construction, bad enough to necessitate my condemning the property, only exists in a very few cases, but there are a very large number of cottages of such a miserable character that they must be detrimental to the moral and bodily health of the occupants.

I was particularly struck by the want of attention to such matters as the provision of good rain-water shooting and down pipes, and good sills to the doors, the absence of which does so much to make the houses damp, and by the number of houses where the windows, especially in the living rooms, were so constructed that they could not be opened. These defects were most noticeable on the property of Miss Jarrett, and in some houses at Tunley owned by Mr. J. Moon.

I am of opinion that more houses are required. I made careful inquiries at every house I went to whether they would like something better, and the answer was in the affirmative in a large number of cases.

Camerton pit employs about 400 men. I was told that many of them have to walk two to three miles to their work.

Dunkerton pit, just outside the parish, employs a large number of men, I believe about 600, Some of these live in Camerton, and I am informed that more would do so if they had houses to go into. The Dunkerton Colliery Co. erected a block of houses for their employés, but the men, I am told, do not like taking them, as, if they leave the Colliery employ for any reason, they have to leave their house as well. I was also told that many young people wishing to marry, though at work in the parish, have to seek a dwelling outside, and this would seem to be correct, as in the older parts of Camerton I did not find a single habitable house void. I think 50 houses could be put up with the certainty of their being occupied at once, and I believe that this number would have to be quickly increased.

Excellent sites exist in the neighbourhood of Red Hill. It appears to me there is a crying necessity for better accommodation.

The majority of the old houses are on the estate of Miss Jarrett; other owners of unsatisfactory house property are Messrs. J. Gullock, Geo. Gibbons, Job Moon, Wm. Smith, all at Tunley; Newth at Carlingcott; Whittaker at Peasedown; and some of the dwellings are among the worst in this or any other Sanitary District.

2

Every working man's house should have, in my opinion, 3 bedrooms, living room, kitchen and wash-house.

You will see by the accompanying list that few houses in Old Camerton fulfil this requirement. I enclose a detailed list of all the houses in the Parish. The number of inmates is correct to date.

I have made no comment on remediable defects, such as bad drainage, defective closets, absence of ash pits, etc. I found them in large numbers; some have evidently remained unabated for years, probably since the last inspection, which for Old Camerton was six years ago. This state of things is common to the rest of the district, and must continue until a sufficient staff is provided to deal with the matter effectively.

Your obedient Servant,

R. H. BREW.

To the rear of the bus shelter, behind the hedge line; is 'Slate' field part of the site of where the condemned cottages once stood. In recent years this piece of land which also runs alongside Priston lane was used as a builders yard and a plant depot.

Builder's yard and plant depot

The land has now been cleared and planning permission has been granted for the construction of two new houses.

Ground being prepared ready for construction to commence

Remains of old cottages have been revealed.

Almost opposite the junction to Priston lane, are two adjoining houses on your left; the two houses before field break.

No:1 and No: 2 Tunley View, were built by Major Cayzer as Tied houses for his farm workers.

No: 2 Tunley View is currently the home to Elenor Biggs and her late husband Tony Biggs, they moved in when the houses were brand new in 1964.

Tony was a farm labourer and worked on Tunley farm like his father did before him, Tony worked on the farm for 55 years and was a much loved and respected man.

No: 2 Tunley View

No.1 Tunley View is currently owned by Dave and Nick Offer, they purchased the Tied house from the Jones family in 2005, and it is now a private dwelling.

These houses were built in the gardens of No. 1 and No. 2 Tunley Hill, these would have stood on the road edge, in front of the above houses. Ernie and Doris Sellars and their daughter Hilary lived in No. 1 Tunley Hill and Fred and Florrie Box lived in No. 2 Tunley Hill (old cottages).

Chapter 3

Passing the two cottages on the opposite side of the road, you will see a large stone building hidden behind some trees, adjacent to Priston lane. This is Tunley Farm House, built from white lias stone that would have been quarried locally and is believed to have been built in the late 1700's.

Tunley Farm House 2014

A beautiful view looking up to Tunley Farm in the distance

Tunley Farm stands proud on the top of Tunley hill and is surrounded by beautiful shades of green fields, with sheep and cattle grazing; edged with hedgerows; stretching out like a patchwork quilt as far as the eye can see.

Tunley house was examined in 1984 by a conservation officer who found two borrowed light windows in stone frames with small ogee mouldings, a late 17th century style in NE Somerset.

The map below is dated 1770, you can clearly see Tunley Farm, reference number: MM1 and NN1.

1770 Map of North East Somerset

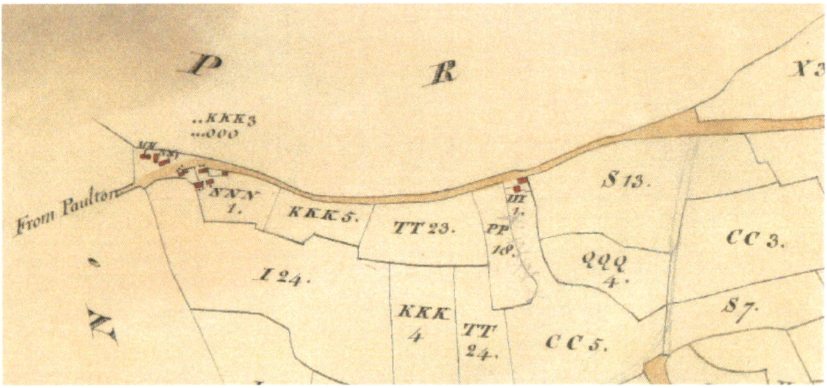

Reverend John Skinner carried out many excavations and found a variety of important archaeological finds. He lived in the Old Rectory near St Peter's Church, Camerton from 1800 to 1839. He was a learned antiquarian, an artist, a poet and scholar. He kept a diary of everyday life, his diary became his confidant but most of all he was a dutiful county priest (please see volume no: 5).

An ancient Camp used to be on the site of the Tunley estate.

An early map of Camerton Parish sketched by Rev John Skinner in the early 1800's.

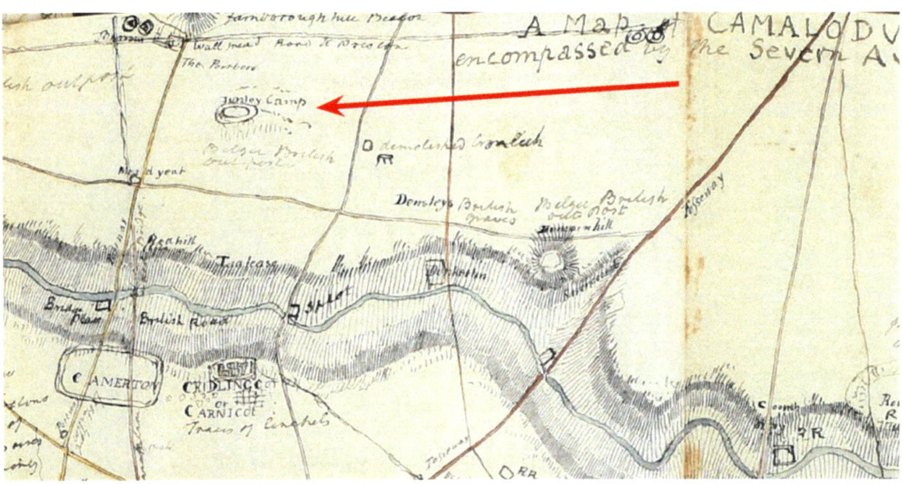

Tunley Hill Camp/Fort

Local sketches and early ordnance survey maps of Camerton parish, show a circular shape, representing a Camp/Fort that used to be located on the top of Tunley Hill.

Tunley Hill is the highest point in Camerton parish and is believed to be the site of an Iron Age Hill Fort. During the 1950's and1960s, several archaeologists carried out excavations, no surface finds or artefacts were discovered. The remains of this hill fort are now so meagre that it is difficult to assess its original form. It has been considerably ploughed down and only its Western side consisting of a scarp up to 4.9 m high is well defined.

Ordnance survey map dated 1817

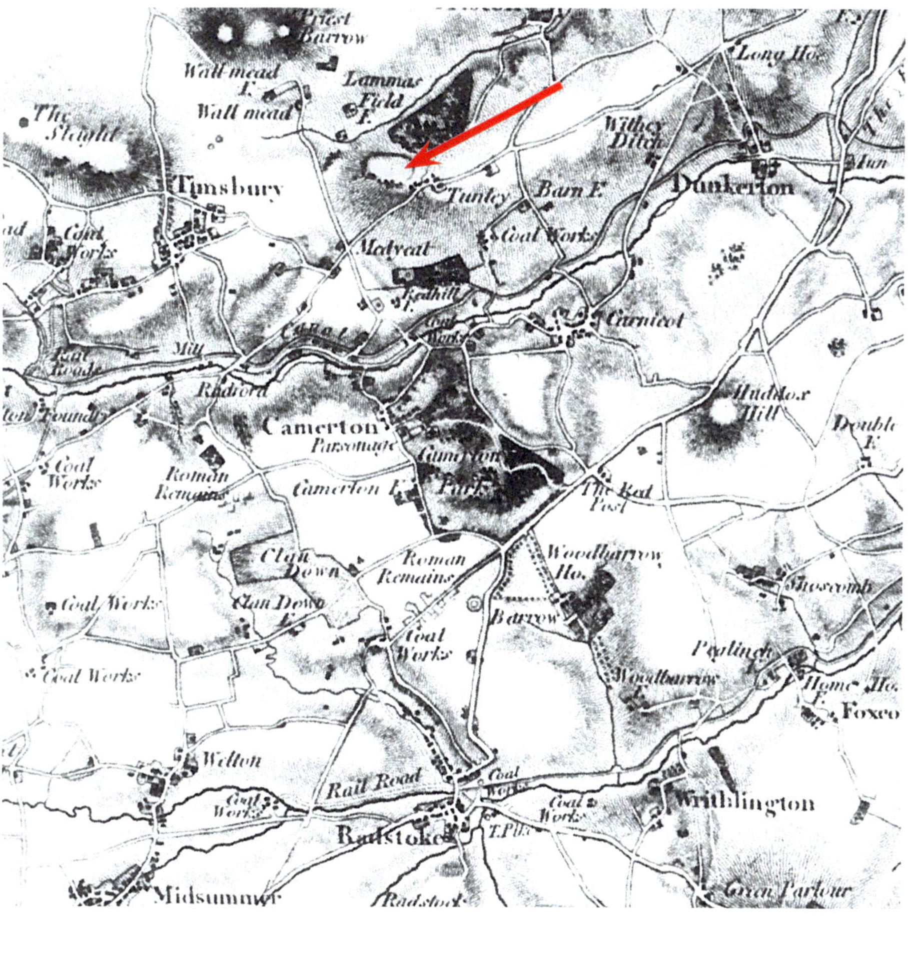

Some of the later ordnance survey maps show either a camp or a fort, also double dotted lines indicating where a 'Prehistoric track' used to lead from and to.

Ordnance survey map dated 1969

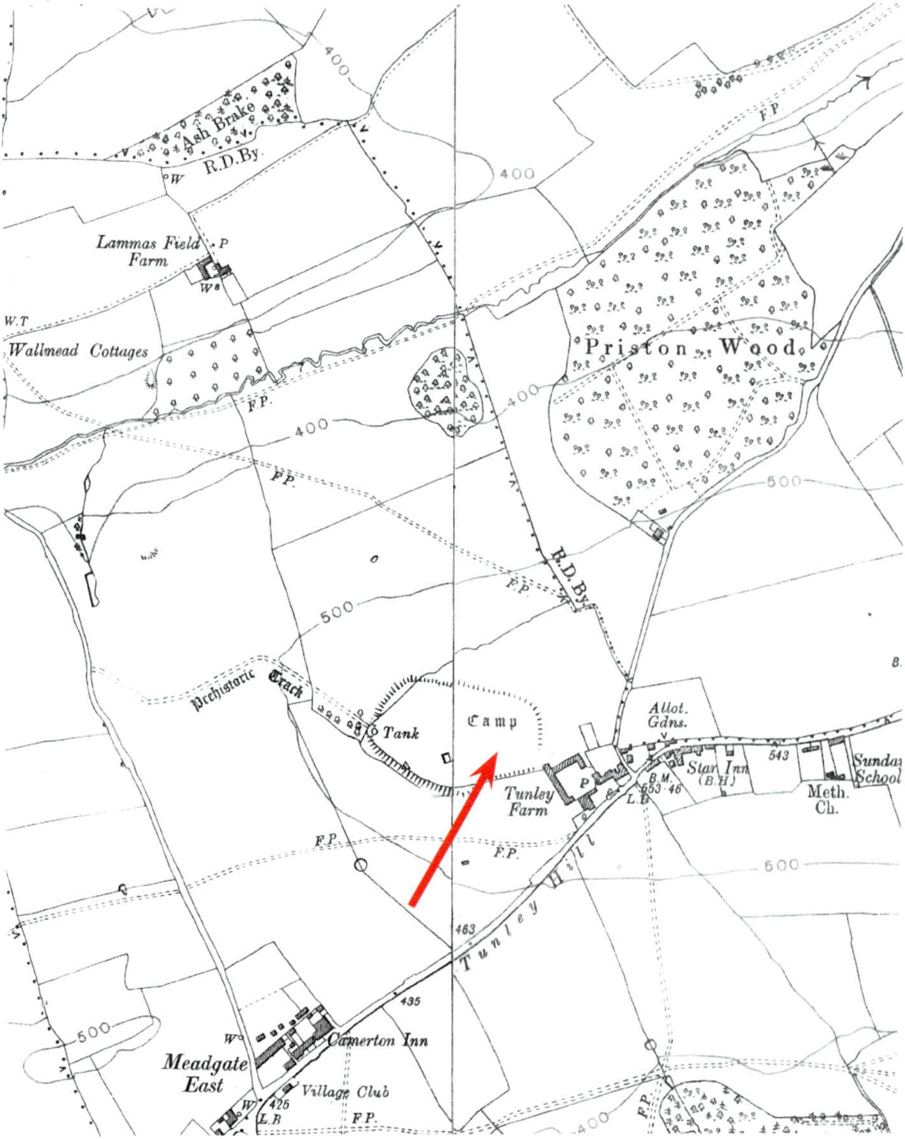

The Kembery Family – have farmed the land around Camerton for over 200 years. Records show some members of the family as being 'Overseers' covering Camerton and surrounding villages. Also other members being 'Sidesmen' for St Peters Church in Camerton.

The handwritten letter below has been in the family for over 200 years.

1793 Letter to the Churchwardens and the Overseers

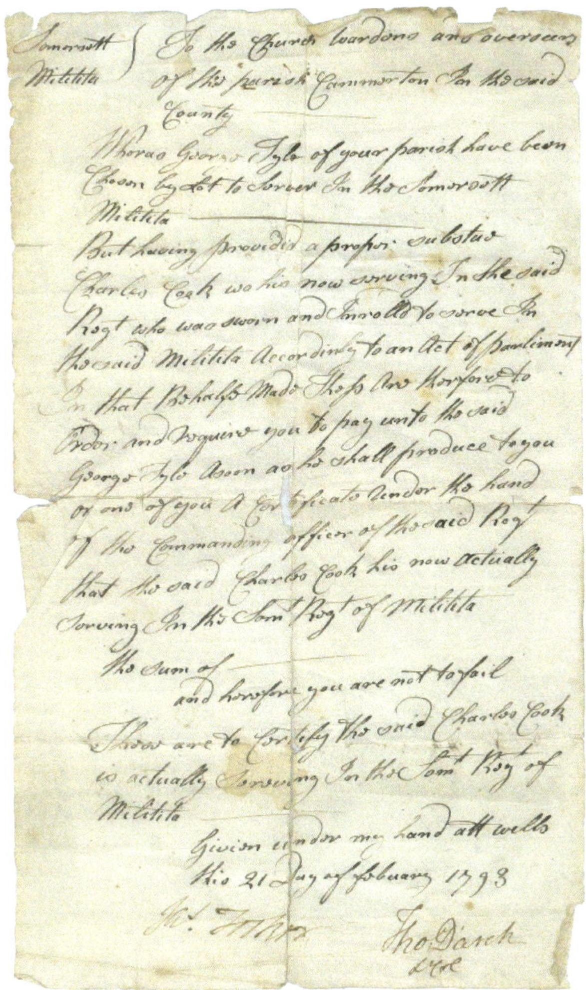
Somersett Militia } To the Church wardens and overseers of the parish Cammerton In the said County

Wheras George Tyle of your parish have been Chosen by Lot to Server In the Somersett Militia

But having providid a proper substu Charles Cook wo his now serving In the said Regt who was sworn and Inrolled to serve In the said Militia According to an Act of parliament In that Behalf Made These Are therfore to Order and require you to pay unto the said George Tyle Assoon as he shall produce to you or one of you A Certificate under the hand of the Commanding officer of the said Regt that the said Charles Cook his now Actually Serving In the Somt Regt of Militia

the sum of
and herefore you are not to fail

These are to Certify the said Charles Cook is actually Serving In the Somt Regt of Militia

Given under my hand att wells this 21 Day of febuary 1793

[illegible] Tho Darch

The above letter was written to the Church Wardens and Overseers of the Parish of Camerton. It confirms George Tyler and Charles Cook being chosen to volunteer for the Militia in Somerset.

The Camerton estate was owned by James Stephens Esq, he was the squire of the day and lived in the old mansion house that stood near St Peter's Church.

In 1799 James Kembery leased Tunley Farm from James Stephens Esq. James Kembery was 45 years of age, his first wife Mary having died, he remarried Sarah Young who was (19 years his junior). Records show James had one daughter 'Susanah' who in 1799 was 9 years of age but there is uncertainty as to whose daughter she was, Mary or Sarah.

Below is a copy of the lease agreement dated 14th October 1799

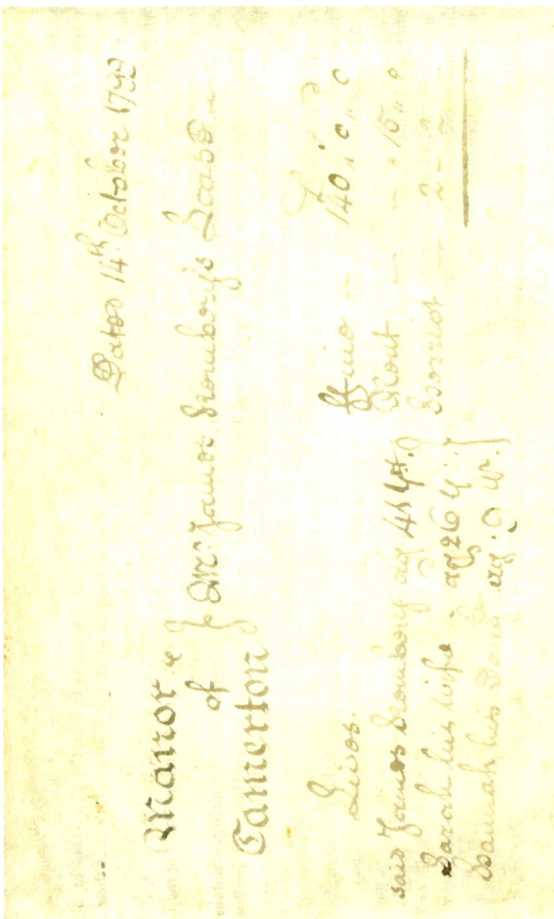

Indenture – this was made up during the reign of George the third, an agreement made between James Stephens Esq of Camerton House in the County of Somerset and James Kembery of Tunley Farm in the said parish of Camerton and County of Somerset.

Extracts from inside the Lease

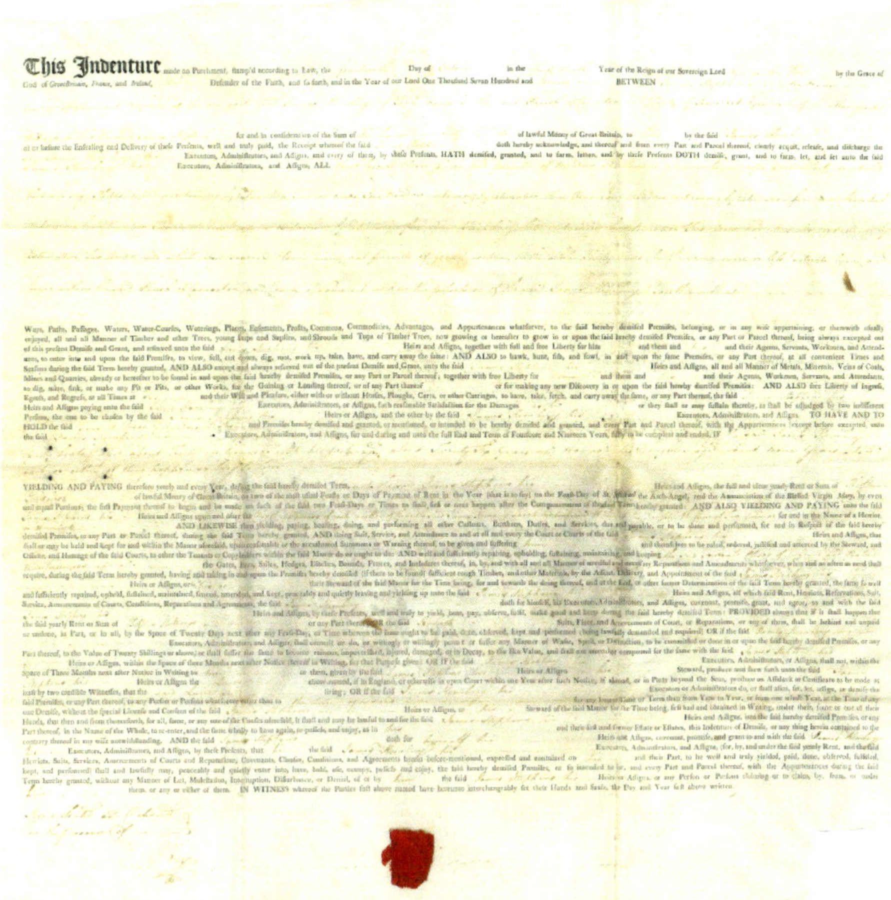

Wax seal and signature of James Stephens Esq

There was limited access to banks as we know today, often if people needed money they would ask a friend or neighbour.

On 19th October 1799 James Kembery agreed a loan between Susanna Haynes and himself for the sum of £400, a considerable sum of money at that time.

A bond agreement made up during the reign of George III

One Penny Pr Sheet
G.R

Know all Men by these presents That I James Kembery of Tonley Farm in the parish of Cameton in the County of Somerset Yeoman am held and firmly bound to Susanna Haynes of the parish of Westbury under the Plain in the County of Wilts Widow in the penal Sum of Eight Hundred Pounds of Good and lawfull Money of Great Britain To be paid to the said Susanna Haynes or her certain Attorney Executors Administrators or Assigns For the true payment whereof I bind myself my Heirs Executors and Administrators and every of them firmly by these Presents Sealed with my Seal Dated this nineteenth Day of October in the thirty ninth Year of the Reign of our Sovereign Lord George the Third by the grace of God of Great Britain France and Ireland King Defender of the Faith and so forth and in the Year of our Lord One Thousand Seven hundred and Ninety nine

The Condition of this Obligation is such That if the above Bounden James Kembery his Heirs Executors or Administrators shall and do well and truly pay or Cause to be paid unto the above named Susanna Haynes her Executors Administrators or Assigns the full Sum of Four hundred pounds of Good and lawfull Money of Great Britain with lawful Interest for the same at and after the rate of five pounds by the hundred by the Year on the nineteenth day of April next ensuing the date hereof clear of all Taxes and Deductions whatsoever without Fraud or further delay Then this Obligation to be void and of none effect or else to remain in full force and Virtue

Sealed and Delivered being first duly stamped in the presence of

James Kembery

[illegible]

Henry Broad[illegible] his Clerk

James Kembery and his family ran a dairy farm at Tunley Farm, the herd would have been 'British Short Horn' cattle producing milk, cheese and butter. There would have been some sheep, a few pigs and some hens on the farm. The local soil is clayey, subsoil is various, the greater portion being oolite and lias stone.

A typical British Short Horn Bull for this period pictured below:

In case of an invasion by Napoleon's French army, Samuel Day Esq, the deputy lieutenant was instructed to raise a militia, Reverend John Skinner took control and formed a group of volunteers. He drew up a list of volunteers from Camerton village on 6 December 1803.

Below is a copy of the handwritten letter by Reverend John Skinner to Samuel Day Esq (Deputy Lieutenant (Division of Somerset).

Front of letter

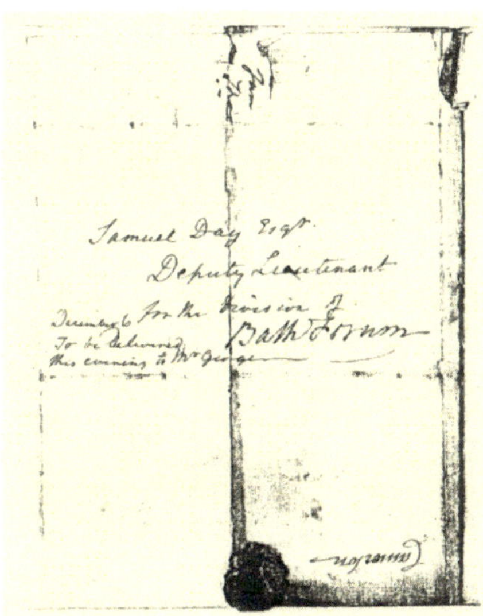

Samuel Day Esqr.
Deputy Lieutenant
for the Division of
Bath Forum
December 6
To be delivered
this evening to Mr George

James Kembery is listed as No: 4 (Overseer of Waggons)

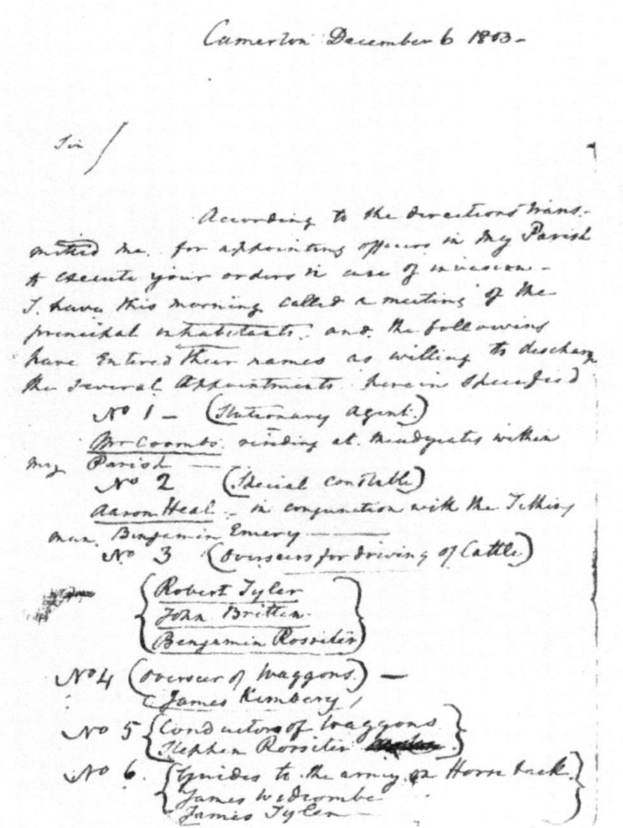

Camerton December 6 1803

Sir/

According to the directions transmitted me for appointing officers in my Parish to execute your orders in case of invasion. I have this morning called a meeting of the principal inhabitants and the following have entered their names as willing to discharge the several appointments herein specified.

No 1 – (Stationary Agent)
Mr Coombs. Residing at Meadgates within my Parish.

No 2 (Special Constable)
Aaron Heal:- in conjunction with the Tything man, Benjamin Emery.

No 3 (Overseers for driving of Cattle)
Robert Tyler
John Britten
Benjamin Rossiter

No 4 (Overseer of Waggons)
James Kembery

No 5 (Conductor of Waggons)
Stephen Rossiter

No 6 Guides to the army on horseback
James Widcombe
James Tyler

No 7 Baker
William Gould bakes about a sack of flour a week and is the only one who bakes for sale.

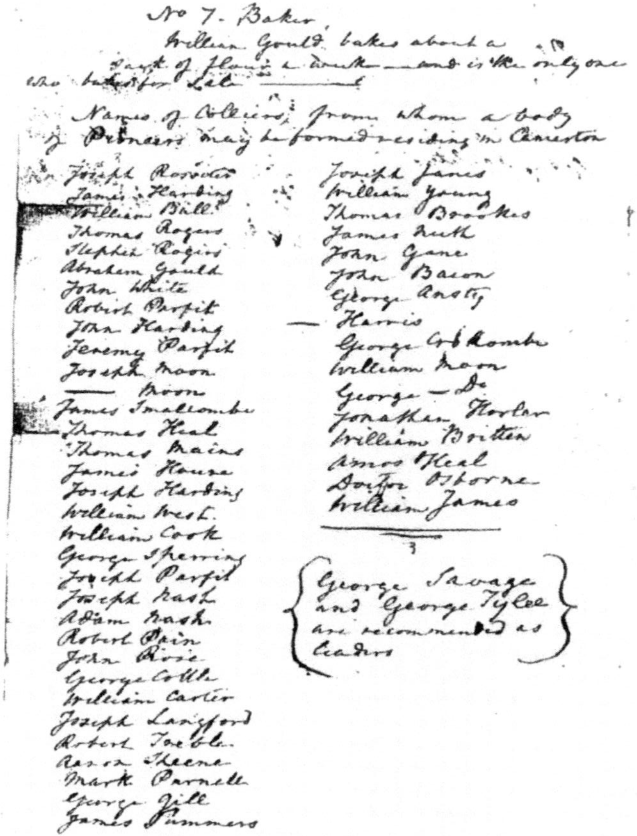
No 7. Baker
William Gould bakes about a sack of flour a week — and is the only one who bakes for sale

Names of Colliers from whom a body of Pioneers may be formed residing in Camerton

Joseph Rossiter	Joseph James
James Harding	William Young
William Ball	Thomas Brooks
Thomas Rogers	James Nuth
Abraham Gould	John Gane
John White	John Bacon
Robert Parfit	George Ansty
John Harding	______ Harris
Jeremy Parfit	George Crocombe
Joseph Moon	William Moon
______ Moon	George ditto
James Smallcombe	Jonathan Horler
Thomas Heal	William Britten
Thomas Mains	Amos Heal
James House	Doctor Osborne
Joseph Harding	William James
William West	
William Cook	
George Sperring	
Joseph Parfit	
Joseph Nash	George Savage
Adam Nash	and George Tyler
Robert Pain	are recommended as
John Rose	leaders.
George Cottle	
William Carter	
Joseph Langford	
Robert Treble	
Aaron Sheene	
Mark Purnell	
George Gill	
James Summers	

PS. I shall certainly attend in the Town Hall at the stated time tomorrow and should there be any further arrangements or alteration I will endeavour to execute them to the best of my abilities.

I remain Sir
Your most obedient Servant

John Skinner.

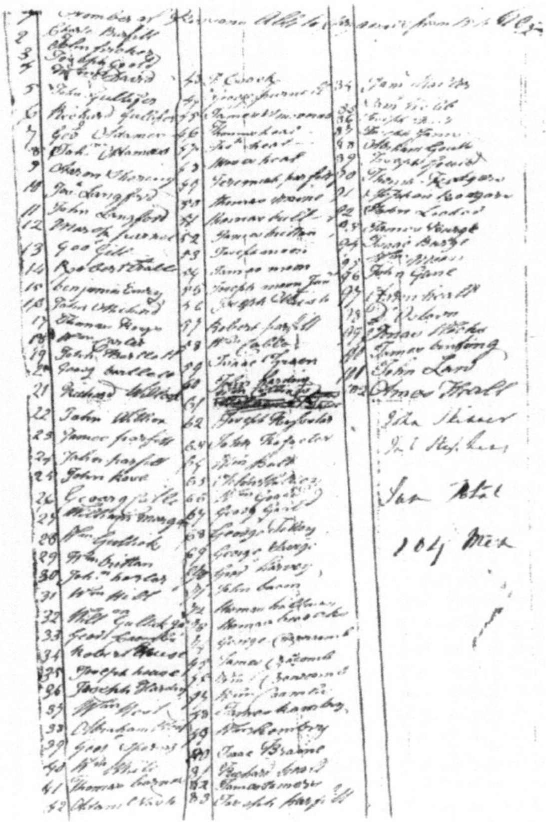

CAMERTON : DEFENCE OF THE REALM
NUMBER OF PERSONS ABLE TO CARRY ARMS FROM 15 TO 60

1	Charles Burfitt	50	Thomas Maine	99	Jonas Weekes
2	Joh Fricker ?	51	Thomas Bull	100	Ja Binding
3	Joseph Goold	52	James Brittan	101	John Lard
4	Wm David	53	Joseph Moon	102	Amos Heall
5	John Gullifer	54	James Moon		
6	Richard Gullifer	55	Joseph Moon Jnr		John Skinner
7	Geo Adames	56	Joseph Naish		
8	Joh[n] Adames	57	Robert Parfitt		Ja ? Stephens
9	Aaron Shering	58	Wm Coble		
10	Jas Langford	59	Isaac Green		
11	John Langford	60	John Harding		In total
12	Mark ? Parnel	61	Wm Collins		104 men
13	Geo Gill	62	Joseph Rossitor ??		
14	Robert Trabie ??	63	John Rossitor ??		
15	Benjamin Emry	64	Wm Bull		
16	John Michard	65	JohnWolley		
17	Thomas Roys	66	Wm Goold		
18	Wm Carter	67	George Gould ?		
19	John Bartlett	68	George Tiley		
20	Georg Barlett	69	George Savage ??		
21	Richard Willcox	70	Geo Harvey		
22	John Willcox	71	John Baron		
23	James Parfitt	72	Thomas Hillman		
24	John Parfitt	73	Norman ?? Crooks		
25	John Rove ?	74	George C...rumb ???		
26	Geoarg Cotle	75	James Croscomb		
27	William Morgan	76	Wm Barnscomb ??		
28	Wm Gullick	77	Wm Coambes		
29	Wm Brittan	78	James Kembry		
30	Joh[n] Horler	79	Wm Kembry		
32	Wm Hill	80	Isaac Braine		
32	Will[m] Gullick	81	Ricard Heall		
33	Geor Caombs	82	James Somers		
34	Robert House	83	Joseph Parfitt		
35	Joseph House	84	Jam[s] Waller		
36	Joseph Harding	85	Sam[l] Webb		
37	Wm West	86	Joseph Webb		
38	Abraham West	87	Joseph James		
39	Geor Spering	88	Abram Gould		
40	Wm White	89	Joseph Gould		
41	Thomas Carnet ?	90	Thomas Rodgers		
42	Adam Vauh ???	91	Stephen Rodgers		
43	J. Coock	92	John Loker		
44	George Parnell	93	James Burge		
45	James Smoombs ??	94	Isaac Burge		
46	Thomas Heal	95	Wm Moon		
47	Jas[s] Heal	96	John Gane		
48	Moses Heal	97	Aron Heall		
49	Jeremiah Parfitt	98	D[r] Osborn [=Doctor?]		

THIS TRANSCRIPTION HAS SOME ERRORS.

There are many local Camerton men that volunteered for the defence of the realm and their names are listed by Reverend John Skinner, many of these families still live in the parish of Camerton today.

End of letter by Reverend John Skinner showing his signature

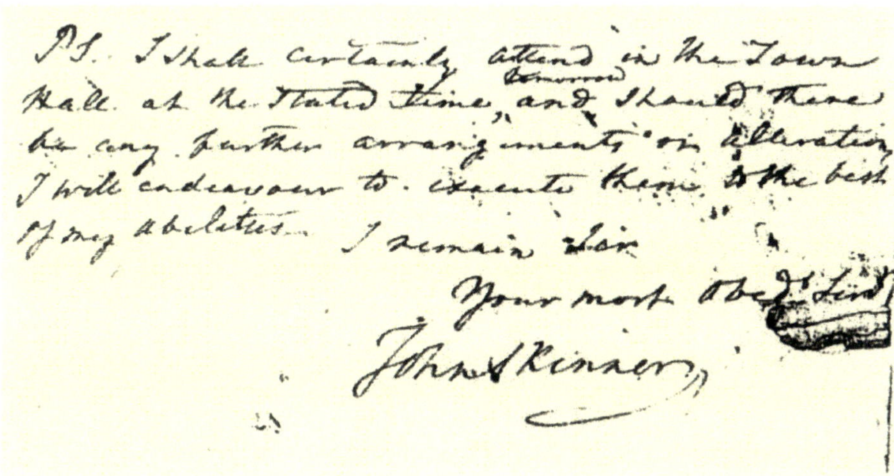

P.S. I shall certainly attend in the Town Hall at the Stated time, tomorrow and should there be any further arrangements or alteration, I will endeavour to execute them to the best of my abilities. I remain Sir

Your most Obedt Servt

John Skinner

The Threatened Invasion

July 1803 – Revd John Skinner wrote the following in his diary:

"I received a letter from Mr Briant Clerk of the General meetings, dated, Ilminster, July 9th 1803; requesting me to summon my parishioners and lay before them plans adopted for the internal defence of the country in case of invasion. Schedules were also delivered which were to be filled up with the names of those willing to serve, either as volunteers in arms, or as overseers of waggons, or guides on horse –back to conduct the army, or as pioneers; the live and dead stock of the parish was also required to be returned by the farmers, with the number of their waggons and teams, and the names of the servants who might conduct them.

Accordingly I gave notice for the assembling of the inhabitants, and as Mr Stephens was at home, with the office of Deputy Lieutenant for the division (Bath Forum) I thought the gentleman would be the proper person to take the lead in the business. We met at his house, and the schedules were filled up according to the directions we had received.

I therein entered my name as a volunteer in the ranks, supposing I could render my country more effective service in this manner than in any other. Mr Stephens and about a dozen besides, having also enrolled their names as willing to bear arms, but there was no return made of Pioneers. Some days afterwards I received letter from the Bishop, wherein he advised the Clergy to remain quiet at their Livings and take upon them the measures to be adopted in their several parishes. This mode of procedure, furthered by the advice of General Simes, his Lordship recommended as the best the Clergy of the Diocese could follow. I therefore withdrew my name from the list of volunteers, and resolved to render myself as serviceable as possible in the more pacific office which might be allotted me; nevertheless resolving privately to lern the Broad Sword exercise, to be prepared in case of emergency".

Sunday, July 17

"I called a General Meeting of the inhabitants of Camerton (by notice which I read in Church) for the following day at 10 o'clock, but, as there happened to be a field day for the Volunteers at the same time, only three of the parishioners attended. Not being able to enter upon business with so small a number I adjourned the meeting til the following day at the same hour. In the interim I rode around the parish, calling at the farmer's houses to request they would attend the meeting, otherwise it would be impossible for me to make the requisite returns.

In the evening I called to Mr Stephens to speak concerning a body of pioneers, as the colliers did not put themselves forward as they had done at Radstock and elsewhere. Mr Stephens argued that he had no power to appoint a Company of pioneers from his own Volunteers, and that he thought would be sufficient. I did not agree with him first, because his own complement (which according to the proposals he made to the Government was to be full 600 men) would thereby, be diminished; secondly, if the Volunteers were to be ordered from home, the Pioneers amongst them could afford no local service, supposing the approach of an enemy.

I therefore resolved at the meeting to endeavour to persuade a Corps of pioneers to enrol themselves from amongst the colliers to be prepared to act on the spot in case of emergency."

Number of Persons between the ages of Fifteen and Sixty willing to serve with Arms

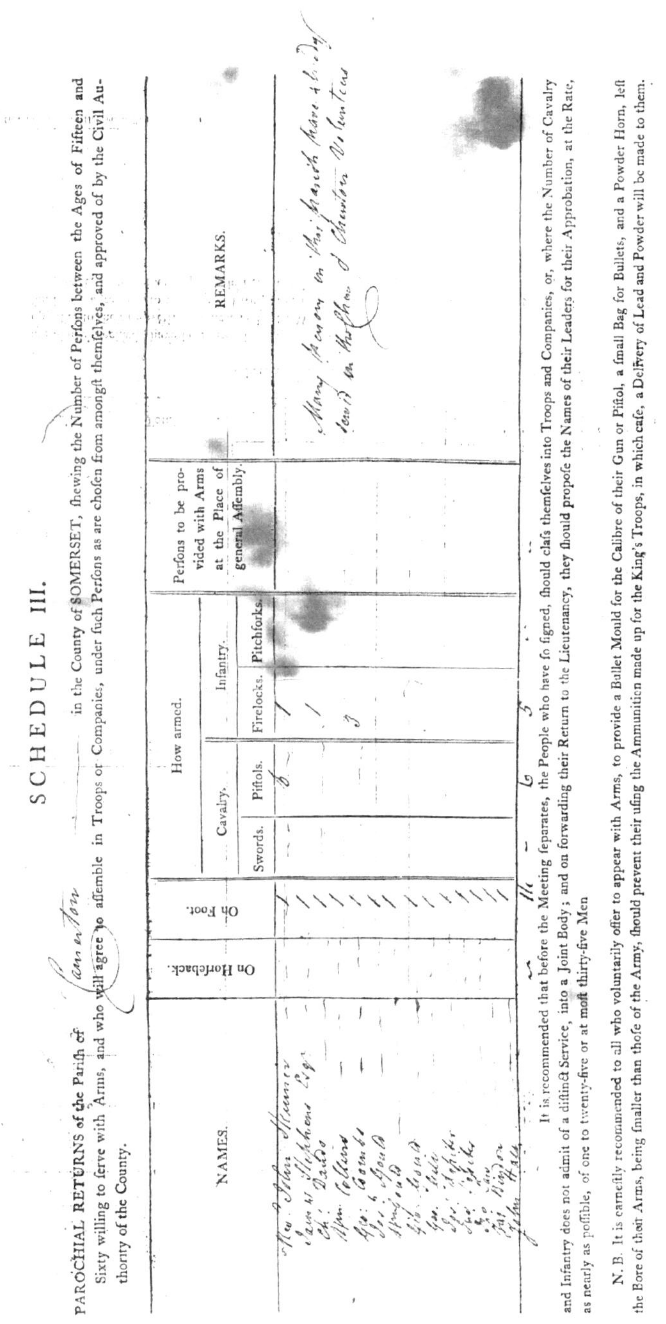

SCHEDULE III.

PAROCHIAL RETURNS of the Pariſh of Camerton in the County of SOMERSET, ſhewing the Number of Perſons between the Ages of Fifteen and Sixty willing to ſerve with Arms, and who will agree to aſſemble in Troops or Companies, under ſuch Perſons as are choſen from amongſt themſelves, and approved of by the Civil Authority of the County.

NAMES.	On Horſeback.	On Foot.	How armed. Cavalry. Swords.	Piſtols.	Infantry. Firelocks.	Pitchforks.	Perſons to be provided with Arms at the Place of general Aſſembly.	REMARKS.
Rev. John Skinner		1		6	1			
Saml. Stephens Esq.		1			1			Many persons in this parish have [illegible] serv'd in the [illegible] & Chewton Volunteers
Ch: Dando		1						
Wm. Collins		1			3			
Geo: Coombs		1						
Jos. Gould		1						
Wm. Gould		1						
Gil. Gould		1						
Geo. [illegible]		1						
Jos. Sopiter		1						
Jno. Sopiter		1						
Jno. [illegible]		1						
Jas. Bingdon		1						
John Hall		1						
		14		6	5			

It is recommended that before the Meeting ſeparates, the People who have ſo ſigned, ſhould claſs themſelves into Troops and Companies, or, where the Number of Cavalry and Infantry does not admit of a diſtinct Service, into a Joint Body; and on forwarding their Return to the Lieutenancy, they ſhould propoſe the Names of their Leaders for their Approbation, at the Rate, as nearly as poſſible, of one to twenty-five or at moſt thirty-five Men

N. B. It is earneſtly recommended to all who voluntarily offer to appear with Arms, to provide a Bullet Mould for the Calibre of their Gun or Piſtol, a ſmall Bag for Bullets, and a Powder Horn, leſt the Bore of their Arms, being ſmaller than thoſe of the Army, ſhould prevent their uſing the Ammunition made up for the King's Troops, in which caſe, a Delivery of Lead and Powder will be made to them.

Kembery - Family continued:

22nd September 1805 Bond loan for £100 between Mr James Kembery Esq and Mr Hon Richmond Hill

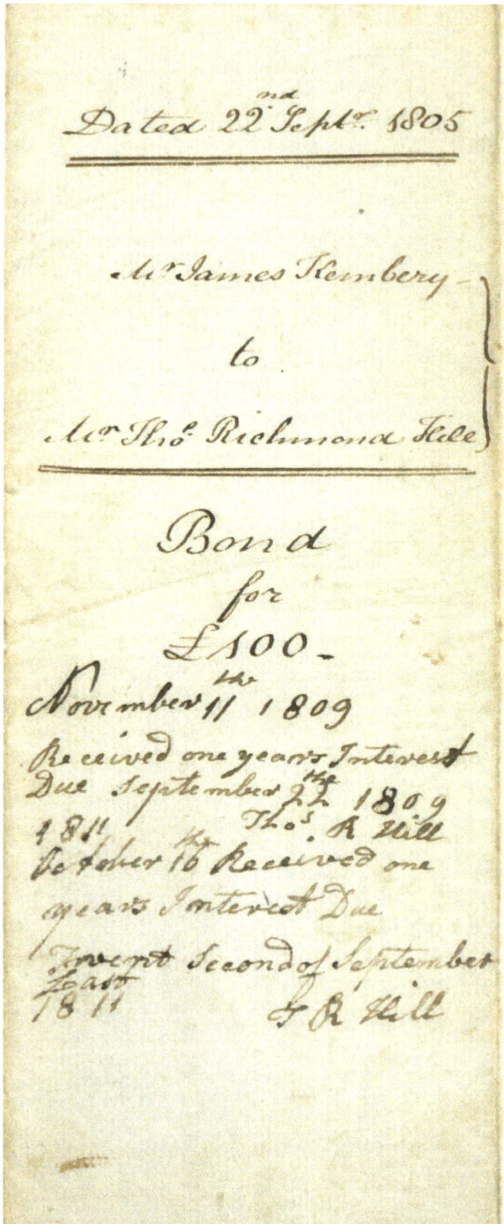

Dated 22nd Septr. 1805

Mr James Kembery

to

Mr Thos. Richmond Hill

Bond
for
£100 -

November 11th 1809
Received one years Interest
Due September 22nd 1809
Thos. R Hill

1811
October 16th Received one
years Interest Due
Twenty Second of September
Last
1811 T R Hill

A hand written letter to the land owner from a tenant asking for clarification on the conditions of their tenancy. This letter has been handed down to generations of the Kembery family and believed to be in connection to Tunley Farm. Unfortunately the signature is too illegible to establish the name of the tenant.

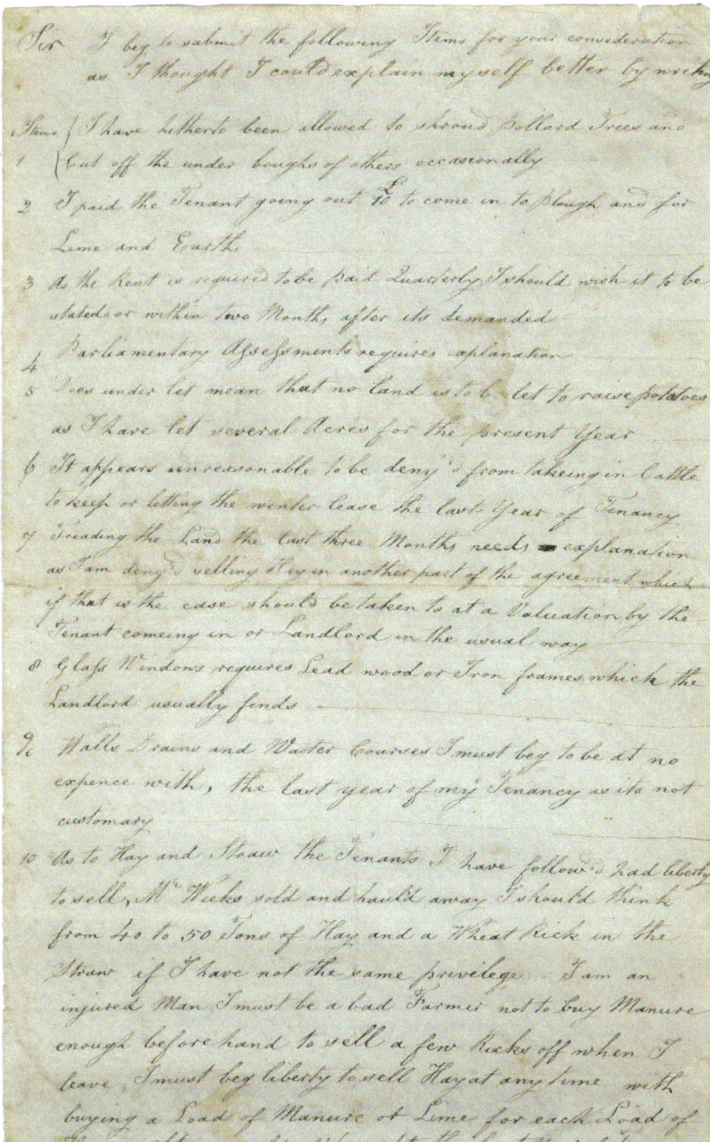

Sir I beg to submit the following Items for your consideration as I thought I could explain myself better by writing

Items 1 { I have hitherto been allowed to shroud Pollard Trees and Cut off the under boughs of others occasionally

2 I paid the Tenant going out £10 to come in to plough and for Lime and Earth

3 As the Rent is required to be paid Quarterly I should wish it to be stated or within two Months after its demanded

4 Parliamentary Assessments requires explanation

5 Does under let mean that no land is to be let to raise potatoes as I have let several Acres for the present Year

6 It appears unreasonable to be deny'd from takeing in Cattle to keep or letting the winter lease the last Year of Tenancy

7 Treading the Land the last three Months needs explanation as I am deny'd selling Hay in another part of the agreement which if that is the case should be taken to at a Valuation by the Tenant comeing in or Landlord in the usual way

8 Glass Windows requires Lead wood or Iron frames which the Landlord usually finds

9 Walls Drains and Water Courses I must beg to be at no expence with, the last year of my Tenancy as its not customary

10 As to Hay and Straw the Tenants I have follow'd had liberty to sell, Mr Weeks sold and hauld away I should think from 40 to 50 Tons of Hay and a Wheat Rick in the Straw if I have not the same previlege I am an injured Man I must be a bad Farmer not to buy Manure enough before hand to sell a few Ricks off when I leave, I must beg liberty to sell Hay at any time with buying a Load of Manure or Lime for each Load of Hay or Straw sold off (except the last Year of Tenancy

Letter side 2

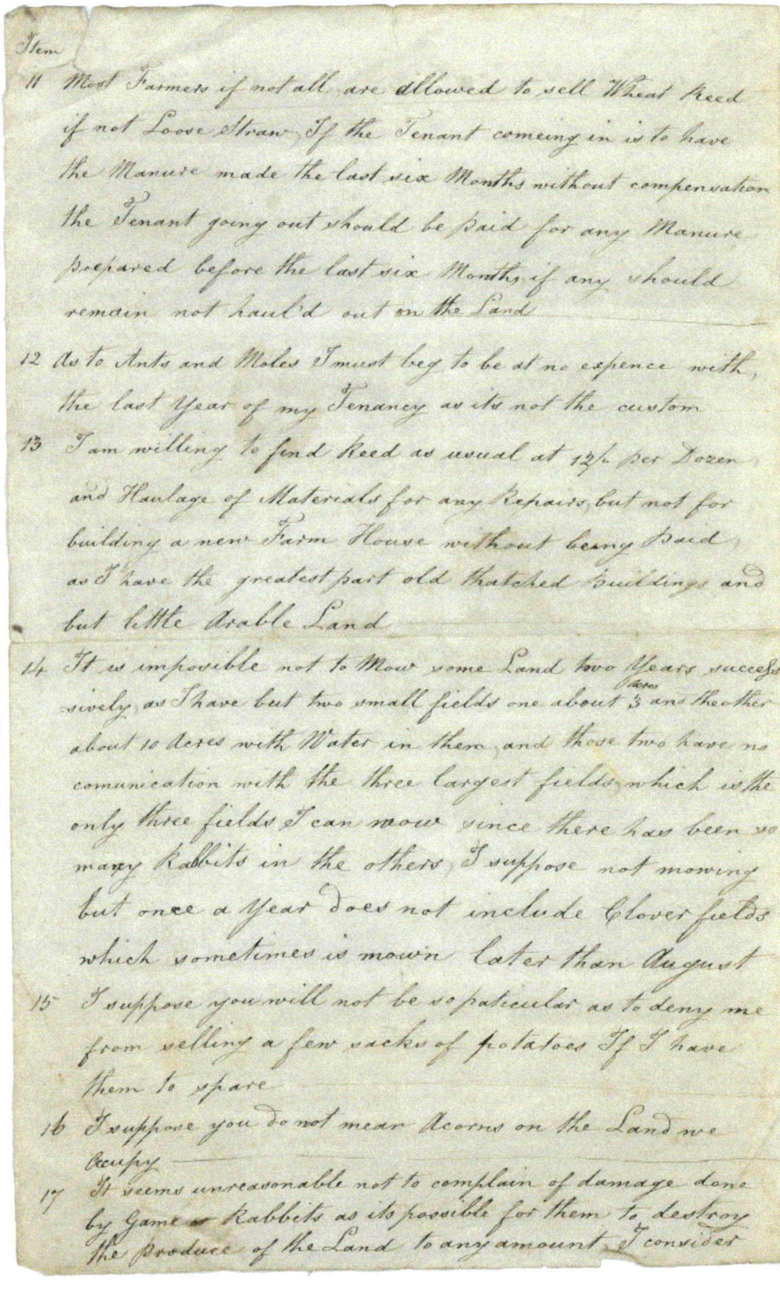

Item

11 Most Farmers if not all are allowed to sell Wheat Reed
if not Loose Straw If the Tenant comeing in is to have
the Manure made the last six Months without compensation
the Tenant going out should be paid for any Manure
prepared before the last six Months if any should
remain not haul'd out on the Land

12 As to Ants and Moles I must beg to be at no expence with,
the last Year of my Tenancy as its not the custom

13 I am willing to find Reed as usual at 12/- per Dozen
and Haulage of Materials for any Repairs, but not for
building a new Farm House without being paid,
as I have the greatest part old thatched Buildings and
but little Arable Land

14 It is impossible not to Mow some Land two Years succes-
-sively as I have but two small fields one about 3 acres and the other
about 10 Acres with Water in them, and those two have no
comunication with the three largest fields which is the
only three fields I can mow since there has been so
many Rabbits in the others I suppose not mowing
but once a Year does not include Clover fields
which sometimes is mown later than August

15 I suppose you will not be so paticular as to deny me
from selling a few sacks of potatoes If I have
them to spare

16 I suppose you do not mean Acorns on the Land we
Occupy

17 It seems unreasonable not to complain of damage done
by Game or Rabbits as its possible for them to destroy
the produce of the Land to any amount I consider

James Kembery died in 1806 and left his second wife Sarah a young widow and mother to Susannah 16 yrs, Robert 7 yrs and James 3 yrs. Sarah remarried John Hicks Esq and moved to Sheephouse Farm, the farm is hidden over the hill to your left as you proceed down Tunley Hill. It is adjacent to the old 'Batch', the name (Batch) was a local name for spoil heaps in the Somerset coalfield, also known as a slag heap.

Picture of Fields and the Batch

The Stephens

Although some properties were owned by individuals, a large portion of Cameton parish including farms, cottages, gardens, fields etc from the 1750s were owned by the Stephens family.

Stephens and the Jarretts - James Stephens had a daughter Anne who married Herbert Newton Jarrett in 1801, they had a son, John Jarrett who was born in 1802. In 1811 Herbert Jarrett died leaving Anne a young widow. In 1816 James Stephens died leaving the Camerton estate to his heir and daughter Anna Jarrett (formerly Stephens). The Jarrett family were wealthy in their own right, their wealth derived from the sugar plantations in the Orange Valley, Jamaica.

Jarrett Family – John Jarrett proposed to Anna Waller but she would not accept his proposal of marriage until he agreed to her conditions; under no circumstances was John's mother to reside with them. John and Anna married in 1823 but moved to a property in Hale, Hampshire. Although mother and son lived separately they worked together as Landlady / lord (please see volume no: 6).

Tunley Farm - It would appear that in 1823 George Sperring had a special arrangement with Anne Jarrett (Widow) and mother to John Jarrett. A sum of £72.10 excluding mining rights to lease Tunley farm for 2000 years by pepper corn law.

Front cover of Indenture agreement dated 1823 below:

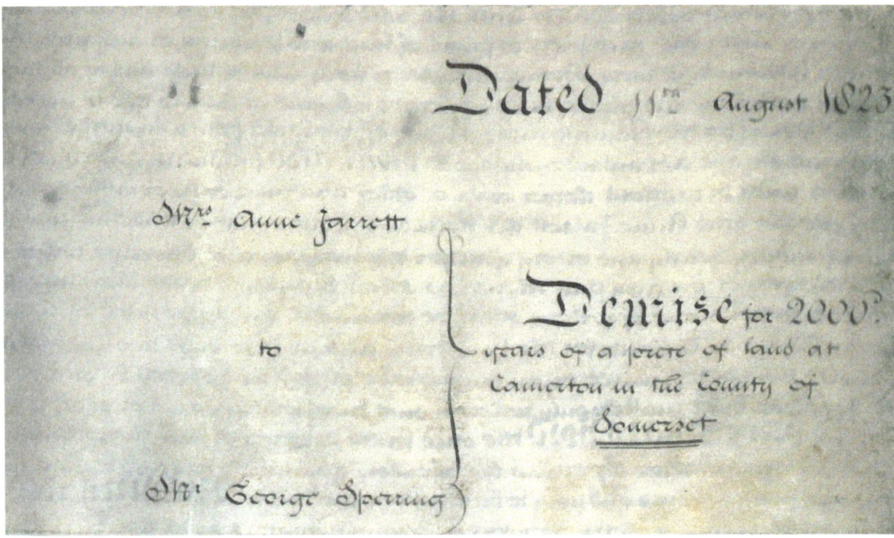

Dated 11th August 1823

Mrs Anne Jarrett

to

Mr George Sperring

Demise for 2000 years of a piece of land at Camerton in the County of Somerset

The signature of Anne Jarrett with wax seal

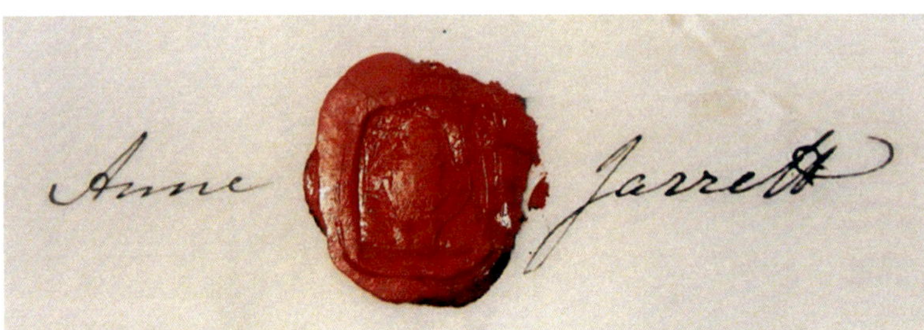

On the 27th December 1823 George Sperring had a partnership with James Holbrook, they took out a mortgage for the sum of £150.

Front cover of Mortgage Agreement below:

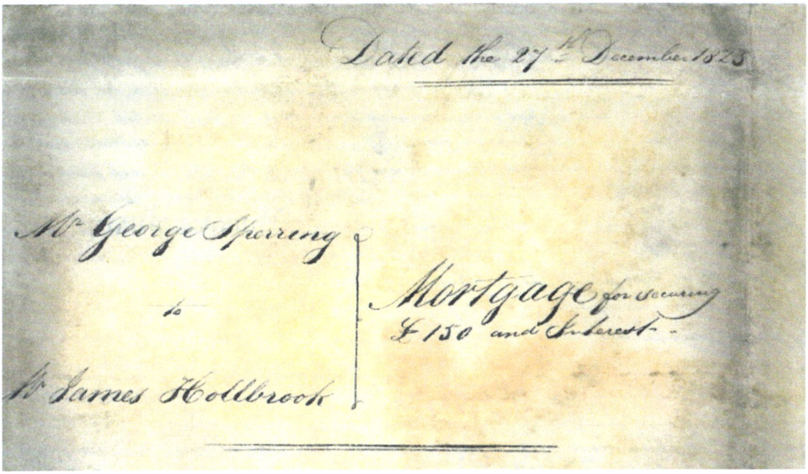
Dated the 27th December 1823

Mr George Sperring

to

Mr James Hollbrook

Mortgage for securing £150 and Interest.

Signature of George Sperring and wax seal

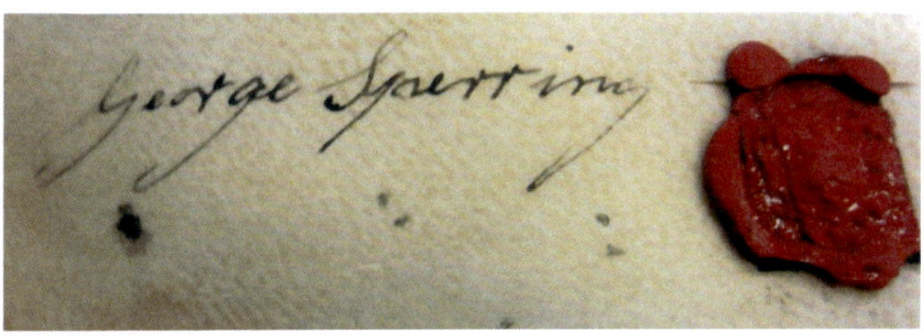

George Sperring and James Holbrook wanted to build 2 houses, they needed a further sum of £350.00 and went into partnership with Henry Bridget-Smith (3 way partnership).

Henry Bridget-Smith's signature and wax seal below:

On the 17th February 1826 George Sperring and James Holbrook paid off their debt to Henry Bridget-Smith with a final instalment of £150 + £50.

George Sperring took out Fire cover to insure Tunley Farm for the amount of £600, he paid one pound and one shilling back in 1827.

Receipt of a Fire certificate below:

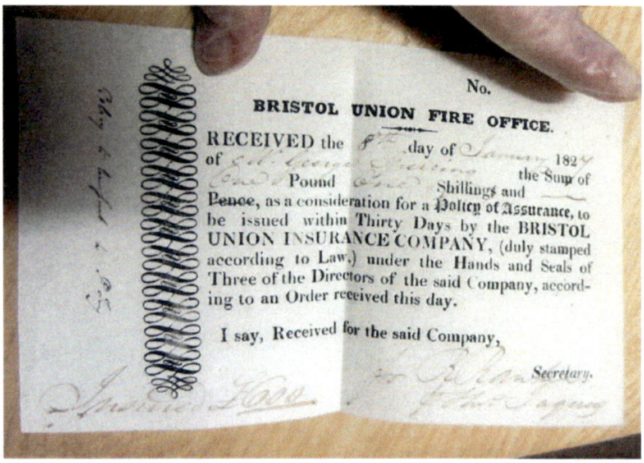
No.

BRISTOL UNION FIRE OFFICE.

RECEIVED the 8th day of January 1827 of Mr George Sperring the Sum of One Pound One Shillings and — Pence, as a consideration for a Policy of Assurance, to be issued within Thirty Days by the BRISTOL UNION INSURANCE COMPANY, (duly stamped according to Law,) under the Hands and Seals of Three of the Directors of the said Company, according to an Order received this day.

I say, Received for the said Company,

Secretary.

Insured £600

On the 2nd January 1827 a legal bond showing a sum of £500 being paid to John Jarrett Esq. On the 30th April 1828 a further agreement was made between George Sperring to transfer the farm, land, cottages and buildings back to John Jarrett Esq, Anne Jarrett was witness to the signatures. A payment of £628 was agreed and paid to George Sperring by John Jarrett esq allowing for a handsome profit.

Front cover of Agreement

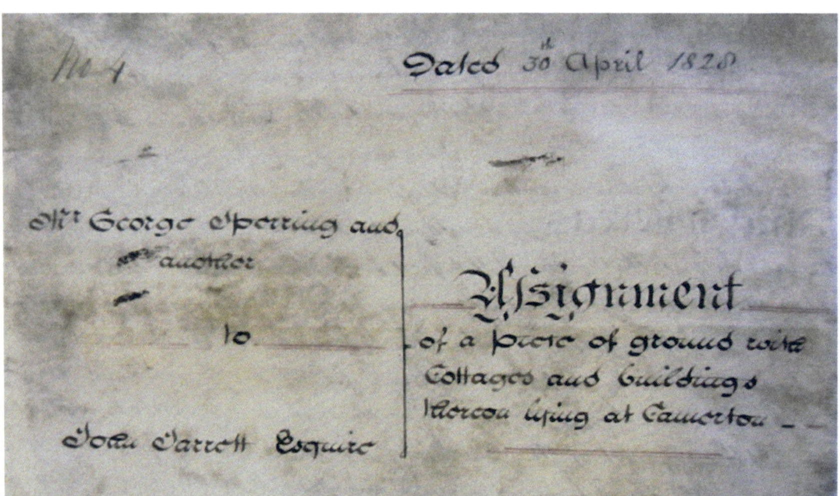
No 4

Dated 30th April 1828

Mr George Sperring and another

to

John Jarrett Esquire

Assignment

of a piece of ground with Cottages and buildings thereon lying at Camerton

Jarrett family continued - In 1830 Mrs Anne Jarrett died at the Old Manor House. Her son John Jarrett inherited the Camerton estate; he and his wife Anna moved into the old manor house. John found plans of a new house his mother had drawn up whilst she was alive. Unfortunately his mother clashed with the local rector, the Reverend John Skinner and dearly wished to live further away from him, the old rectory and the church. To honour his mother's wishes, John invited the family friend and architect George Stanley Repton, to help him design a new house for his wife and himself.

1833 Lease dated 9th January - Inn Mead adjoining Park land

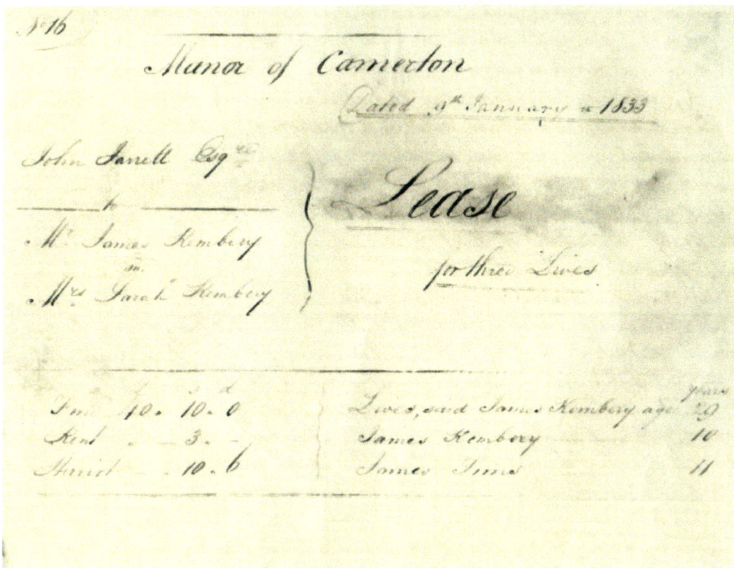

No 16

Manor of Camerton

Dated 9th January 1833

John Jarrett Esqre
to
Mr James Kembery
and
Mrs Sarah Kembery

Lease
for three Lives

	£	s	d
Fine	10.	10.	0
Rent	.	3.	–
Heriot	.	10.	6

Lives, said James Kembery aged	years 29
James Kembery	10
James Sims	11

An agreement between John Jarrett Esq and Mrs Sarah Kembery (widow) her son James, her grandson James and James Simes.

John Jarrett's signature and wax seal

G.S Repton Esq and John Jarrett Esq signatures

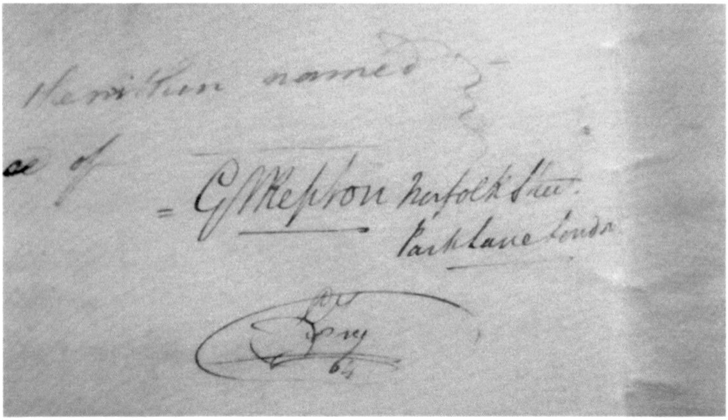

The above witness signature is G.S Repton, he was a personal friend to John Jarrett and today is remembered as a well known architect.

John Jarrett's wife Anna wrote to her brother Wathen monthly, he was a diplomat abroad and Anna enjoyed telling him of all her news. On the 13th May 1833 she wrote him a letter saying "Our house goes on charmingly", "and the first stone was laid yesterday by John". They had almost 2 years of disruption, spending their time travelling around the country visiting relatives and friends. They returned to Camerton for visits and squeezed themselves into what was left of the old house (which was being pulled down so that some materials could be re-used). In the Autumn of 1834 John and Anna (Lord and Lady) moved into their new house; they named it 'Camerton Court'.

News of a baby – After 14 years of being childless, Anna Jarrett felt she had been blessed, she gave birth to a little girl on the 25th January 1838, she was so grateful for a healthy baby and named her Anna Mary. To Anna's surprise and delight she gave birth 2 years later to another daughter, early December 1840, she was named 'Emily Eliza' (please see volume no:5).

Handwritten letter from Anna to her brother Wathen dated 18th October 1837

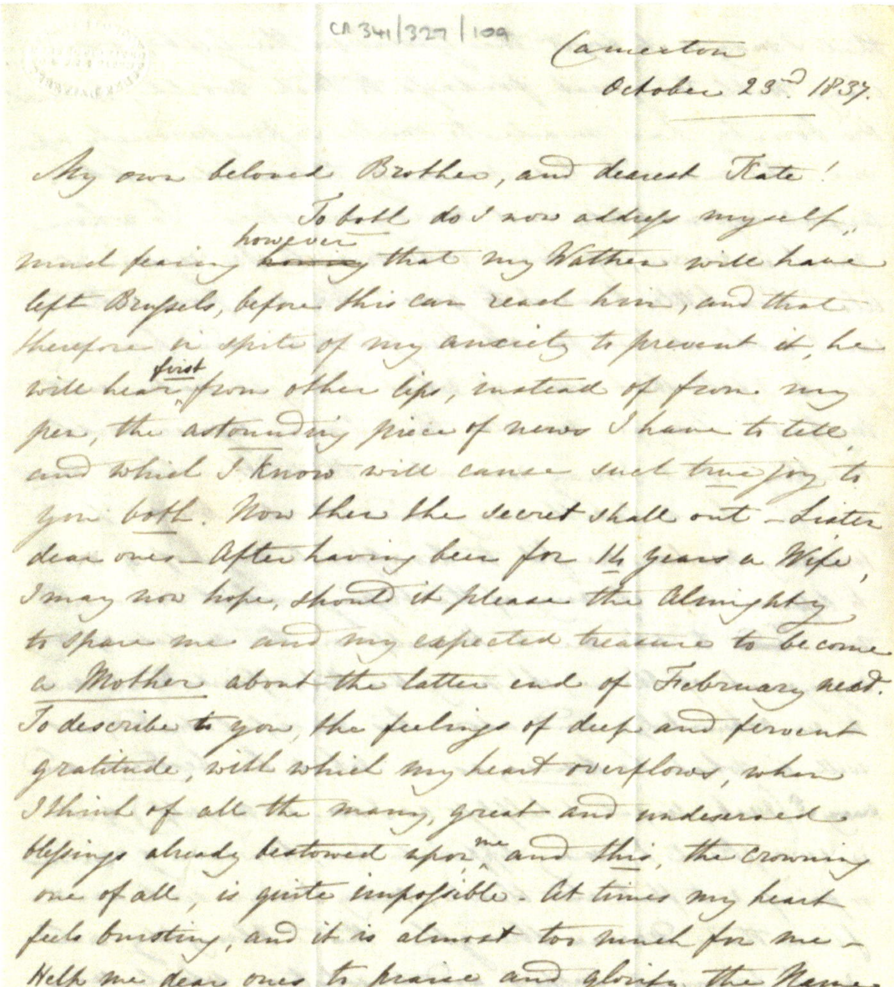

Camerton
October 23rd 1837.

My own beloved Brother, and dearest Kate!

To both do I now address myself, most fearing however that my Wathen will have left Brussels, before this can reach him, and that therefore in spite of my anxiety to prevent it, he will hear first from other lips, instead of from my pen, the astounding piece of news I have to tell, and which I know will cause such true joy to you both. Now then the secret shall out – Listen dear ones – After having been for 14 years a Wife, I may now hope, should it please the Almighty to spare me and my expected treasure to become a Mother about the latter end of February next. To describe to you, the feelings of deep and fervent gratitude, with which my heart overflows, when I think of all the many, great and undeserved blessings already bestowed upon me and this, the crowning one of all, is quite impossible – At times my heart feels bursting, and it is almost too much for me – Help me dear ones, to praise and glorify the Name of that Gracious and Heavenly Father, who has thus abundantly blessed me, and pray for me too that I may become daily less unworthy of his benefits.

Extract from page 2 - Would you could see my darling husband's happy face, and hear his joyous voice.

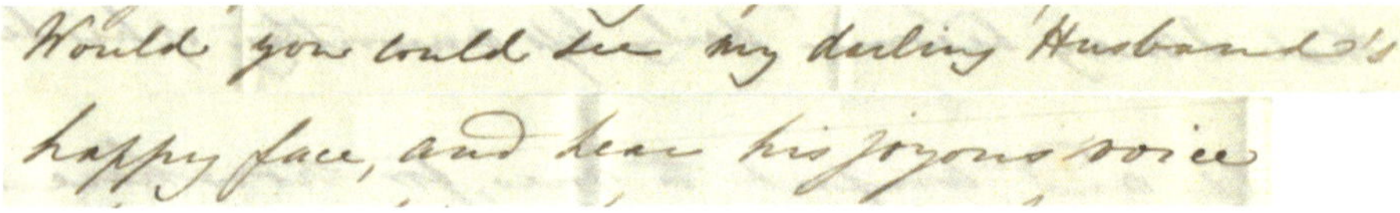
Would you could see my darling Husband's happy face, and hear his joyous voice

Extract from page 3 - My dearest and kind friend Lady Elizabeth has promised to be with me, in my hour of trial.

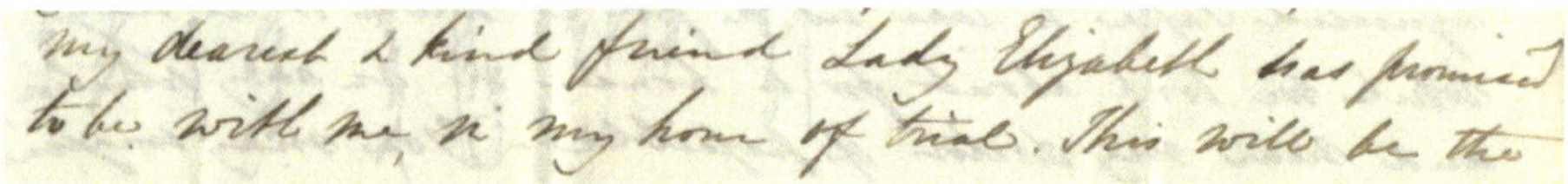
my dearest & kind friend Lady Elizabeth has promised to be with me in my hour of trial. This will be the

Extract from page 4 - I have requested Papa to take us in for a week or ten days, for a house, in an easy situation, and near my doctor if possible. You may imagine the multitude of letters we have to write so, I will say no more than God forever bless and preserve you darling Babe.

Your most affectionate and happy sister, Anna

settled by the earliest days

requested Papa to take us in for a week or ten days

while we look about for a house in an easy situation

and near my doctor if possible - You may imagine

the multitude of letters we have to write

so I will say no more than God for ever bless and preserve

you both and your darling Babe. Your most affectionate and happy Sister Anna

Tunley Farm marked on Camerton's Tithe Map 1844

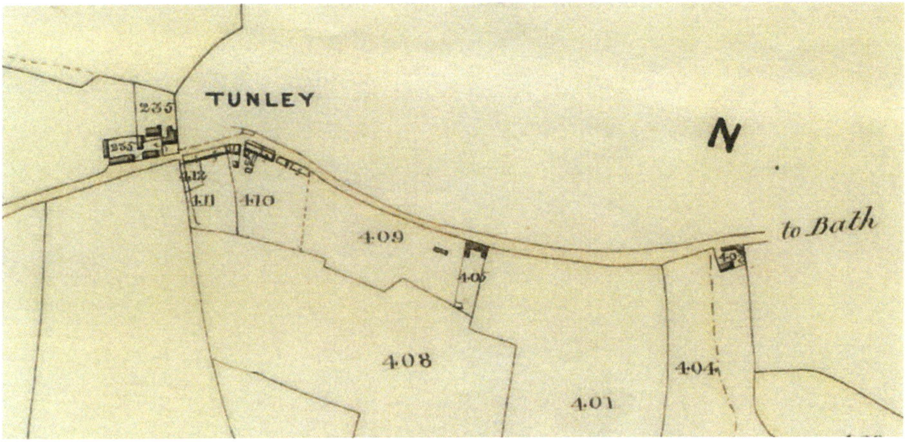

According to the Tithe apportionment book, John Jarrett Esq (Lord of the Manor) owned Tunley Farm, the occupier at this time was Benjamin Wooley.

Tunley Farm reference numbers: 232 to 251 on the map

	384	Long mead	pasture	2	.	39	.	11	7
	385	Orchard	pasture Orchard	.	3	8	.	6	.
	386	Cottage and Garden		.	.	27	.	.	9
Benjamin Woolley	232	Robins Close and Tunley close	pasture	7	2	6	1	19	7
	233	Under Tunley	pasture	14	2	24	3	5	11
	235	House Outbuildings Barton and garden		.	3	.	.	3	9
	236	Slight or plain ground	Arable	14	.	26	4	17	5
	239	Collins's mead and short mead	pasture	20	.	2	5	2	1
	246	Fearney wood	pasture	18	2	34	4	4	3
	247	Great wood	pasture	20	3	36	4	8	1
	249	Lower wood	pasture	15	1	13	2	19	8
	250	Lower wood	pasture	6	.	3	1	2	7
	251	Hargrove	pasture	3	3	26	.	14	9
Henry Robins	27	Cottage and garden		.	.	4	.	.	.

The Jarrett Family Leave Camerton – For some unknown reason, in the 1850s the Jarrett family decided to move from their lovely new house in Camerton, to Warwickshire.

Watercolour painting of Anna and Emily Jarrett

Maybe John and Anna thought their daughters Anna and Emily would be more likely to make the acquaintance of eligible young men in the social circles of Warwickshire; rather than quiet isolation of Camerton. John Jarrett died in 1863 and his wife Anna died 5 years later.

George Gibbons ran the farm around 1861 to about 1915 under lease from the Jarrett family.

Below is a copy of the original entry in the Farm Lands of Camerton Manor record book, by kind permission of Mr and Mrs. M. Holbrook.

1864 – Tunley Farm – G Gibbons (Tenant)

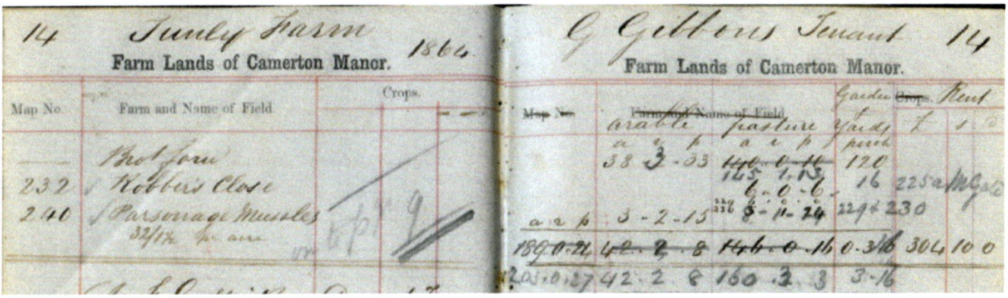

In 1865 entries shows George Gibbons paying rent to lease Tunley farm from the Camerton Manor estate (Jarrett family).

1865 Entries from the Camerton Manor, Page No's: 17 & 18

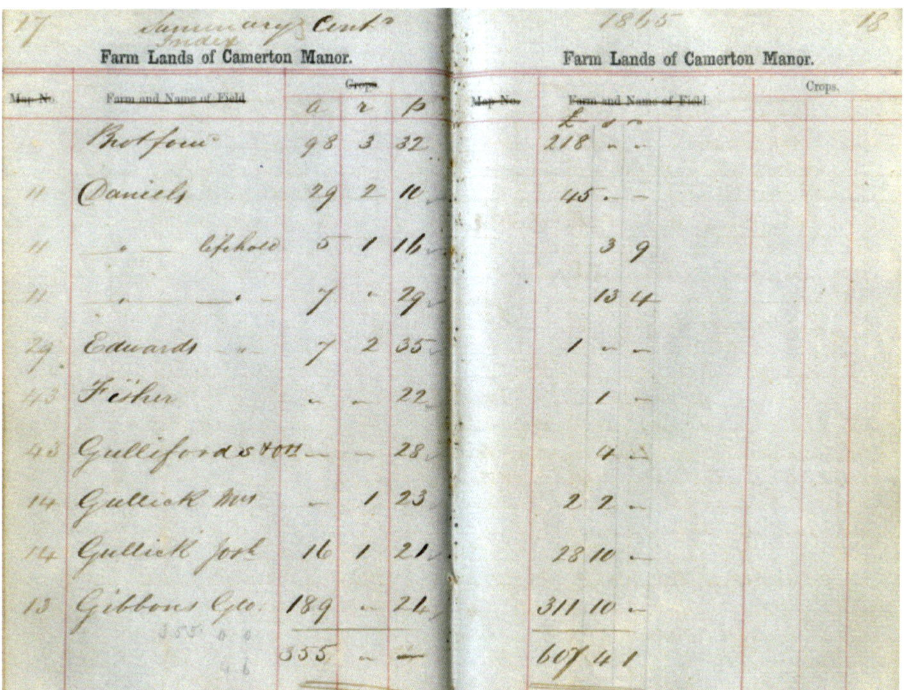

1865 Entries from the Camerton Manor, Page No's 23 & 24

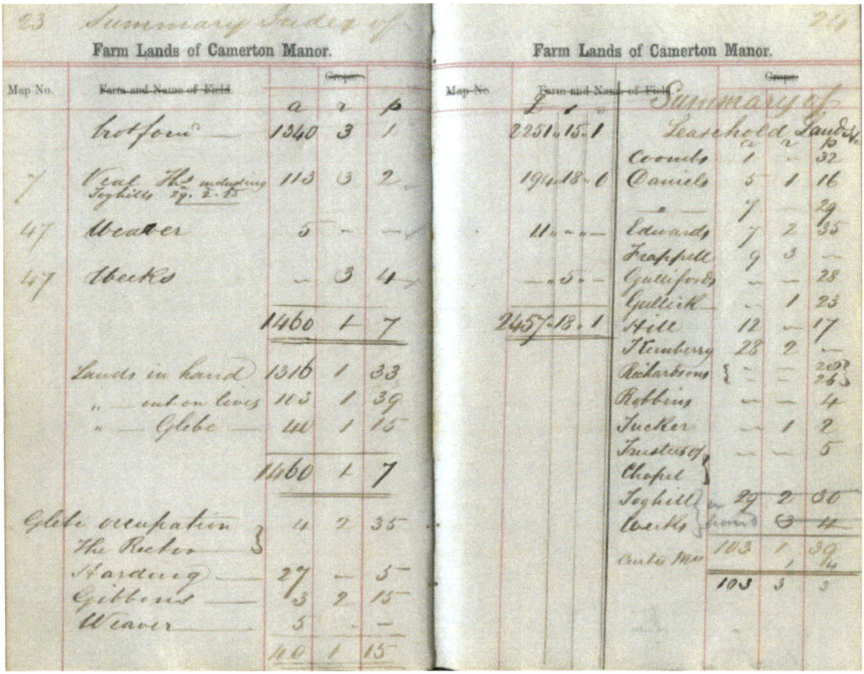

23 Summary Index of

Farm Lands of Camerton Manor.

Map No.	Farm and Name of Field	a	r	p
	Crofton	1340	3	1
7	Veal Ths including Tyning Fig. 2. 15	113	3	2
47	Weaver	5	–	–
47	Weeks	–	3	4
		1460	1	7
	Lands in hand	1316	1	33
	" out on lives	103	1	39
	" Glebe	40	1	15
		1460	1	7
	Glebe occupation The Rector	4	2	35
	Harding	27	–	5
	Gibbons	3	2	15
	Weaver	5	–	–
		40	1	15

24

Farm Lands of Camerton Manor.

Summary of Leasehold Lands

£ s d	Name	a	r	p
2251.15.1				
	Coombs	1	–	32
1914.18.1	Daniels	5	1	16
		7	–	29
11.–.–	Edwards	7	2	35
	Frappell	9	3	–
–.5.–	Gulliford	–	–	28
	Gullick	–	1	23
2457.18.1	Hill	12	–	17
	Stumbury	28	2	–
	Richardsons	–	–	20 / 26
	Robbins	–	–	4
	Tucker	–	1	2
	Trustees of Chapel	–	–	5
	Tyning	29	2	30
	Weeks	[illegible]	3	4
	Carried	103	1	39
		103	3	3

The Jarrett sisters return to Camerton - According to the 1871 Census, Anna and Emily returned to Camerton. As grown women, they proceeded to run the estate with great success! (please see volume No. 5).

George Gibbons was mainly a producer of dairy; milk, cheese and butter, he was also a seed merchant and grower.

Advert dated 1875

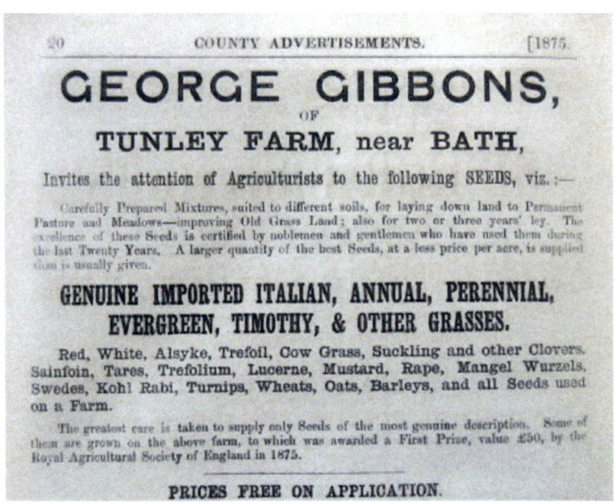

20 COUNTY ADVERTISEMENTS. [1875.

GEORGE GIBBONS,

OF

TUNLEY FARM, near BATH,

Invites the attention of Agriculturists to the following SEEDS, viz.:—

Carefully Prepared Mixtures, suited to different soils, for laying down land to Permanent Pasture and Meadows—improving Old Grass Land; also for two or three years' ley. The excellence of these Seeds is certified by noblemen and gentlemen who have used them during the last Twenty Years. A larger quantity of the best Seeds, at a less price per acre, is supplied than is usually given.

GENUINE IMPORTED ITALIAN, ANNUAL, PERENNIAL, EVERGREEN, TIMOTHY, & OTHER GRASSES.

Red, White, Alsyke, Trefoil, Cow Grass, Suckling and other Clovers. Sainfoin, Tares, Trefolium, Lucerne, Mustard, Rape, Mangel Wurzels, Swedes, Kohl Rabi, Turnips, Wheats, Oats, Barleys, and all Seeds used on a Farm.

The greatest care is taken to supply only Seeds of the most genuine description. Some of them are grown on the above farm, to which was awarded a First Prize, value £50, by the Royal Agricultural Society of England in 1875.

PRICES FREE ON APPLICATION.

George specialised in making cheese, in 1878 he was awarded the gold medal for Cheddars in Paris and seven medals at Amsterdam and Copenhagen.

> *Hist*, vol. II). Another distinguished maker is George Gibbons, of Tunly Farm, near Bath, a relative of the Hardings, who, at the International Dairy Show at New York, in 1878, won the two chief prizes with six Cheddars made in his dairy. He was also awarded the gold medal for Cheddars at Paris, and seven medals at Amsterdam and Copenhagen. About 1880 Mrs. Cannon, of Evercreech, highly distinguished herself by her fine Cheddars, which quickly gained her £2,000 in prizes, and achieved a world-wide reputation. So much was thought of her method that it was officially adopted by the Bath and West of England Society when it founded its Cheddar Cheese Schools in 1890. A later system, also of very great excellence,

The 1905 Frome show gives an example of how large some of the cheese truckles would have looked like.

1881 Census

George Gibbons	Head (Corn and Seed Merchant Farmer)
Ellen Gibbons	Wife
Elizabeth Y Gibbons	Daur (Farmer's daughter)
Benjamin Gibbons	Son (Farmer's son)
William Gibbons	Son (Farmer's son)
Sarah Goold	Servant Dairy Maid
Fanny Hayes	Servant Domestic Servt

1881 Poor Rate Book ref no: 23

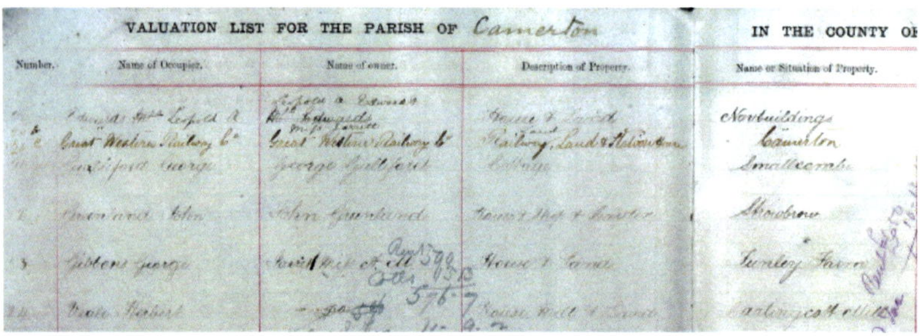
VALUATION LIST FOR THE PARISH OF Camerton IN THE COUNTY OF

Number.	Name of Occupier.	Name of owner.	Description of Property.	Name or Situation of Property.
[illegible]	Edwards Ltd Leopold A	Leopold A Edwards	House & Land	Newbuildings
[illegible]	Great Western Railway Co	Great Western Railway Co	Railway Land & [illegible]	Camerton
[illegible]	Gifford George	George Gifford	Cottage	Smallcombe
[illegible]	Greenland Ellen	John Greenland	House Shop & Garden	[illegible]
[illegible]	Gibbons George	[illegible]	House & Land	Tunley Farm
[illegible]	Hale Robert	[illegible]	House, Mill & Land	Carlingcott Mill

1881 Poor Rate Book show George Gibbons as an overseer

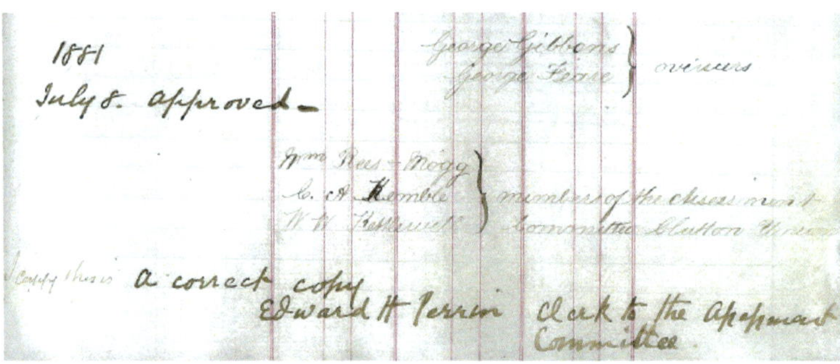
1881
July 8. approved —

George Gibbons
George Feare } overseers

Wm Rees-Mogg
C. A. Kemble
W. W. Hellewell } members of the assessment committee Clutton Union

I certify this is a correct copy
Edward H Perrin Clerk to the Assessment Committee

1887 Poor Rate Book

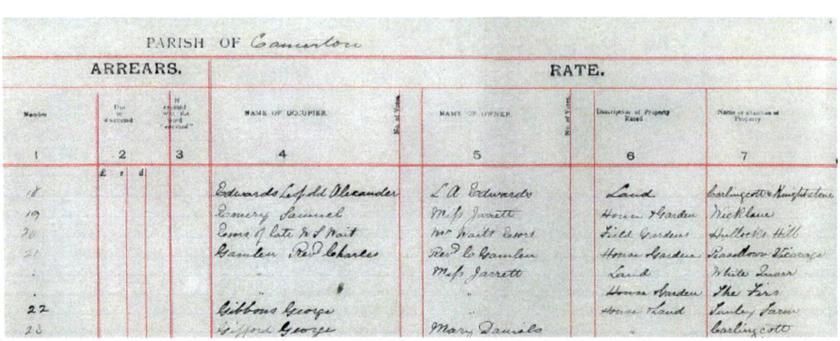
PARISH OF Camerton

ARREARS.			RATE.			
Number	Due or Excused	If excused with the word "excused"	NAME OF OCCUPIER	NAME OF OWNER	Description of Property Rated	Name or Situation of Property
1	2	3	4	5	6	7
18			Edwards Leopold Alexander	L A Edwards	Land	Carlingcott & Knightstone
19			Emery Samuel	Miss Jarrett	House Garden	Wick Lane
20			Exors of late W S Wait	Mr Wait Exors	Field Gardens	Hullocks Hill
21			Gamlen Revd Charles	Revd C Gamlen	House Garden	Camerton Vicarage
				Miss Jarrett	Land	White Quarr
					House Garden	The Firs
22			Gibbons George		House Land	Tunley Farm
23			Gifford George	Mary Daniels		Carlingcott

Anna Jarrett had a special programme printed with a diary of her 50th birthday celebrations including the following pages.

January 1888 – Front Page of Anna Jarrett's birthday celebrations

Inside Cover

So many of my people have asked me for "the words to keep" that I have printed for private circulation amongst them a short account of the Festivities, etc., which have taken place here lately on the occasion of my 50th Birthday.

A. M. JARRETT.

Camerton Court,
February 3rd, 1888.

Introduction page

On Tuesday, the 24th January, a dinner was given in the Dining Room at the Court, to which the tenant farmers of the Estate, with their families, the Clergy of Camerton and Peasedown S. John and some members and friends of the family were invited; amongst whom were Mrs. Charles Jarrett, Miss Hippisley, and Mr. and Miss Horton. Immediately after dinner Miss Honnywill, Miss Holland, Mrs. Gamlen and Mrs. Tisdall also came in to join the company. Before dinner, when all were assembled in the Drawing Room, a very handsome Necklace and Locket were presented to Miss Jarrett by the Steward and Tenants of the

Page 4

Estate. Mr. Gibbons who presented the gift on behalf of the above, said, "May it please you, Miss Jarrett, I have had the honour done me by the Tenantry on your Camerton Estate, of being deputed to ask your acceptance of a small token of the high esteem and regard they entertain towards you as their Landlord. It consists of a diamond Collarette Necklace and Locket set in gold, designed after the pattern of an old Celtic one found some years ago in this neighbourhood. With it Miss Jarrett, may I also ask you to accept our most earnest and sincere wishes that for many years you may be spared to continue the promotion of the comfort, welfare, and happiness of all around you, than which we know nothing gives you greater pleasure."

Page 14 & 15

In the evening the district was illuminated by a bonfire on Tunley Hill, and during the whole day the Church bells rang merrily, and from the tower floated a handsome flag made for Miss Jarrett by Mr. Fear, the Parish Clerk. The Pits also were dressed out with flags, and cannons were fired at intervals by the pitmen."

It is believed the gigantic bonfire photographed below was built to either celebrate Queen Victoria's Jubilee on the 21st June 1887, or Anna Jarrett's 50th birthday in January 1888.

Bonfire – you can just make out the St George's flag flying at the top of the bonfire.

Poachers 1898

Left is George Henry Fry, right is William (Bill) James Fry, local poachers with their greyhound dogs believed to have been used for hare coursing.

An agricultural revolution took place from the 1750s to the early 1900s. An increase in the population had taken place, therefore an increase in the supply of food was needed. Significant changes of the way farmers carried out their farming skills occurred. Domestication of animals took place, the open field system of strip farming was replaced by larger enclosed fields that were hedged and ditched.

The traditional 3 crop rotation was replaced by the Norfolk Four Crop rotation system in the early 1900s, the fallow field was replaced and used for growing turnips or clover, this saved on the wastage land.

Farmers would split an area into four pieces, growing different crops in each section, the crops would be rotated each year, this meant different nutrients were used in each piece and not over used each year.

In the early 1900's the horse was eventually replaced by the tractor, saving on labour and time, these remarkable changes helped to increase a greater production of food.

A boy of fourteen cross-ploughing on a Yorkshire farm.
("Agricultural Gazette" Photograph.)

AGRICULTURAL GAZETTE. 57

A Three Years' Tractor Balance Sheet.

Expenses.

	£	s.	d.
Running Expenses.			
1918. Petrol, 60 gals. at 2/6½	7	12	6
1919. „ 60 „ at 3/3	9	15	0
1920. „ 78 „ at 3/2	12	7	0
1918–19. Paraffin, 1,200 gals. at 1/6	90	0	0
1920. Paraffin, 830 gals. at 1/10	76	1	8
1918–19. Oil, 112½ gals. at 4/–	22	10	0
1920. Oil, 98 gals., at 4/9 ..	23	5	6
1918–20. Grease, 12 lb., at 1/–	0	12	0
	£242	3	8
Tractor Costs.			
12 plugs	3	0	0
4 governor washers	0	14	0
Repairs to clutch	0	5	6
Tyres for rear wheels ..	3	15	0
Fan belt	0	5	0
Overhaul	45	17	6
Carriage on tractor	3	0	0
Carriage when new	1	10	0
Differential bushing	7	0	0
Low-speed pinion	3	10	0
4 piston rings	0	17	6
Front forks	7	0	0
Connecting-rod bearing ..	1	16	0
Bolts	1	10	0
Minor repairs and improvements	10	10	0
	£90	8	6
Wages.			
Equivalent of 908 acres ploughing, at 3/6 per acre ..	£158	18	0
Depreciation.			
Tractor cost, £395; to-day's market value, £195; estimated depreciation ..	£200	0	0
Total expenses ..	£691	10	2

Earnings.

	£	s.	d.
1918–19.			
Ploughing 325 acres, at 25/–..	406	5	0
Cultivating 209 acres, at 7/–..	73	3	0
Corn cutting, 114 acres, at 7/–	39	18	0
Harrowing 61 acres, at 5/– ..	15	5	0
Threshing, 3 days, at £2 ..	6	0	0
1920.			
Ploughing just over 263 acres, at 30/–	394	15	0
Cultivating 150 acres, at 10/–	75	0	0
Corn cutting, 58 acres, at 8/–	23	4	0
Harrowing, 48 acres, at 6/–..	14	8	0
Threshing, 1 day, at £2 ..	2	0	0
Hauling :—			
5 days, 60 loads, 48 miles ..	10	0	0
1 day, 12 loads beans, 10 miles	2	0	0
1 day, 18 loads wheat, 12 miles	2	0	0
Total earnings ..	£1,063	18	0
Total expenses ..	£691	10	2
Balance profit ..	£372	7	10

A hand drawn map by E. M Heppel (colliery manager) dated 1900 clearly showing Tunley Farm.

1900 Map

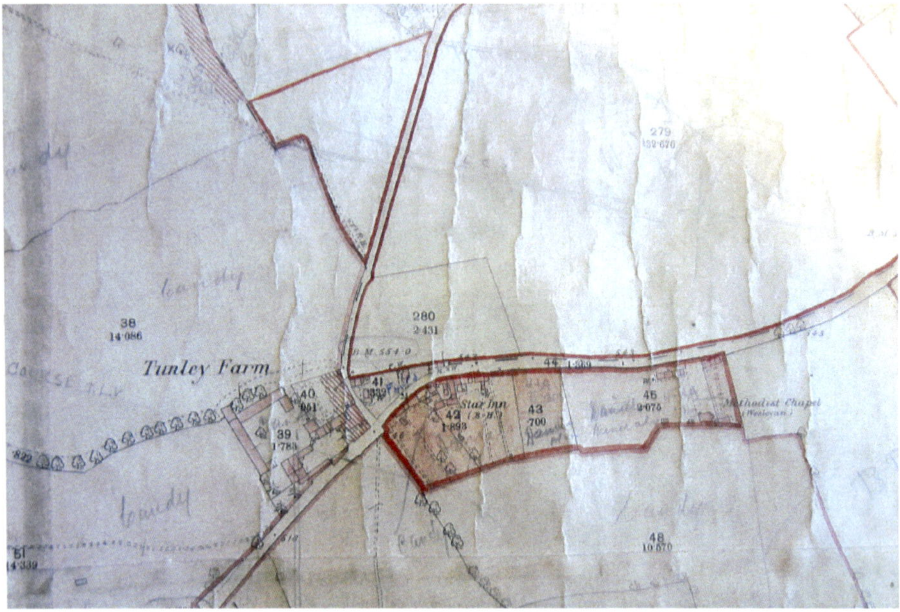

Tunley Hill Reservoir with the new water supply added about 1935

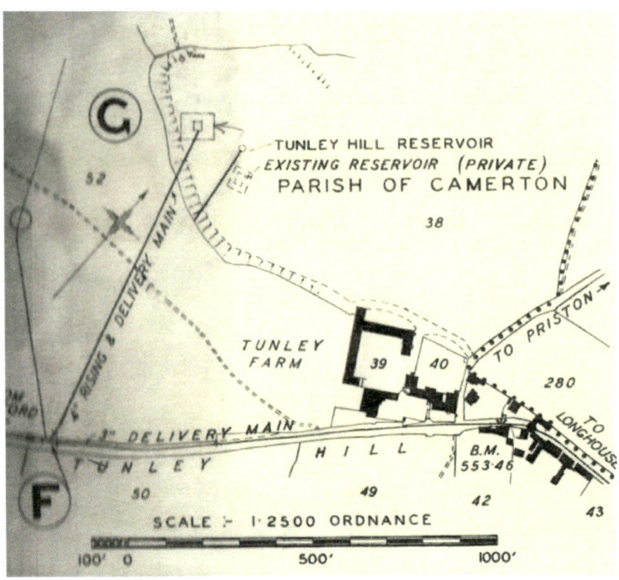

Reservoir Field on Tunley Farm with remains of 3 Reservoirs

Reservoir No: 1 Mushroom Shaped Structure - is in fact a top to a reservoir, natural spring water from 'Rattle Spring', Wallmead would have been pumped by a ram, across the field and up Tunley Hill to the reservoir. Once this reservoir ceased to be used; it was capped. Today a natural stone built, low levelled wall, circular in shape, surrounds it. The domed shaped roof made of steel tiles riveted together, covers it.

Reservoir No: 2 Red Brick Rectangular – The bricks look hand made, larger than your normal sized brick, with smooth sides all the way around (no frog shaped inlay on the top like modern bricks). The author believes these bricks were made in Camerton.

Circular Concrete Tank – Put in around May 1935 by Bathavon Rural District Council, this supplied Camerton and the district with a water supply.

George Arnold (Head Carter/Cowman) on Tunley Farm with a prize winning 'Short Horn Bull' in the early 1900's.

Prize winning 'Short Horn Bull'

The Camerton estate was in the Jarretts hands for nearly 100 years, until Emily's death in 1911. Sadly both sisters remained spinsters, leaving no children to be future heirs, therefore no direct descendants to the leave the estate to. In Emily's will, the whole of the estate was left in the hands of the trustees who were responsible for the future of 'Camerton Court' estate.

A few years later Sir Frank Beauchamp purchased Camerton estate including the local mines. He was a Justice of the Peace for Somerset and a member of the Somerset County Council since 1909; he served on several of the council's committees. He was a member of the Somerset volunteers and Territorals for 18 years until February 1918, he was attached to Major L.O.M.G.S, southern command, stationed at Salisbury. Previous to this appointment, he was acting O.C, A.S.C at Fovant near Salisbury, he was honoured for public and local services. Major Beauchamp who contested North Somerset twice in the Conservative interest, had been promoted to Colonel. He visited America in 1918 on a mission, on behalf of the war office. He was made a baronet in 1918 and awarded a CBE in 1919.

He turned part of his home into colliery offices that ran Camerton's coal pit. In the early 1920s, Sir Frank Beauchamp was considered to be one of the largest coal owners in the country (please see volume no: 6).

Sir Frank Beauchamp

The Candy family leased Tunley Farm from Sir Frank Beauchamp from around 1919. William Candy built a house in the 1930's in Tunley and named it "Chestnuts".

A letter from Mr W A Candy dated 1930 sent from Tunley Farm

Tunley
Bath

Re Mr H Arnold.

He has worked for me as head Carter 12 years & I have always found him honest & straight & I can say just the same of his wife –

I should think they would make a very good couple for the post to which this refers –

W. A. Candy.

Building a Hay Stack in 1940.

A Haystack at Tunley Farm with a few local men, George Arnold in the middle and Bacco Biggs on the left. There is a conveyer powered by an old Lister engine.

During the 2nd World War a mobile search light was stationed on top of Tunley Hill, in Reservoir field, Tunley Farm. The position is at the highest point in the locality. Residents can recall a lorry catching fire one evening and rumour has it that some young ladies visited the soldiers and a cigarette caused the fire.

Pictured below is the location believed to be where the search light once stood.

Corner of Reservoir field

View from the bottom of the hill looking up the hill

When there was an air-raid, the search light could be seen all over, it would merge with other search lights e.g High Littleton, Lansdown in Bath and from Bristol. When the enemy aircraft flew overhead they could be easily seen by our armed forces for shooting down.

Gloucestershire Regiment, the 4th City of Bristol Battalion in 1938

The above regiment was converted to a 'Searching Unit' in 1938, they became part of the Royal Artillery in August 1940. Their new title was 66th (Gloucesters) Searching Regiment; it is believed they were based in Bristol. Some members of the ATS were in the same unit and came from Old Market, Bristol.

Francis Joshua Harris is believed to be stood on Tunley Farm, he was in the 447 Coy regiment, 4th BN; the Gloucestershire regiment (66th Searchlight Regiment) T.A pictured below:

Francis Joshua Harris

Tunley Hill – Jack Cavill in control of the beautiful shire horses and cart in the field running up towards Tunley Farm; Trevor Biggs eldest brother to Tony running behind the trailer in the early 1940s.

Camerton and Woodborough Estate Auction took place in 1948
Lot 33 (Tunley Farm, in the parish of Camerton)
Still in the hands of the Candy family

LOT 33

(*Coloured Pink on Plan*)

TUNLEY FARM

in the Parish of Camerton

Tenants : Mr. W. A. Candy. **Rental** (apportioned), £400 per ann.

Tenancy : Yearly Ladyday.

Bathavon Rural District Council (site of Reservoir), Rental £5 per ann.

A FIRST-RATE DAIRY FARM

Situate at the North end of the Estate on Tunley Hill, adjoining Tunley Village and intersected by a metalled Parish Road, from which there is direct access to the house and buildings.

THE FARMHOUSE

is substantially built of stone with slated roof and contains :—

On the Ground Floor. **Hall** with tiled floor and staircase ; Large **Dining** and **Drawing Rooms,** both with open fire ; **Small Office or Study;** Secondary Hall, fitted wash basin ; **Kitchen,** fitted Triplex range, "Aga" cooker and "Beeston" Domestic boiler ; Pantry ; Dairy ; Cooling and Sterlising Rooms ; Old Dairy and Cheese Room ; Outside W.C.

Above, approached by main and secondary stairs are **Nine Bedrooms,** Bathroom (h. & c.), separate W.C. ; heated linen cupboard ; Housemaid's Pantry, fitted sink.

Water Supply pumped from Camerton Colliery to private reservoir on the hill to the rear of the house, whence it gravitates to house and buildings.

Main Electricity. Drainage to Cesspool.

EXCELLENT FARM BUILDINGS

mainly brick and/or stone built, with slated or tiled roofs around a large stock yard with water piped to a central tank, comprising Two "Accredited" Cow Houses with tyings for about 70 cows, tubular fittings, automatic drinking bowls and electric light installed by Tenant. Full length Hay Loft over; Barn; Four Boxes; Stabling for 3; Mixing House; Implement House; Timber and galvanised 5-bay Cart Shed; Garage for 1 car.

TUNLEY FARM COTTAGES

are situate almost opposite the Homestead, in O.S. No. pt. 42 and comprise a Block of Three stone-built Cottages with gardens, one containing Two Bedrooms and Two small Ante-rooms, Sitting Room, Living Room, Scullery with copper and two with Two Bedrooms, Living Room and Scullery. Each has outside E.C. Main Water Supply from standpipe in the gardens.

THE LAND

for the greater part is situate on a well-drained Southern slope and is divided into convenient enclosures of nearly uniform size. It comprises about 150 acres of excellent pasture land and about 54 acres of arable, in all approx.

214a. 2r. 27½p.

in accordance with the following

33

W.A Candy and his family were tenants of Sir Frank Beauchamp until 1948, the Camerton and Woodborough estates including Tunley Farm were put up for sale at auction. The Candy family purchased the farm at the auction in Bath.

Sir Frank Beauchamp died just a few years later on the 17th June 1950; he was 83 years of age and is buried in St Peter's Church yard, Camerton.

In 1952 the Candy family sold Tunley Farm at auction and shortly after sold the dairy, beef cattle, agricultural implements, working horse and a Fordson tractor.

Front cover of sale catalogue

TUNLEY FARM

TUNLEY

5 miles from Bath, off the main Bath-Radstock Road.

SALE OF

90

DAIRY and BEEF CATTLE

viz.:

47 Shorthorn and Cross Bred Heifers and Young Dairy Cows with calves at side, in full milk, or in milk and in calf; 4 Ayrshire Bulling Stirks; 20 forward Beef Cattle; 7 yearling and 11 weaning Heifer calves and Pedigree Shorthorn Bull.

WORKING HORSE

AGRICULTURAL IMPLEMENTS

FORDSON TRACTOR

TILLEY & CULVERWELL (BATH)

In conjunction with

KING, MILES & Co.

---

have been favoured with instruction from Mr. W. A. Candy (the farm having been sold), to sell the above by Auction. upon the premises on

THURSDAY, 16th OCTOBER, 1952, commencing at 11.30 a.m. promptly

Catalogues of the Auctioneers at their offices:

14, New Bond Street, Bath (Tel. Bath 3150).
Farrington Gurney (Tel. Temple Cloud 211).

Fyson & Co., Ltd., Printers, Bath

Agricultural Equipment for sale:

HARVESTING EQUIPMENT

96 **"Bamford" Tractor Mowing Machine.**
97 "Albion" Tractor Mowing Machine.
98 "Albion" Horse Mowing Machine.
99 ,, ,, ,,
100 "Martin" Swatheturner and side delivery Rake.
101 Tedding Machine.
102 ,,
103 **Tractor Hay Sweep.**
104 "Albion" expanding Rake.
105 "Bamford" Horse Rake.
106 **"Wallace" Tip Elevator.**
107 "Hired Man" $2\frac{1}{4}$ h.p. Engine on trolley.
108 Hay Loader.
109 McCormick 5 ft Binder.
110 Knife Stand.
111 Tractor 4 Wheel Trailer on rubbers with H.T. Ladders and side boards.
112 Tractor 4 wheel Trailer on irons with H. Ladders.
113 4 wheel Waggon on rubbers.
114 4 wheel Trolley.
115 Tip Cart on rubbers.

Names of Dairy and Beef Cattle :

DAIRY & BEEF CATTLE

1	Young Shorthorn Cow	"Phyllis" with calf at side.
2	Young Shorthorn Cow	"Lily" with calf at side.
3	Young Shorthorn Cow	"Anne 2nd" with calf at side.
4	Shorthorn Heifer	"Joey" with calf at side.
5	Young Shorthorn Cow	"Audrey" with calf at side (3 qrts.)
6	Young Friesian × Cow	"Blackie" with calf at side (3 qrts.)
7	Young Shorthorn Cow	"Bunty" in full milk (not served).
8	Young Shorthorn Cow	"Filpail" in full milk (not served).
9	Young Shorthorn Cow	"Poppy" in full milk (not served).
10	Young Shorthorn Cow	"Lucy" in full milk (not served).
11	Young Shorthorn Cow	"Flower" (not served) (3 qrts.)
12	Shorthorn × Heifer	"Alice" in full milk (not served).
13	Friesian × Heifer	"Smart" in full milk (not served).
14	Shorthorn × Heifer	"Elsie" in full milk (not served).
15	Shorthorn × Heifer	"Milkmaid" springing to calf.
16	Young Shorthorn Cow	"Pansy" ,, ,,
17	Young Shorthorn Cow	"Iris" ,, ,,
18	Young Shorthorn Cow	"Snowball" ,, ,,
19	Young Shorthorn Cow	"Tiny" ,, ,,
20	Young Ayrshire × Cow	"Peach" ,, ,,
21	Young Shorthorn Cow	"Topsy" ,, ,,
22	Young Guernsey × Cow	"Fat" ,, ,,
23	Young Shorthorn × Cow	"Mabel" ,, ,,
24	Young Friesian × Cow	"Dinah" in milk, served 30th April
25	Young Shorthorn Cow	"Rose" in milk, served 5th May.
26	,, ,,	"Ann" in milk, served 15th May.
27	,, ,,	"Countess 2nd" in milk. served 4th June.
28	,, ,,	"Valerie" in milk, served 7th June.
29	,, ,,	"Viola" in milk, served 21st June.
30	,, ,,	"Mary" in milk, served 23rd June.
31	,, ,,	"Star" in milk, served 2nd July.

Tunley farm had been in the hands of the Candy family for over 30 years.
Mr William Candy and his wife moved to Chestnuts, Tunley to spend the rest of their days.

Major Bernard Gilbert Stancomb Cayzer - purchased Tunley Farm in the Autumn of 1952. Major Cayzer's family were ship owners and were very wealthy in their own right. He lived in a Regency style built house in Timsbury (Grade II listed building), it was built in 1816 by Captain John Parish and is therefore known locally as 'Parish's House'.

This house was up for sale in 2006 and caused a bit of a stir as rumours were flying around that Johnny Depp (Actor) was going to buy the house. T.V cameras and the media arrived in the village creating excitement until it was confirmed that the house was in fact purchased by another family.

Local people fondly remember Major Cayzer because he took great care of Tunley Farm, ran it like clock-work. People would actually drive miles to Camerton, just to see it.

Major Cayzer was a pillar of the community and a very generous man. He provided the money to build Conygre hall, Timsbury as well as giving generously in other quarters of Timsbury village. The hall is hired out for all sorts of events and activities including rugby tots, Jude Lee Filer aged 5 years old pictured below.

Foundation Stone

Conygre Hall was designed and built by J Crozier Ltd and was officially opened on May 26th 1972.

Brass Plaque dedicated to Major B.G.S Cayzer inside the hall

In addition to Major B.G.S Cayzer's local generosity, he is more widely known for having given No: 1 The Royal Crescent, to Bath's Preservation Society. The house was on the market for sale in 1967, he bought the property in order for it to become a historic house museum.

The struggle for the protection and conservation of Bath's architectural heritage was particularly fierce in the 1960's and 70's, many properties were under threat. Major Cayzer was a great supporter of Bath Preservation Trust and it's work, he generously gave the house to the Trust along with funds for it's restoration and conversion into a museum.

Extensive restoration and refurbishment took place between 1968-70. The internal refit and decoration was overseen by a committee and Major Cayzer himself was Chairman. Other committee members included the architect Phillip Jebb, the interior designer Jean Munro and Peter Thornton who was the keeper of the furniture and wood work at the Victorian and Albert museum. The most noticeable external work during the 1960's was the raising of the first floor windows back to their original 18th century levels.

His initiative and generosity inspired the restoration and furnishing of this magnificent Georgian Town House. It was built between 1767 and 1774 to the design of architect John Wood. It represents the highest point of palladian architecture in Bath; No:1 was the first house to be built in the Crescent; it provided luxury accommodation for the aristocracy that visited Bath.

Major B.G.S Cayzer stood outside No:1 Royal Crescent in Bath

Photograph below is copyright to 'Bath Preservation Trust'

Above is a plaque made of Bath stone, placed on the inside right hand wall to the main entrance door of No:1 Royal Crescent, dedicated to Major B.G.S Cayzer.

The late **Tony Biggs** worked for Major Cayzer in the mid 1970s and was well known for being able to drive his tractor well and could turn it on a sixpence. Whilst working on Tunley farm, the wheel of his tractor nearly went down an old air shaft; believed to be an old mine.

Tony investigating the near miss he had

Major B.G.S Cayzer put Tunley Estate up for sale at a Bath auction on the 18th May 1977. The estate included two well equipped modern dairy and corn farms; Tunley Farm, Tunley and Church Farm, Priston.

The front cover of the Tunley's estate sales brochure below:

Near Bath in the County of Avon

THE TUNLEY ESTATE

comprising

TWO WELL EQUIPPED AND PRODUCTIVE DAIRY AND CORN FARMS

extending to

205 HECTARES

(506 ACRES)

FOR SALE BY AUCTION

at

FORTT'S RESTAURANT, MILSOM STREET, BATH

on

WEDNESDAY 18th MAY 1977

With Vacant Possession (except certain units of accommodation)

KING MILES & Co

Chartered Surveyors *Established circa 1752*

25 Market Place and 60 High Street, Wells, Somerset

Telephone: Wells (0749) 73002

Tunley Farm Estate shaded in pink on the map below:

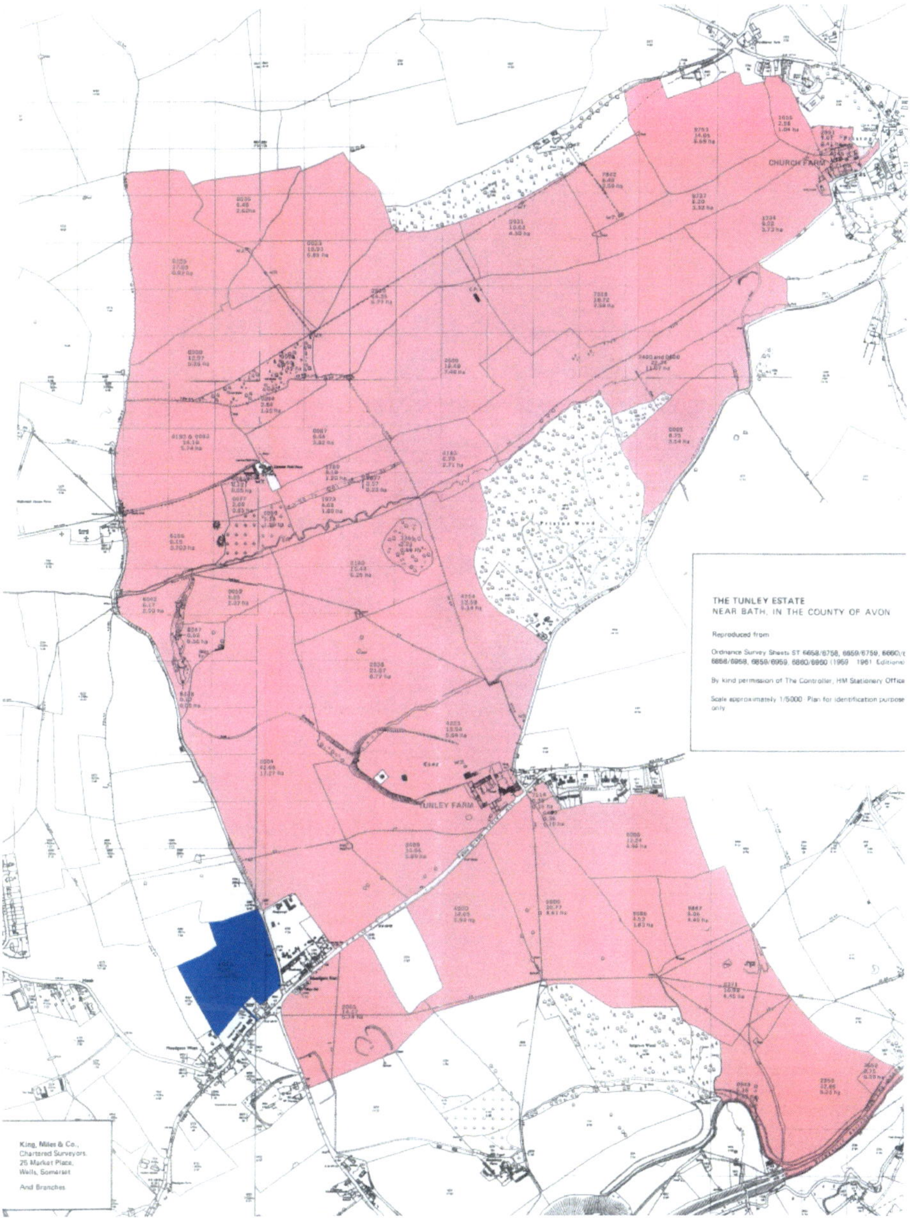

The next owner of this farm was Mr David Jones and family, they ran a dairy farm (Vaindre farm) in St Melons, Cardiff; until the Cardiff City Council compulsorily purchased it in 1976.

Mr David Jones, his wife Dorothy and family had to look for an alternative farm but not many farms were available on the market of any significant size. They discovered Tunley Estate up for sale at auction and purchased it in 1977.

The Jones family

In 1977 Rhyddian Jones and his cousin Howard Jones moved from Wales to Tunley and Priston, they ran both dairy farms; Tunley Farm, Tunley and Church Farm, Priston. Rhyddian is fondly remembered by locals as a gentle soul, he took great pride and care in looking after his animals. Unfortunately due to the poor rate paid for milk, it was not viable to keep the dairy herd, it broke Rhyddian's heart to have to sell the herd.

In 1983 Rhyddian's parents, David and Dorothy Jones with his sister Heather moved to Mead Cottage in Priston.

In I989 a family decision was made, to sell the farm house separate to the farm buildings and surrounding land.

Dennis Cundick and his wife Ruth purchased the house in the same year. They moved from Bath with their children to their dream house 'Tunley Farm House'.

Aerial shot of Tunley Farm House in 1989

'Tunley Farm House' partly hidden behind a high garden wall, the view is as you would see it as you pass from the main road pictured below:

Dennis Cundick jointly ran a business with his partner, it was called Cundick & Gore; the partnership dissolved and the business name changed to Cundick Transport.

Cundick's Transport Van

In 1990 Rhyddian's brother Stephen commuted from Wales to join his sister Heather, they had the task of reorganising both farms. To help generate an income, they turned Tunley farm's cow sheds and barn buildings into business units, today it houses B1 and B2 light industrial units and is an industrial estate.

Tunley Farm's Industrial Estate

The farm also ran horse riding lessons for local children for several years, pictured below is Craig Benn aged 10 years of age in 1990.

Stephen Jones took the initiative to join an environmental scheme in the early 1990's, hence lots of brown hares, roe deer and muntjac deer are on the increase in the area, they have shorter legs than the Roe deer.

Roe Deer **Muntjac Deer** **Hare**

In the late 1990s Stephen and his sister Heather, decided to plan corporate days out and developed a first class shoot for local people.

People with sticks ready to beat the ground in 1998

The late Tony Biggs, above right drove the beaters around in a purpose built trailer pulled by his tractor.

The start of a shoot 2004

Local People from left to right: Mike Crew, Simon and Fiona? John Wyatt, Bob Hughes, Andy Mach, Alan Carter, Martin Mathison, John Fry, Roger Taylor, Bob ? Brian Scurlock and the handsome Springer Spaniel.

In 2003 Stephen Jones was very pleased to discover that Barn Owls had nested in one of his Barns on Tunley Farm.

Owlets

Partridge Eggs

Above left, Stephen Jones holding a few of the baby owlets.

The late Don Jones, above right (former gamekeeper of Tunley Farm) worked for the Jones family for roughly 14 years. He is holding a tray of 'Partridge eggs' he had in his care in 2004.

Tunley estate is one of only two sites in the West Country used by RAF Odiam for Chinook Navex landings. In 2006 an RAF Odiham based chinook landed behind the farm in a field called 'Yew Ground'; the pilot and Stephen Jones stood near by.

RAF Chinook with the pilot and Stephen Jones

Tunley estate has planted Miscanthus (Elephant Grass) which is grown and sold for fuel. It also acts as a good wind break and cover for the pheasants.

Malkham Mathisen (former Game Keeper for the Badminton estate) is currently the Game Keeper for the Tunley estate and has worked there for about 8 years. He is stood by the Miscanthus plant/Elephant grass to give you an idea how tall it is.

Malkham stood by the Miscanthus Plants in 2013

Tunley Farm House as you can see it today!

Pictured below is believed to be William Lye holding the reins to his pony and trap outside Tunley Farm House on Tunley Hill. Around the early 1900's the Lye family butchers believed to have had a slaughter house and a butcher's shop in the village of Tunley.

Chapter 4

As you approach the bottom of Tunley Hill, to your left there is a field known as 'Glebe Ground' this land was once owned by St Peter's Church. The field provided an income for the church.

During the second world war a small military encampment was set up in this enclosed area. Local residents can recall wooden huts standing in this field and the strong military presence.

Glebe Ground/Church Field (shaded blue)

The whole community helped the men and women serving in the armed forces in one way or another, a few examples are written in articles printed in a local church magazine dated October 1940 below:

Camerton Comforts Fund Oct 1940

CAMERTON COMFORTS FUND.

Work has recommenced and we are glad to have some new names on our list of helpers. There have been several letters received from those who have recently received 2 pairs of socks together with 2/6 (the sum of £2/10/0 received from the P.C.C. has been divided amongst the 20 Camerton men and women serving in H.M. Forces).

We would like to remind you that the money received from the sale of the paper, sent to the Depot at 1, Bridge Place will be spent on purchasing wool for the making of woollen comforts for Camerton men and women on active service. Please continue to collect for this good cause.

Poppy Appeal/Working Party Dec 1943

POPPY DAY COLLECTIONS were up by £2/5/0 this year. Details have been printed in the press showing a grand total of £15/12/5½.

WORKING PARTY

The efforts of the working party will result in each Camerton man & woman serving in H.M. Forces receiving a Christmas Gift of £1. The village collections and donations and the entertainments arranged have brought in £20 and £14 to date. THANKS TO ALL who have helped.

St Peter's Camerton Parish magazine

Camerton Spitfire Fund

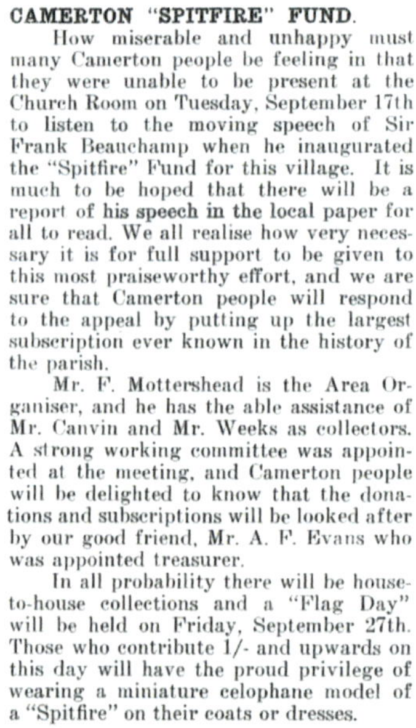

CAMERTON "SPITFIRE" FUND.

How miserable and unhappy must many Camerton people be feeling in that they were unable to be present at the Church Room on Tuesday, September 17th to listen to the moving speech of Sir Frank Beauchamp when he inaugurated the "Spitfire" Fund for this village. It is much to be hoped that there will be a report of his speech in the local paper for all to read. We all realise how very necessary it is for full support to be given to this most praiseworthy effort, and we are sure that Camerton people will respond to the appeal by putting up the largest subscription ever known in the history of the parish.

Mr. F. Mottershead is the Area Organiser, and he has the able assistance of Mr. Canvin and Mr. Weeks as collectors. A strong working committee was appointed at the meeting, and Camerton people will be delighted to know that the donations and subscriptions will be looked after by our good friend, Mr. A. F. Evans who was appointed treasurer.

In all probability there will be house-to-house collections and a "Flag Day" will be held on Friday, September 27th. Those who contribute 1/- and upwards on this day will have the proud privilege of wearing a miniature celophane model of a "Spitfire" on their coats or dresses.

The army camp was in close proximity of the local pub at the bottom of Tunley hill, the (Camerton Inn) . The photograph below was taken from Glebe ground otherwise known as Church field early evening (Autumn 2013).

The Camerton Inn

Locals can remember the soldiers having many a good scrap with the gypsies that camped nearby.

The cropped field on the right hand side, just before the boundary fence of the Old Camerton Inn's car-park is called Seventy Acres South.

(Seventy Acres South - Field)

In the 1960s, Steam Traction Engine Rallys became popular and a group of local people in Camerton decided to organise a fundraising event; this was the start of the Camerton's own Steam Rallies.

The first Rally took place in 1967 and was held in Seventy Acres South, by kind permission of the Tunley Estate land owner, Major B.G.S Cayzer. All profits made during this event were donated to the restoration of St Peter's Church. This event proved popular and was an unusual way of drawing the crowds; people travelled from all over to see the Steam Rallies.

Camerton 1967 Traction Engine Rally Programme

The Rallies continued each year, some times at different locations raising hundreds of pounds for worthy causes. The last few Rallies raised money to help build the new Camerton Recreation Centre. The last Steam Rally took place in 1982 at Rounhill field by kind permission of W. F Wells Esq. The Rallies ran for 15 years
Camerton 1982 Traction Engine Rally Programme.

At the bottom of Tunley Hill is an area called Meadgate, in the early 1800s it was known as Medyate. Over a period of time it has been split into two parts, Meadgate East and Meadgate West. In 1791 there were only three houses in Medyate.

View from Tunley Hill (Meadgate East)

A hand drawn map of Meadgate East

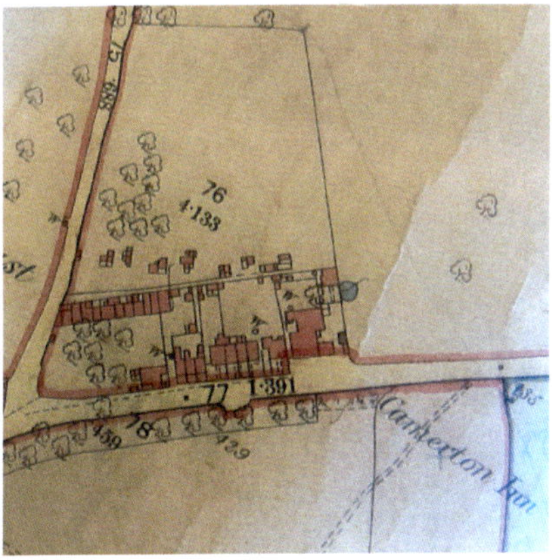

Above is a beautifully illustrated coloured map by Mr E. M Heppel dated 1900. Mr E M Heppel – used to be the General Manager of Camerton Collieries.

Meadgate Cottage

At the rear of the old Camerton Inn, slightly to the right and at the top of the car park, stands an old cottage. It is a natural stone built cottage that has been extended over the years. It has a wooden gate leading you into a pretty walled garden in front of the cottage (south facing). Although this cottage is known today as No: 29 Meadgate and Windmill Cottage, it was once known as 'Meadgate Cottage'.

In the 1846 Poor Rate Book it records Joseph Tucker being the owner of the cottage and garden and John Cook as the occupier.

Reference No: 222

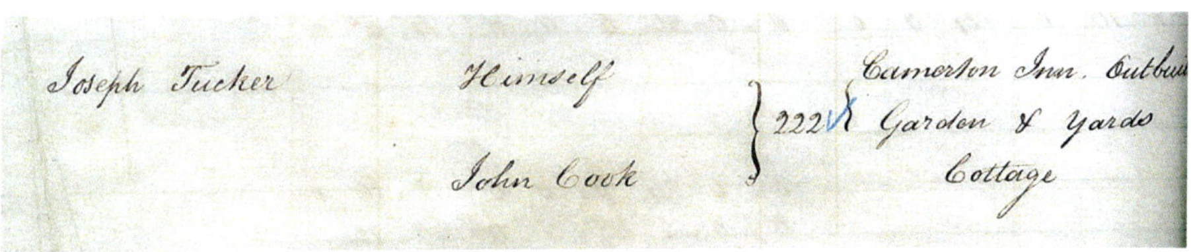

Joseph Tucker Himself
John Cook
222 Camerton Inn. Outbui
Garden & Yards
Cottage

The Windmill Family lived in Meadgate cottage for many years, in the 1884 poor rate book, Issac Windmill is recorded as being a tenant for Thatcher Breweries at Meadgate East, cottage with a garden, Issac was a coal miner, married to Fanny (nee Clarke), they had four children; Henry, Albert, Hilda and Arthur.

1884 Poor Rate Book

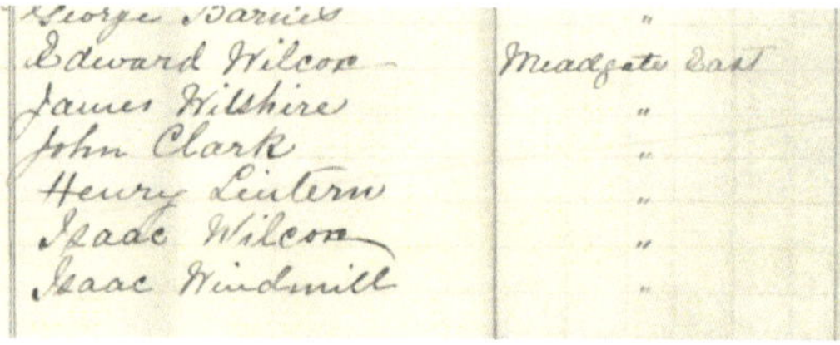

George Barnes	"
Edward Wilcox	Meadgate East
James Wiltshire	"
John Clark	"
Henry Linterm	"
Isaac Wilcox	"
Isaac Windmill	"

Meadgate Cottage about 1907 with the Windmill family

Left to right: Henry (Harry), Hilda, Issac and Fanny holding their youngest son Arthur. Their second eldest son Albert was away when this photo was taken.

Albert was born in 1889, he left school and undertook a blacksmith apprenticeship at Camerton colliery. In the spring of 1909 he decided to leave the colliery and joined the Army for a 12 year service; he was 20 years of age. Albert served as a Gunner with the 5th Mounted Battery, Royal Garrison Artillery.

Pictured below is Albert Windmill in his uniform

Albert left England in 1911 and spent 3 years in Jutogh, India and was present at the Delhi Durbar to celebrate the coronation of King George V.

A silk embroidered hanky (over 100 years old)

War broke out in Europe, Albert and the 5th Mounted Battery of the Royal Garrison Artillery were shipped back to Britain arriving in the Summer of 1914. After a period of time on leave he re-equipped for European conditions, the unit left for France and Flanders on 9th December 1914. He continued in action for a further 9 months and then instantly killed by enemy shellfire in the Ypres Salient on the 15th August 1915.

Albert Windmill was a brave soldier who gave his life for his country, he was 26 years of age and blown to pieces in a trench by a German shell in action south of Ypres Salient.

1914 – 1915 Star Medal

A bronze plaque was sent to all families of a member of the imperial forces who were killed, they died for freedom and honour.

Bronze Plaque – with Albert Windmill's name inscribed.

The plaque was locally known as the 'Death Penny'; although a lot larger than an old penny, it was actually 5" across and quite weighty.

The Sign – was a Parochial magazine that covered Camerton and Peasedown St John.

Below is an article written by the rector of St Peter's Church, Camerton; Arthur M Dewing. There is an interesting piece about Albert Windmill in it.

September 1915

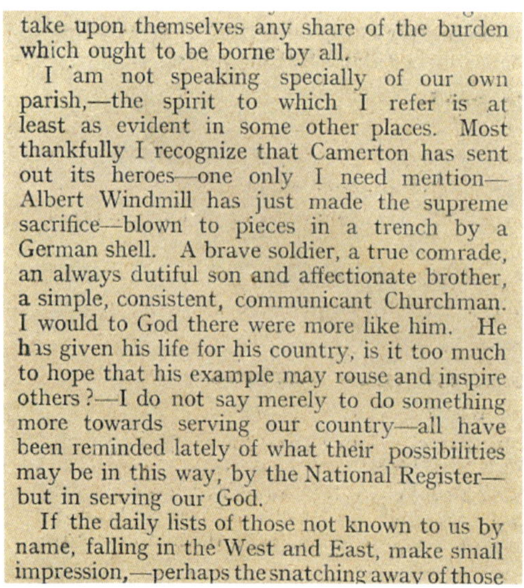

take upon themselves any share of the burden which ought to be borne by all.

I am not speaking specially of our own parish,—the spirit to which I refer is at least as evident in some other places. Most thankfully I recognize that Camerton has sent out its heroes—one only I need mention—Albert Windmill has just made the supreme sacrifice—blown to pieces in a trench by a German shell. A brave soldier, a true comrade, an always dutiful son and affectionate brother, a simple, consistent, communicant Churchman. I would to God there were more like him. He has given his life for his country, is it too much to hope that his example may rouse and inspire others?—I do not say merely to do something more towards serving our country—all have been reminded lately of what their possibilities may be in this way, by the National Register—but in serving our God.

If the daily lists of those not known to us by name, falling in the West and East, make small impression,—perhaps the snatching away of those

In 1936 Albert's brother, Arthur worked as a miner down Camerton new pit. When the late Ken Biggs was about 8 years old, he could clearly remember his mother telling him about a terrible accident. Unfortunately Arthur's hand got stuck in a winding machine at the bottom of the pit, the only way to free his arm was by having his hand amputated. Dr Crook from Timsbury carried out the amputation under the light of a miner's lamp. Ken can recall Arthur having a stub with a hook at the end, said "He was a grafter, he would catch hold of the spade with his hook and work like a Trojan". Arthur's daughter, May said "Dad had an artificial hand but seldom used it".

Arthur Windmill (Miner)

Arthur and his wife Elsie had 5 children, May, Don, Joyce, Jimmy and Bert. Jimmy Windmill set up his own engineering business called Springfield Surfacing, his brother Don worked along side of him. The business has been handed to their children Paul and Richard who continue to run the successful family business. Issac Windmill remained at Meadgate Cottage until he sold it in the late 1940s.

Meadgate Cottage changed hands a few times, Mr and Mrs Ron and Bette Ashman owned the cottage and named it Windmill Cottage. Bette was well known in the village for being the principle fundraiser and the driving force behind trying to raise funds to build the Camerton Recreation Centre.

Bette was also secretary to Camerton Church School and well loved by the children.

The late Bette Ashman

The current owners, Glen and Kirsty Honeybun purchased the cottage in 1997 from Ron and Bette Ashman. (please see volume no. 2).

No: 29 Meadgate/Windmill cottage as seen today!

To the left of the No:29 Windmill Cottage stands a large proud building, it used to be the local pub known as the Camerton Inn. It is believed to have been built in the early 1800s with local traditional white lias stone. The last tenants were Camerton's Tandoori Indian Dining and Takeaway.

Indian Dining and Takeaway (2013)

Doctor Coombes kept a gallon house and sold beer in 1825. Reverend John Skinner, rector of St Peter's Church kept a diary of every day life in Camerton during the early 1800s; his diary became his confident.

On April 1825, Reverend John Skinner wrote about the Coombes family in his diary, he states that the father of Coombes the priest who lived at Meadyates, had a chapel in his house, he was a blacksmith of Camerton, who went by the name Doctor Coombes; apparently he added tooth drawing and inoculation to his manual exercises on the anvil. The latter part of his life Dr Coombes kept a gallon house and sold beer at Meadyates.

Mr Coombes embraced the Catholic faith, this branch of the Coombes family did much to re-establish the Catholic religion at Bath, Downside and Shepton Mallet.

In the 1841 census it records Joseph Coombes 40 years of age, his wife aged 35 and their 8 children living at the Camerton Inn and records Joseph as being the publican.

1841 Census

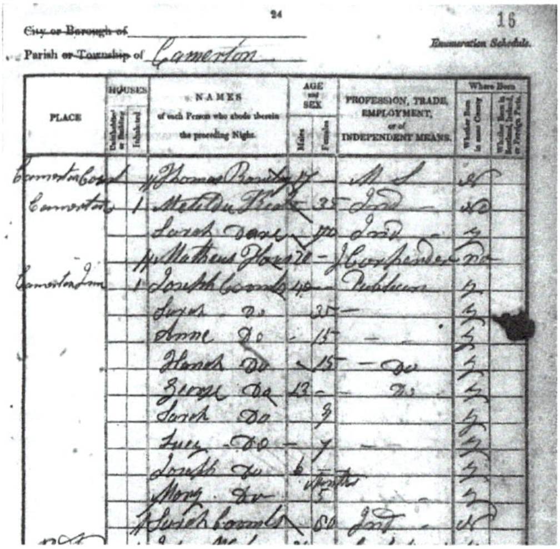

The Coombes family were renowned for good beer in the area, they had their own brewery (Coombes Brewery) that was based in nearby Clandown. The landlord would only let a new customer have 1 pint and a local 2 pints, it was very strong! (please see volume no. 3)

1844 Tithe Map No: 222

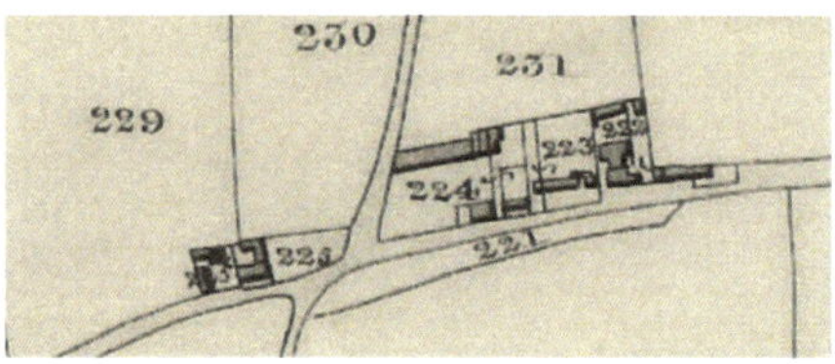

In 1846 it is recorded in the poor rate book as Joseph Tucker was the owner of the Camerton Inn, outbuildings, garden, yard and Meadgate Cottage. The occupier (Landlord) of the public house was also Joseph Tucker. John Cook is recorded as being the tenant of Meadgate Cottage.

1846 Poor Rate Book

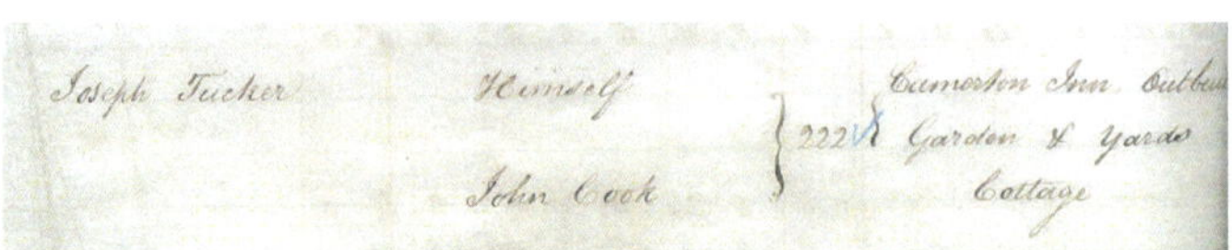

The Camerton Inn

In the 1881 census, records Benjamin Weaver 67 years of age, the head of the family and a licenced victualler. His wife, Elizabeth Weaver was 59 years of age; their son was Benjamin Weaver and recorded as being a cattle dealer. They lived in the Camerton Inn, Meadgate.

Poor Rent Book Entry 1887

Entry Number 66 – Benjamin Weaver is the landlord of the Camerton Inn, owned by Thatcher Breweries.

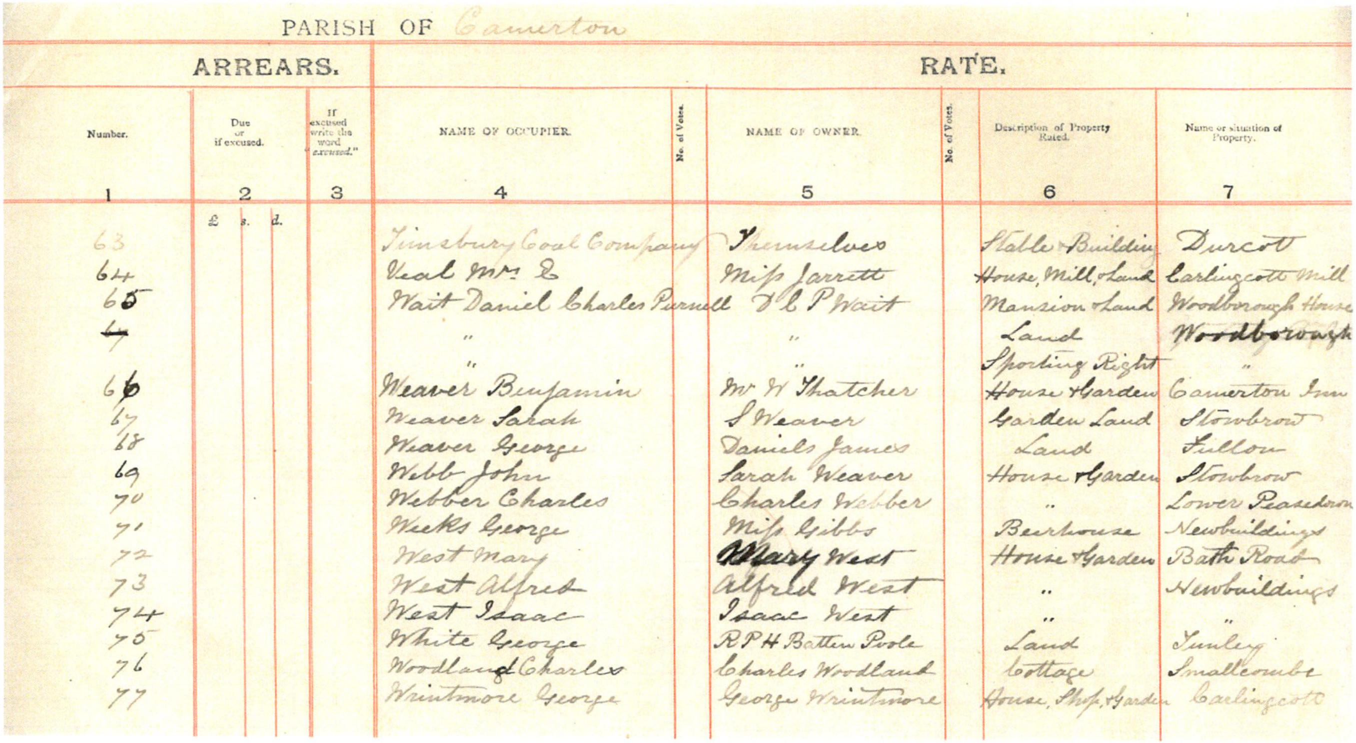

PARISH OF Camerton

ARREARS.			RATE.					
Number.	Due or if excused.	If excused write the word "excused."	NAME OF OCCUPIER.	No. of Votes.	NAME OF OWNER.	No. of Votes.	Description of Property Rated.	Name or situation of Property.
1	2	3	4		5		6	7
	£ s. d.							
63			Timsbury Coal Company		Themselves		Stable & Building	Durcott
64			Veal Mrs E		Miss Jarrett		House, Mill, & Land	Carlingcott Mill
65			Wait Daniel Charles Parnell		D C P Wait		Mansion & Land	Woodborough House
4			"		"		Land	Woodborough
			"		"		Sporting Right	"
66			Weaver Benjamin		Mr W Thatcher		House & Garden	Camerton Inn
67			Weaver Sarah		S Weaver		Garden Land	Stowbrow
68			Weaver George		Daniels James		Land	Fullow
69			Webb John		Sarah Weaver		House & Garden	Stowbrow
70			Webber Charles		Charles Webber		"	Lower Peasedown
71			Weeks George		Miss Gibbs		Beerhouse	Newbuildings
72			West Mary		Mary West		House & Garden	Bath Road
73			West Alfred		Alfred West		"	Newbuildings
74			West Isaac		Isaac West		"	"
75			White George		R P H Batten Poole		Land	Tunley
76			Woodland Charles		Charles Woodland		Cottage	Smallcombe
77			Wrintmore George		George Wrintmore		House, Shop, & Garden	Carlingcott

Records show Benjamin Weaver was the landlord of the Camerton Inn from 1861 to the early 1890's.

Records from Kelly's Diary show from 1893 to 1896 Walter Davies was the Landlord of the Camerton Inn.

Poor Rate Book dated 1893

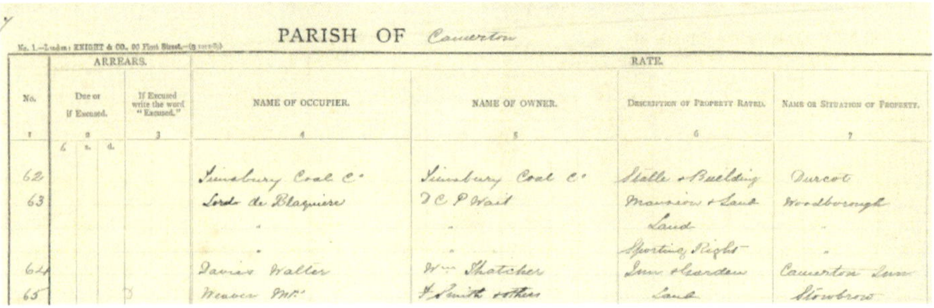

No. 1.—London: KNIGHT & CO., 90 Fleet Street.

PARISH OF Camerton

No.	ARREARS. Due or if Excused. £ s. d.	If Excused write the word "Excused."	RATE. Name of Occupier.	Name of Owner.	Description of Property Rated.	Name or Situation of Property.
1	2	3	4	5	6	7
62			Timsbury Coal Co	Timsbury Coal Co	Stalls & Building	Durcot
63			Lords de Blaquiere	J C P Wait	Mansion & Land	Woodborough
			"	"	Land	"
			"	"	Sporting Right	"
64			Davies Walter	Wm Thatcher	Inn & Garden	Camerton Inn
65			Weaver Mrs	J Smith & others	Land	Stowbrow

In 1897 - The landlord of the Camerton Inn was Alfred Nicholls.

Photograph of the Camerton Inn in the late 1800's

Pictured above you can see how the young boys wore caps and ladies with long aprons, one boy sat on a pony and another boy on a bicycle. The road was a track not yet surfaced. Changes were starting to take place with regards to getting from place to place.

Alfred Nicholls - was landlord of the Camerton Inn

Alfred Nicholl's first wife, Ameilia died in 1882, he remarried in the spring of 1896 to Ann Elizabeth Cooper who was 20 years his junior.

Marriage Certificate - Alfred Nicholls and aged 45 years and Ann Elizabeth Cooper aged 25 years.

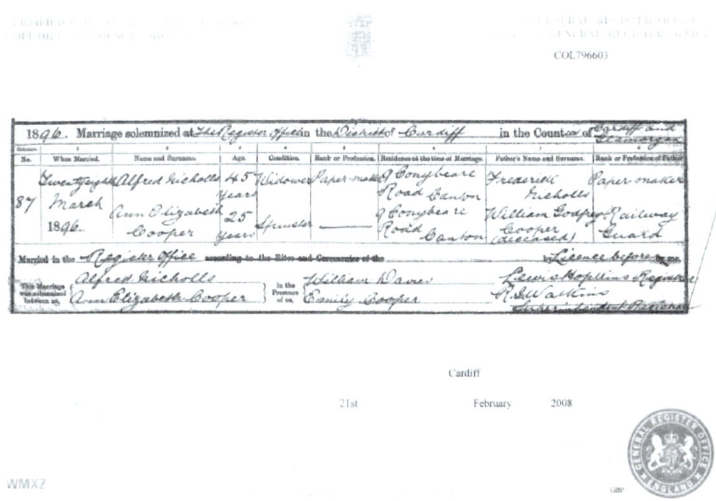

COL796603

1896. Marriage solemnized at The Register Office in the District of Cardiff in the County of Cardiff and Glamorgan

No.	When Married.	Name and Surname.	Age.	Condition.	Rank or Profession.	Residence at the time of Marriage.	Father's Name and Surname.	Rank or Profession of Father.
87	Twentyeighth March 1896	Alfred Nicholls	45 years	Widower	Paper-maker	9 Conybeare Road Canton	Frederick Nicholls	Paper-maker
		Ann Elizabeth Cooper	25 years	Spinster	—	9 Conybeare Road Canton	William Godfrey Cooper (deceased)	Railway Guard

Married in the Register Office ~~according to the Rites and Ceremonies of the~~ by Licence before ~~by~~ me.

This Marriage was solemnized between us, Alfred Nicholls, Ann Elizabeth Cooper; in the Presence of us, William Dawe, Emily Cooper; Lewis Hopkins Registrar, R. J. Watkins Superintendent Registrar

Cardiff

21st February 2008

WMXZ

Alfred and Ann had a son named Arthur Edward Nicholls, he was born on 27th June 1896. The family moved from Cardiff to Meadgate, Camerton; about 1897; Alfred became the landlord of the Camerton Inn.

In 1901 Ann gave birth to a daughter in the Inn, they named her Edith Gwendoline. In 1902 another daughter arrived and was named Nora Phylis. In 1905 Ethel Winifred arrived but sadly died soon after her birth.

The Camerton Inn - was also the headquarters for Meadgate football team.

In August 1911 printed in the local "Sign' magazine is an article on the AGM of the Camerton Football Club. Ann ran the Camerton Inn from 1907 to the Autumn of 1911.

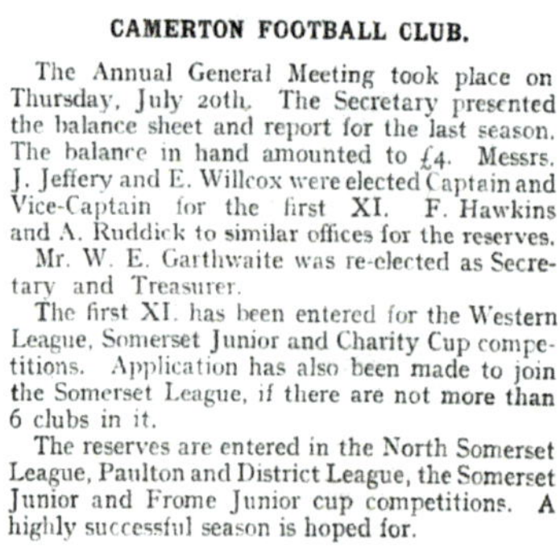

CAMERTON FOOTBALL CLUB.

The Annual General Meeting took place on Thursday, July 20th. The Secretary presented the balance sheet and report for the last season. The balance in hand amounted to £4. Messrs. J. Jeffery and E. Willcox were elected Captain and Vice-Captain for the first XI. F. Hawkins and A. Ruddick to similar offices for the reserves.

Mr. W. E. Garthwaite was re-elected as Secretary and Treasurer.

The first XI. has been entered for the Western League, Somerset Junior and Charity Cup competitions. Application has also been made to join the Somerset League, if there are not more than 6 clubs in it.

The reserves are entered in the North Somerset League, Paulton and District League, the Somerset Junior and Frome Junior cup competitions. A highly successful season is hoped for.

In 1907 the Camerton Inn was owned by Thatcher's Breweries, the occupier Alfred Nicholls, the landlord leased the pub and garden from the brewery.

The Poor Rate Book around 1907 – (Entry No: 72)

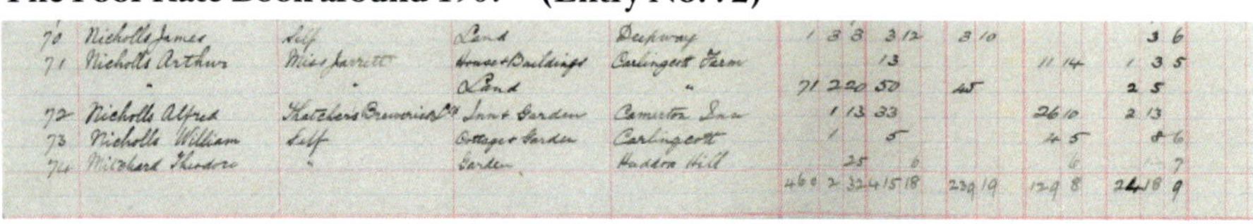

No.	Occupier	Owner	Description	Situation
70	Nicholls James	Self	Land	Deepway
71	Nicholls Arthur	Miss Jarrett	House & Buildings	Carlingcott Farm
	"	"	Land	"
72	Nicholls Alfred	Thatchers Breweries Co	Inn & Garden	Camerton Inn
73	Nicholls William	Self	Cottage & Garden	Carlingcott
74	Mitchard Theodore	"	Garden	Haddon Hill

Alfred died at the age of 58 on the 20th November 1907, leaving Ann a widow, he left her £473 and 18 shillings in his will.

Poor Rate Book 1913

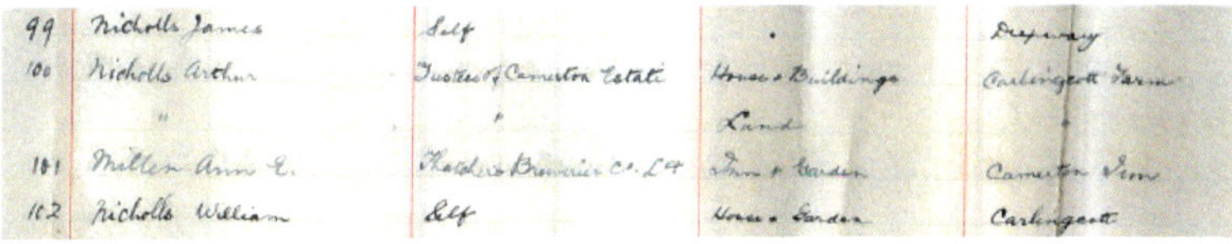

99	Nicholls James	Self	.	Dispensary
100	Nicholls Arthur	Trustees of Camerton Estate	House & Buildings	Carlingcott Farm
	"	"	Land	"
101	Millen Ann E.	Thatchers Breweries Co. Ltd	Inn & Garden	Camerton Inn
102	Nicholls William	Self	House & Garden	Carlingcott

Ann was courting William Millen he was a local Game Keeper for the Priston estate, he was employed by Captain Vaughan-Jenkins who owned both the Priston and Tunley estates.

William with his faithful companions and gun

Shooting Season involved a great deal of hard work, the estate received many trespassers from the mining districts and often resulted in court proceedings.

The season also spread a lot of joy as it was real sporting days, the bags were sometimes small but the spirit of the hunt was with the men, their dogs and guns. Whilst being a game keeper, William used to give locals the odd rabbit, this was always well received; especially to large families on a low wage. It was also a good show of Game for his employer.

Captain Vaughan Jenkins (Landowner)

Pictured above, Captain Vaughan Jenkins is sat in the chair with William Millen stood to the left of him.

Ann aged 36 years married William Millen aged 26 years, 10 years her junior, in secret during the Autumn of 1911.

1911 Wedding Certificate

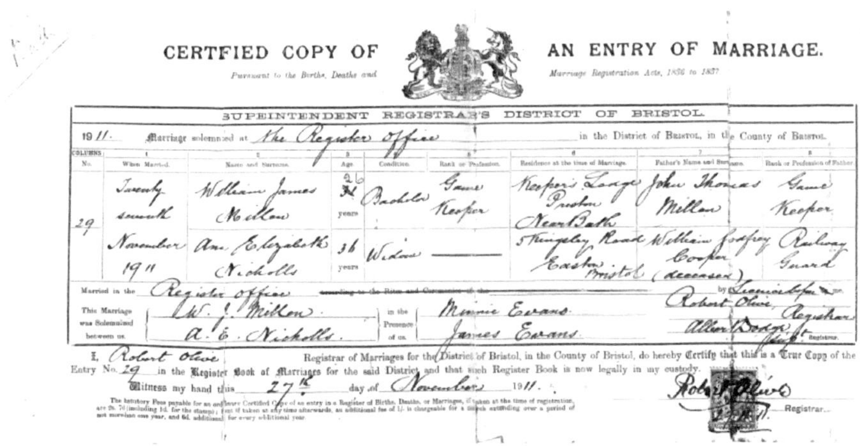

CERTFIED COPY OF AN ENTRY OF MARRIAGE.

Pursuant to the Births, Deaths and Marriage Registration Acts, 1836 to 1837

SUPEINTENDENT REGISTRAR'S DISTRICT OF BRISTOL.

1911. Marriage solemnized at The Register Office in the District of Bristol, in the County of Bristol.

No.	When Married.	Name and Surname.	Age.	Condition.	Rank or Profession.	Residence at the time of Marriage.	Father's Name and Surname.	Rank or Profession of Father.
29	Twenty seventh November 1911	William James Millen	26 years	Bachelor	Game Keeper	Keeper's Lodge Preston Near Bath	John Thomas Millen	Game Keeper
		Ann Elizabeth Nicholls	36 years	Widow	———	5 Kingsley Road Easton Bristol	William Godfrey Cooper (deceased)	Railway Guard

Married in the Register Office ~~according to the Rites and Ceremonies of the~~ by Licence by me.

This Marriage was Solemnized between us, W. J. Millen, A. E. Nicholls. in the Presence of us, Minnie Evans, James Evans. Robert Olive, Registrar. Albert Dodge, Supt. Registrar.

I, Robert Olive Registrar of Marriages for the District of Bristol, in the County of Bristol, do hereby Certify that this is a True Copy of the Entry No. 29 in the Register Book of Marriages for the said District, and that such Register Book is now legally in my custody.

Witness my hand this 27th day of November 1911.

Robert Olive Registrar.

The Statutory Fees payable for an ordinary Certified Copy of an entry in a Register of Births, Deaths, or Marriages, if taken at the time of registration, are 2s. 7d (including 1d. for the stamp); but if taken at any time afterwards, an additional fee of 1/- is chargeable for a search extending over a period of not more than one year, and 6d. additional for every additional year.

William could not continue working as a game keeper and be the landlord of the Camerton Inn, he gave his notice to cease work as a game keeper.

He started a new life with his wife Ann and was stepfather to Ann's 3 children; Arthur was the eldest and at that time a young teenage boy. William and Ann went on to have 4 further children.

Arthur Edward Nicholl's family believe he left home to join the army when he was about 18 years of age. He served as a regular soldier with '9' platoon, 3rd Somerset Light Infantry and was stationed at Crown Hill Barracks, Plymouth.

Pictured below is Arthur Nicholls in his uniform

Army Form W. 3138 Separation allowance showing 18 shillings and 2 pennys; arrears from 21.1.16 to 8.5.16 paid to his mother. It also shows how Arthur had paid into the 'Soldiers, Sailors and Families Association' (SSAFA) the sum of 7 pennies that had already been deducted from his wages.

W.3138 Form dated 9th May 1916 – Separation payment

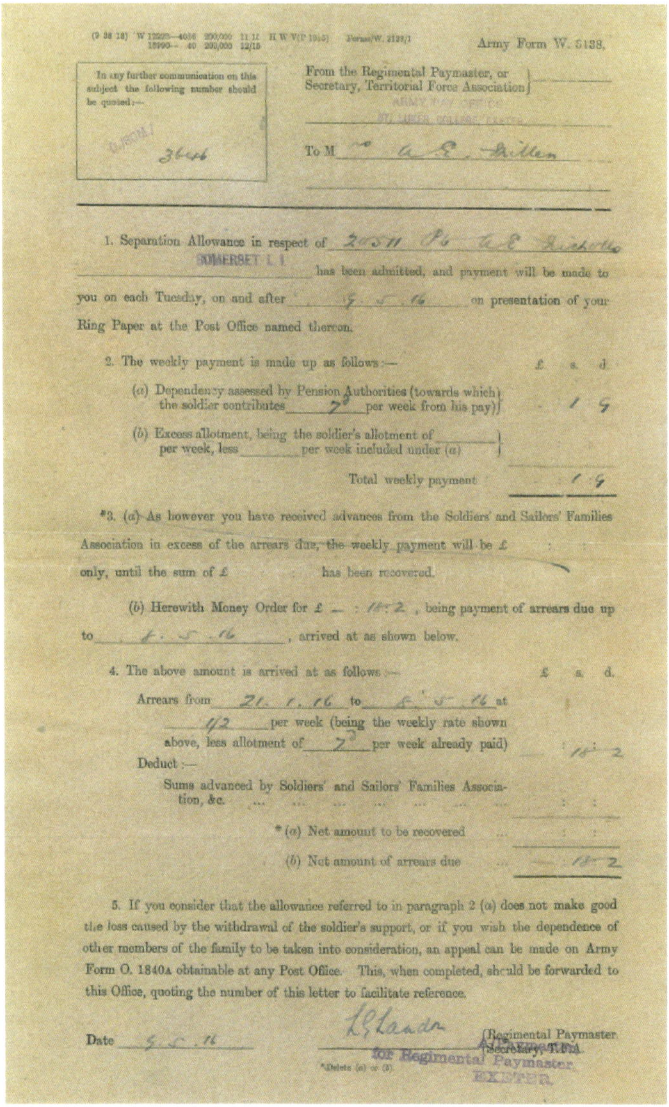

Army Form W. 3138.

In any further communication on this subject the following number should be quoted:— 3646

From the Regimental Paymaster, or Secretary, Territorial Force Association
ARMY PAY OFFICE
ST. LUKES COLLEGE, EXETER

To Mrs A. E. Millen

1. Separation Allowance in respect of 20511 Pte A. E. Nicholls SOMERSET L. I. has been admitted, and payment will be made to you on each Tuesday, on and after 9. 5. 16 on presentation of your Ring Paper at the Post Office named thereon.

2. The weekly payment is made up as follows:—

	£	s.	d.
(a) Dependency assessed by Pension Authorities (towards which the soldier contributes 7d per week from his pay)		1	9
(b) Excess allotment, being the soldier's allotment of ____ per week, less ____ per week included under (a)			
Total weekly payment		1	9

*3. (a) As however you have received advances from the Soldiers' and Sailors' Families Association in excess of the arrears due, the weekly payment will be £ : : only, until the sum of £ : : has been recovered.

(b) Herewith Money Order for £ — : 18 : 2, being payment of arrears due up to 8. 5. 16, arrived at as shown below.

4. The above amount is arrived at as follows:—

	£	s.	d.
Arrears from 21. 1. 16 to 8. 5. 16 at 1/2 per week (being the weekly rate shown above, less allotment of 7d per week already paid)		18	2
Deduct:— Sums advanced by Soldiers' and Sailors' Families Association, &c. ...			
*(a) Net amount to be recovered ...			
(b) Net amount of arrears due ...	—	18	2

5. If you consider that the allowance referred to in paragraph 2 (a) does not make good the loss caused by the withdrawal of the soldier's support, or if you wish the dependence of other members of the family to be taken into consideration, an appeal can be made on Army Form O. 1840A obtainable at any Post Office. This, when completed, should be forwarded to this Office, quoting the number of this letter to facilitate reference.

Date 9. 5. 16 — L. G. Lander, for Regimental Paymaster, EXETER. Regimental Paymaster / Secretary, T.F.A.

*Delete (a) or (b).

May 10th 1916, Arthur went to France, on the 1st June he joined the 1st Battalion who were preparing for the Somme Battle.

Arthur wrote home as often as he could, a sample of one of the many hand written letters to his sister Gwen below:

A Hand Written letter from Arthur to his Sister Gwen

"We had to go through a wood, six paces apart; I had not gone about 20 yards when I went tumbling into a hole about 3ft deep all right"; "Talk about mud, wasn't the name for it!"

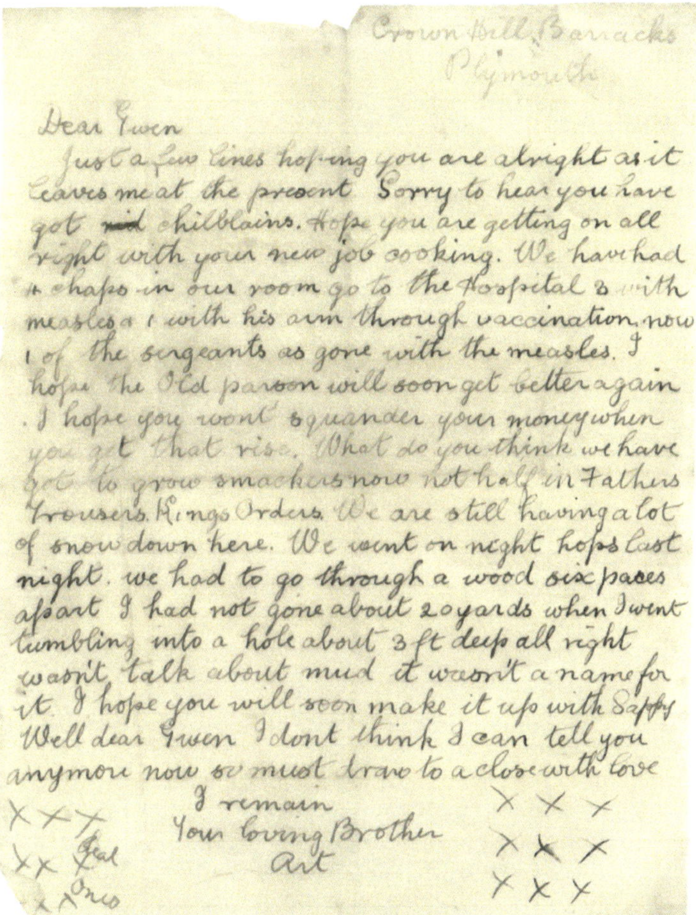

Crown Hill Barracks
Plymouth

Dear Gwen
Just a few lines hoping you are alright as it leaves me at the present. Sorry to hear you have got chilblains. Hope you are getting on all right with your new job cooking. We have had 4 chaps in our room go to the Hospital 3 with measles & 1 with his arm through vaccination, now 1 of the sergeants as gone with the measles. I hope the Old parson will soon get better again. I hope you wont squander your money when you get that rise. What do you think we have got to grow smackers now not half in Fathers Trousers. Kings Orders. We are still having a lot of snow down here. We went on night hops last night. we had to go through a wood six paces apart I had not gone about 20 yards when I went tumbling into a hole about 3 ft deep all right wasn't, talk about mud it wasn't a name for it. I hope you will soon make it up with Saffy. Well dear Gwen I dont think I can tell you anymore now so must draw to a close with love

I remain
Your loving Brother
Art

XXX
XXX
XXX

During Arthur's first action, he would have had his 20th birthday; on 27th June; just less than one week later he was reported missing!

Arthurs's mother, Mrs A Millen gave a photograph to a local newspaper hoping that some light may be shed about her son. Mrs A Millen also wrote a letter to the war office, asking for any news of her son.

Army Form B. 104---83 dated 6th Sept 1916, informing Mrs A Millen a report was received by the War Office stating her son Arthur was posted missing after an engagement by the British Imperial force on 1st July 1916.

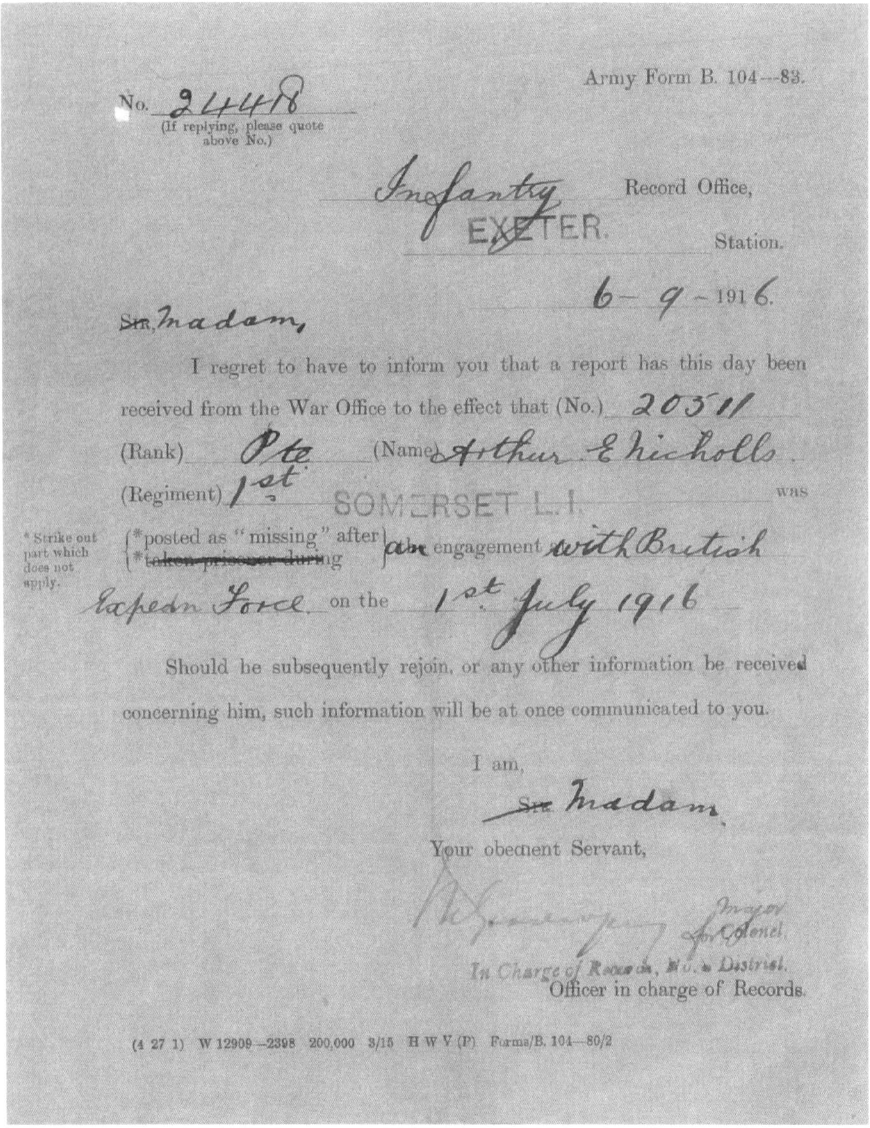

Army Form B. 104---83.

No. 24418
(If replying, please quote above No.)

Infantry Record Office,
EXETER. Station.

6-9-1916.

~~Sir,~~ Madam,

I regret to have to inform you that a report has this day been received from the War Office to the effect that (No.) 20511 (Rank) Pte (Name) Arthur E Nicholls. (Regiment) 1st SOMERSET L.I. was

*posted as "missing" after ~~*taken prisoner during~~ an engagement with British Expedn Force on the 1st July 1916

* Strike out part which does not apply.

Should he subsequently rejoin, or any other information be received concerning him, such information will be at once communicated to you.

I am,
~~Sir~~ Madam
Your obedient Servant,

Major for Colonel,
In Charge of Records, No. District,
Officer in charge of Records.

(4 27 1) W 12909—2398 200,000 3/15 H W V (P) Forms/B. 104—80/2

In the spring of 1917 the battlefields of the Somme and Ancre were cleared by V corps and a number of new cemeteries were made. Number 2 began in May 1917 with burials in plots I and II, Arthur's body was found and remains are now laid to rest in plot I, Grave no: 26, Serre Road, No: 2 cemetery (France)

Arthur Edward Nicholls identity Dog Tag, his Bugle pin badge representing the 1st Battalion Somerset Light Infantry below:

Dog Tag

Bugle Badge

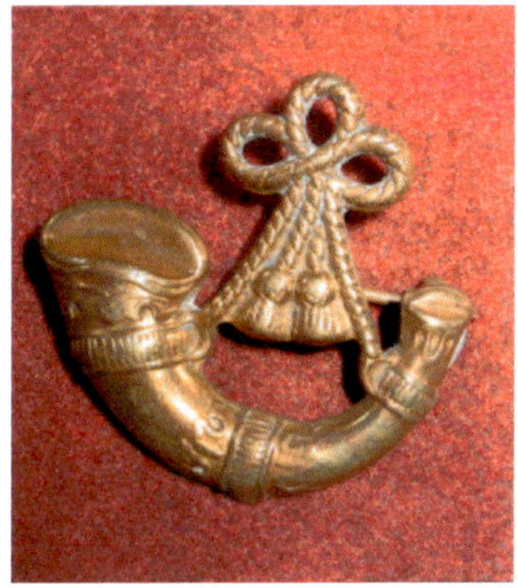

British War Medal

Victory Medal

British Red Cross – a letter dated 16th August 1917 from the British Red Cross to Mrs A Millen below:

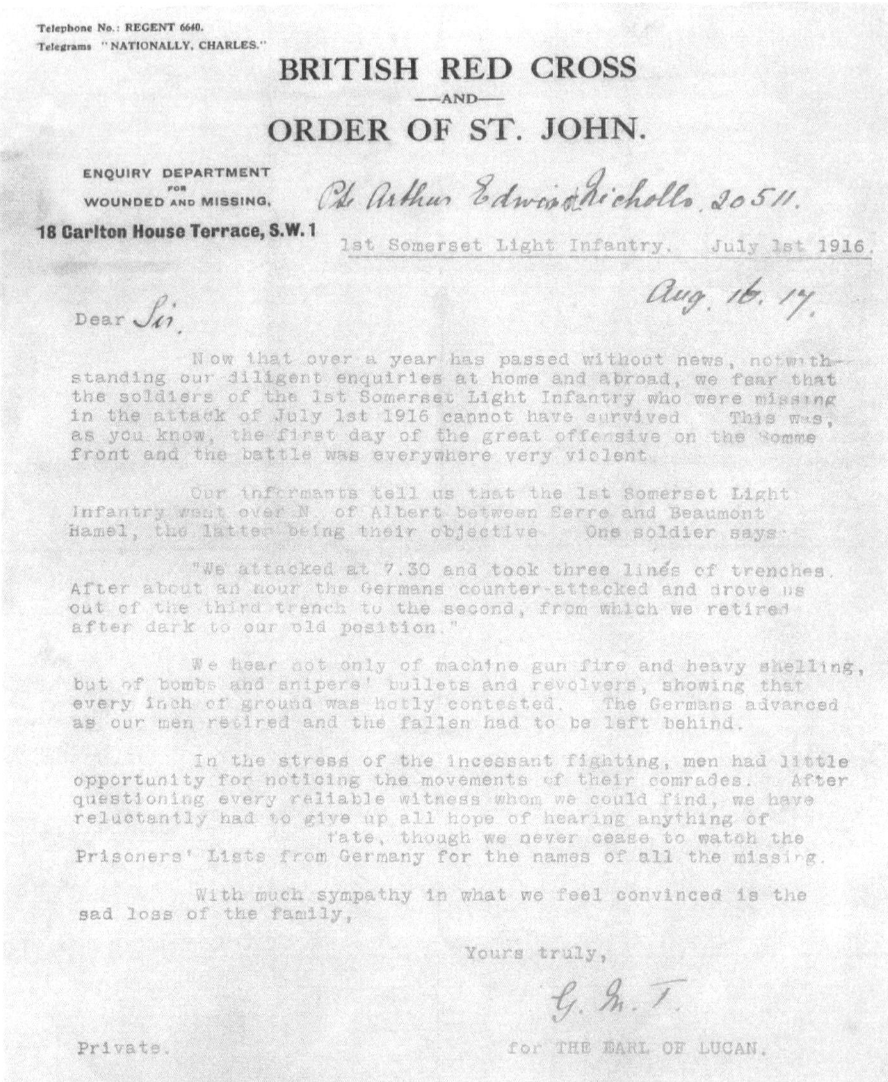

Telephone No.: REGENT 6640.
Telegrams "NATIONALLY, CHARLES."

BRITISH RED CROSS
—AND—
ORDER OF ST. JOHN.

ENQUIRY DEPARTMENT
FOR
WOUNDED AND MISSING,
18 Carlton House Terrace, S.W. 1

Pte Arthur Edwin Nicholls. 20511.
1st Somerset Light Infantry. July 1st 1916.

Aug. 16. 17.

Dear Sir,

Now that over a year has passed without news, notwithstanding our diligent enquiries at home and abroad, we fear that the soldiers of the 1st Somerset Light Infantry who were missing in the attack of July 1st 1916 cannot have survived. This was, as you know, the first day of the great offensive on the Somme front and the battle was everywhere very violent.

Our informants tell us that the 1st Somerset Light Infantry went over N. of Albert between Serre and Beaumont Hamel, the latter being their objective. One soldier says:-

"We attacked at 7.30 and took three lines of trenches. After about an hour the Germans counter-attacked and drove us out of the third trench to the second, from which we retired after dark to our old position."

We hear not only of machine gun fire and heavy shelling, but of bombs and snipers' bullets and revolvers, showing that every inch of ground was hotly contested. The Germans advanced as our men retired and the fallen had to be left behind.

In the stress of the incessant fighting, men had little opportunity for noticing the movements of their comrades. After questioning every reliable witness whom we could find, we have reluctantly had to give up all hope of hearing anything of fate, though we never cease to watch the Prisoners' Lists from Germany for the names of all the missing.

With much sympathy in what we feel convinced is the sad loss of the family,

Yours truly,

G. M. T.

Private. for THE EARL OF LUCAN.

(No Man's Land) – The road out of Maillet to Serre and Pulsieux entered 'No Man's Land' about 1,300 metres south-west of Serre. The 31st and 4th divisions attacked north and south of this road, the land is where thousands of men lost their lives to the battle of the Somme on the 1st July 1916.

A cemetery was designed by Sir Edwin Lutyens, he is referred to as the greatest British architect, the cemetery was extensively increased after the Armistice and finally completed in 1934.

Serre Road Cemetery No: 2 France

SSAFA is an armed forces charity which was formed in 1885 and has been running for nearly 131 years, it is still helping to give life time support for our forces and their families.

SSAFA was formed to help families left behind. Major James Gildea wrote to the Times appealing for funds and volunteers at the time of the second expeditionary forces set sail for Egypt in early 1885. Within 3 months of the Times publishing his letter; the charity known as the (Soldiers, Sailors Association) was set up to help families left behind.

Sir James Gildea, founder of the charity SSAFA

In 1914 Britain entered World War 1, volunteers helped over one million women, children and other relatives across the United Kingdom. SSAFA was the only charity to care for families left behind by soldiers going to the front.

Her Majesty Queen Victoria was patron to SSAFA and the emblem pictured below is showing the HR crown

ssafa

Lifelong support
for our Forces
and their families

HRH Majesty Queen Elizabeth is SSAFA's Patron

HRH Prince Michael is SSAFA's President

SSAFA is a national charity and has been supporting our Forces and their families for more than 130 years. Today they continue to help thousands of people in hundreds of different ways. It gives Lifelong support and looks after all generations of service personnel, gives to individual needs e.g bereavement, befriending, financial, psychological or emotional support.

SSAFA help anyone who has served for a day in uniform of H M Services and their dependents.

If you know of anyone who needs SSAFA's help, please call the SSAFA help line on Tel: 0207 403 8783.

William James Millen was landlord of the Camerton Inn from 1911 to 1923, the sign in the photograph below clearly shows his name.

The Camerton Inn, Meadgate in the early 1900s

William James Millen is stood proud on the end of the back row wearing a cap and very smart appearance.

The group of people are wearing their Sunday best and are either going to a party or waiting for a charabanc bus to take them out on a day trip, perhaps to Weston Super Mare ?

It is hard to believe you could buy a pint and a wad of tobacco for just one penny! It was a hard life so the local Inn was a second home to many, a pint of ale, sat by an old log fire, smoking a pipe. Having a chat with friends used to help them forget their troubles and the harsh reality of life.

The outbuildings at the rear of the pub's garden used to be stables for the horses and a Blacksmith shop for the local smithy. It would have been a hive of activity in it's day, everything was transported by horse and cart.

Used to be Stables and a Blacksmith shop pictured below

Landlords

A W Durham was the landlord of the Camerton Inn from 1923 to the late 1940s his name is clearly seen in the photograph below. Bert Connick and his wife ran the Camerton Inn from about 1949 to the mid 1950s. Mac Mactravers was the landlord of the Camerton Inn from the mid 1950s to 1960. Dennis Rogers was the Landlord of the Camerton Inn from 1960 to 1972. For several years Dennis also worked down the pit as a miner, he was about 30 years of age in the photograph on page 173.

A W Durham's name above the Front Door of the Camerton Inn

Pete Feare about 2 years of age with his father Wil Feare in 1948.

Dennis Rogers with his mining workmates

Publicans/Landlords covering nearly 200 years

Joseph Coombs, Joseph Tucker, Benjamin Weaver, Walter Davies, Alfred Nicholls, Ann Nicholls, William Millen, Bert Connick, Albert Durham, Mac Mactravers, Dennis Rogers, Gus & Lilian Lloyd, John & Peggy, Thelma Dingle, Anne & Ron Fleet and finally Sally Shaw & partner Alan Chambers.

According to local residents in the late 1990s there was a cold blooded murder that took place outside the front of the Camerton Inn. Rumour says, a drug dealer from Bath was sitting outside the pub enjoying a drink one evening; an unknown car with it's window opened; slowly pulled up alongside him. Someone inside the car took aim and shot the drug dealer dead; this caused quite a stir in the sleepy village of Camerton.

The last landlady of the pub was Sally Shaw, she ceased trading and sold the pub to Mr J Gunter in 2007. He in turn renovated the interior of the building changing it from a pub to an Indian restaurant and leased it to the Bombay King. The business changed it's name to Shazar and remained an Indian restaurant.

The Old Pub Sign 'Camerton Inn Freehouse'

The sign was revealed in the Autumn of 2013 for a short while, covered up with a change of business name. It was a nice treat for people to see how the old pub sign would have looked like.

The business name changed again to the Camerton's Tandoori Indian restaurant and takeaway; and was managed by Mr Lutbur Rahman. The building is currently vacant.

Camerton's Tandoori Indian Restaurant and Takeaway as seen in 2014, the front (south view) of the Camerton Inn.

Mr Rahman with his daughter outside the Indian restaurant

View of the Camerton Inn, Meadgate

The Camerton Inn/No. 28 Meadgate - The old pub had a flat on the second floor which is registered as 28 Meadgate.

1910 Claimant William James Gibbons the lodger on the register

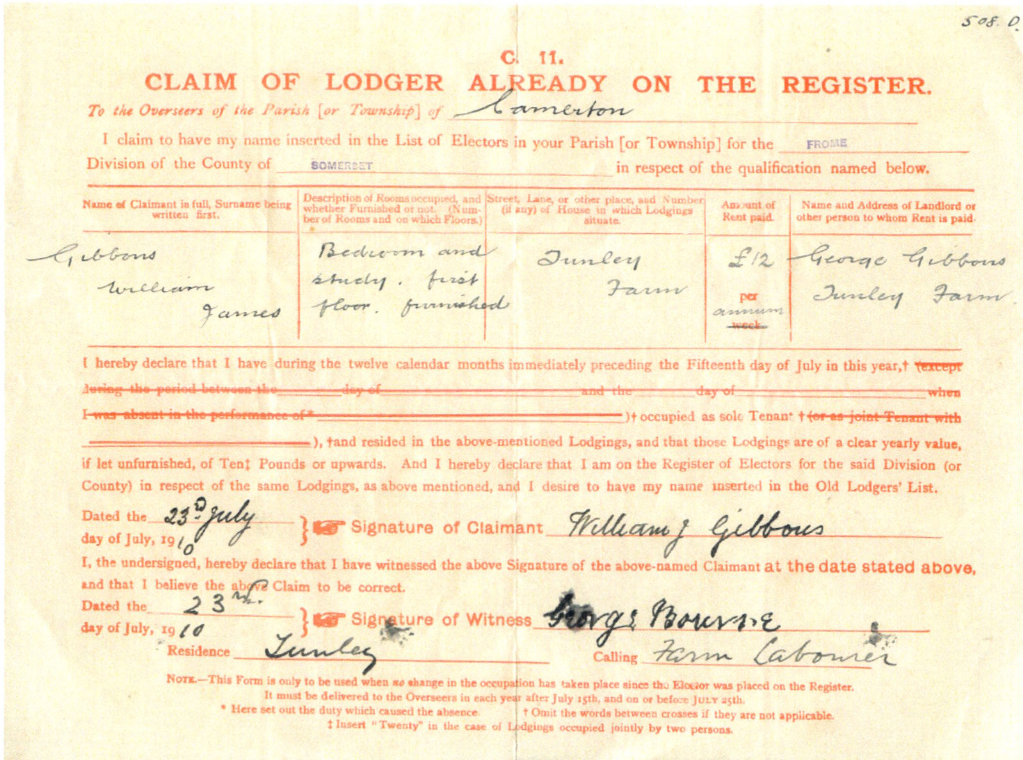

508. O.

C. 11.

CLAIM OF LODGER ALREADY ON THE REGISTER.

To the Overseers of the Parish [or Township] of Camerton

I claim to have my name inserted in the List of Electors in your Parish [or Township] for the FROME Division of the County of SOMERSET in respect of the qualification named below.

Name of Claimant in full, Surname being written first.	Description of Rooms occupied, and whether Furnished or not. (Number of Rooms and on which Floors.)	Street, Lane, or other place, and Number (if any) of House in which Lodgings situate.	Amount of Rent paid.	Name and Address of Landlord or other person to whom Rent is paid.
Gibbons William James	Bedroom and study. first floor. furnished	Dunley Farm	£12 per annum ~~week~~	George Gibbons Dunley Farm

I hereby declare that I have during the twelve calendar months immediately preceding the Fifteenth day of July in this year,† ~~except during the period between the ____ day of ____ and the ____ day of ____ when I was absent in the performance of*~~ ____)† occupied as sole Tenant † ~~(or as joint Tenant with~~ ____), ‡and resided in the above-mentioned Lodgings, and that those Lodgings are of a clear yearly value, if let unfurnished, of Ten‡ Pounds or upwards. And I hereby declare that I am on the Register of Electors for the said Division (or County) in respect of the same Lodgings, as above mentioned, and I desire to have my name inserted in the Old Lodgers' List.

Dated the 23rd July day of July, 1910 } Signature of Claimant William J Gibbons

I, the undersigned, hereby declare that I have witnessed the above Signature of the above-named Claimant at the date stated above, and that I believe the above Claim to be correct.

Dated the 23rd day of July, 1910 } Signature of Witness George Bourne

Residence Dunley Calling Farm Labourer

NOTE.—This Form is only to be used when *no* change in the occupation has taken place since the Elector was placed on the Register. It must be delivered to the Overseers in each year after July 15th, and on or before JULY 25th.

* Here set out the duty which caused the absence. † Omit the words between crosses if they are not applicable.

‡ Insert "Twenty" in the case of Lodgings occupied jointly by two persons.

Chapter 5 - Meadgate East

Meadgate East as seen today pictured below:

Map of Meadgate East (1886)

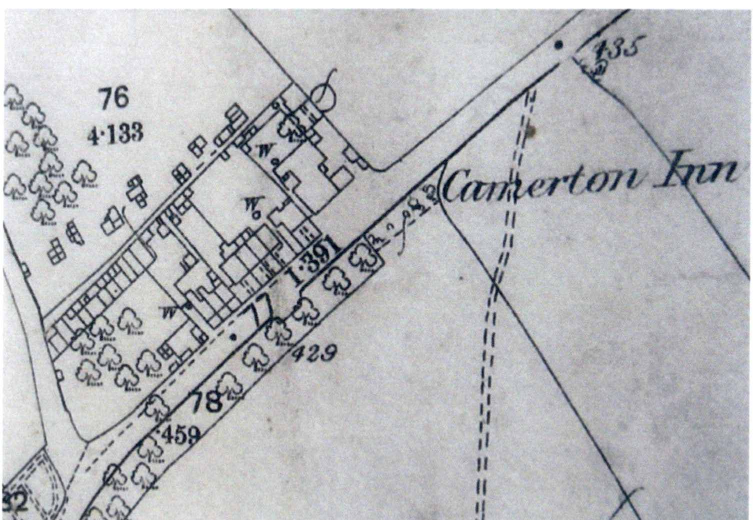

The Jarrett family owned most of the properties in Meadgate and would have rented the cottages out to local families. John Jarrett died in 1863, his wife Anna died 5 years later; leaving their daughters Anna and Emily the Camerton Court estate. Both sisters ran the Camerton estate and the local mine with great success.

Most the families that occupied the cottages in Meadgate East, were mining families, the male head of the family, husband or son(s) worked down the local Camerton and nearby pits.

Entries of Tenants from the 1881 Poor Rate Book (Meadgate East)

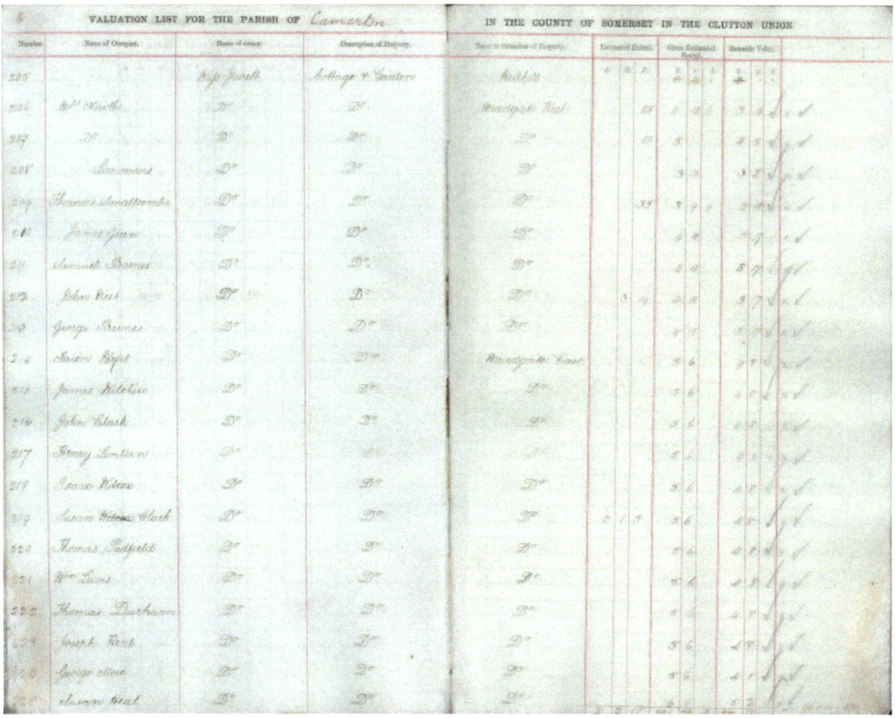

VALUATION LIST FOR THE PARISH OF Camerton IN THE COUNTY OF SOMERSET IN THE CLUTTON UNION

Number.	Name of Occupier.	Name of owner.	Description of Property.	Name or Situation of Property.
205		Miss Jarrett	Cottage & Garden	Radstock
206	Wm North	Do	Do	Meadgate West
207	Do	Do	Do	Do
208	Simmons	Do	Do	Do
209	Thomas Smallcombe	Do	Do	Do
210	James Gian	Do	Do	Do
211	Samuel Barnes	Do	Do	Do
212	John West	Do	Do	Do
213	George Barnes	Do	Do	Do
214	Aaron Payne	Do	Do	Meadgate East
215	James Hitchins	Do	Do	Do
216	John Clark	Do	Do	Do
217	Henry Lenton	Do	Do	Do
218	Isaac Wilcox	Do	Do	Do
219	Susan Wilcox Clark	Do	Do	Do
220	Thomas Padfield	Do	Do	Do
221	Wm Lewis	Do	Do	Do
222	Thomas Durham	Do	Do	Do
223	Joseph West	Do	Do	Do
224	George Moore	Do	Do	Do
225	Susan Heal	Do	Do	Do

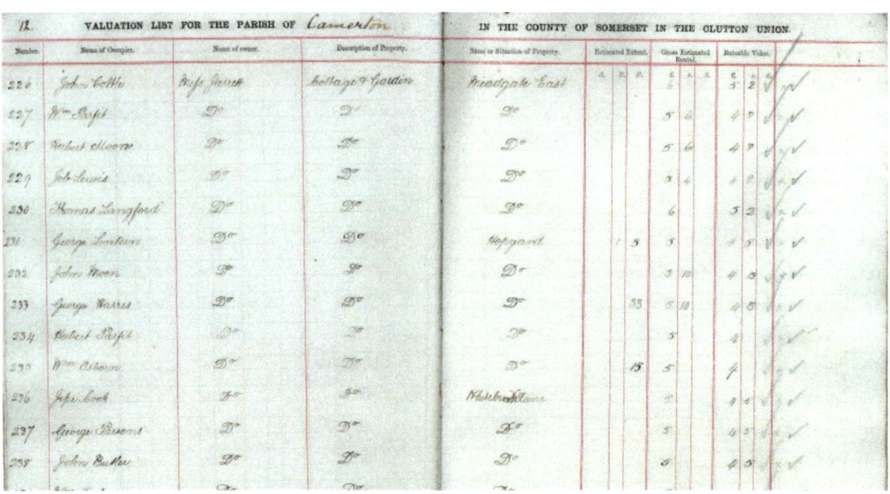

12\. VALUATION LIST FOR THE PARISH OF Camerton IN THE COUNTY OF SOMERSET IN THE CLUTTON UNION

Number.	Name of Occupier.	Name of owner.	Description of Property.	Name or Situation of Property.
226	John Cottle	Miss Jarrett	Cottage & Garden	Meadgate East
227	Wm Parfit	Do	Do	Do
228	Robert Moore	Do	Do	Do
229	Job Lewis	Do	Do	Do
230	Thomas Langford	Do	Do	Do
231	George Lenton	Do	Do	Hopyard
232	John Moon	Do	Do	Do
233	George Harris	Do	Do	Do
234	Robert Parfit	Do	Do	Do
235	Wm Gibson	Do	Do	Do
236	Jesse Cook	Do	Do	Whitebrook Lane
237	George Parsons	Do	Do	Do
238	John Butler	Do	Do	Do

Recorded at the rear of the poor rate book dated the 8th July 1881, there are some interesting signatures; the overseers were local men, George Gibbons and George Fear; they collected a sum of money called a poor rate from people living with in the parish. The money collected was given to people that had fallen on hard times and needed help.

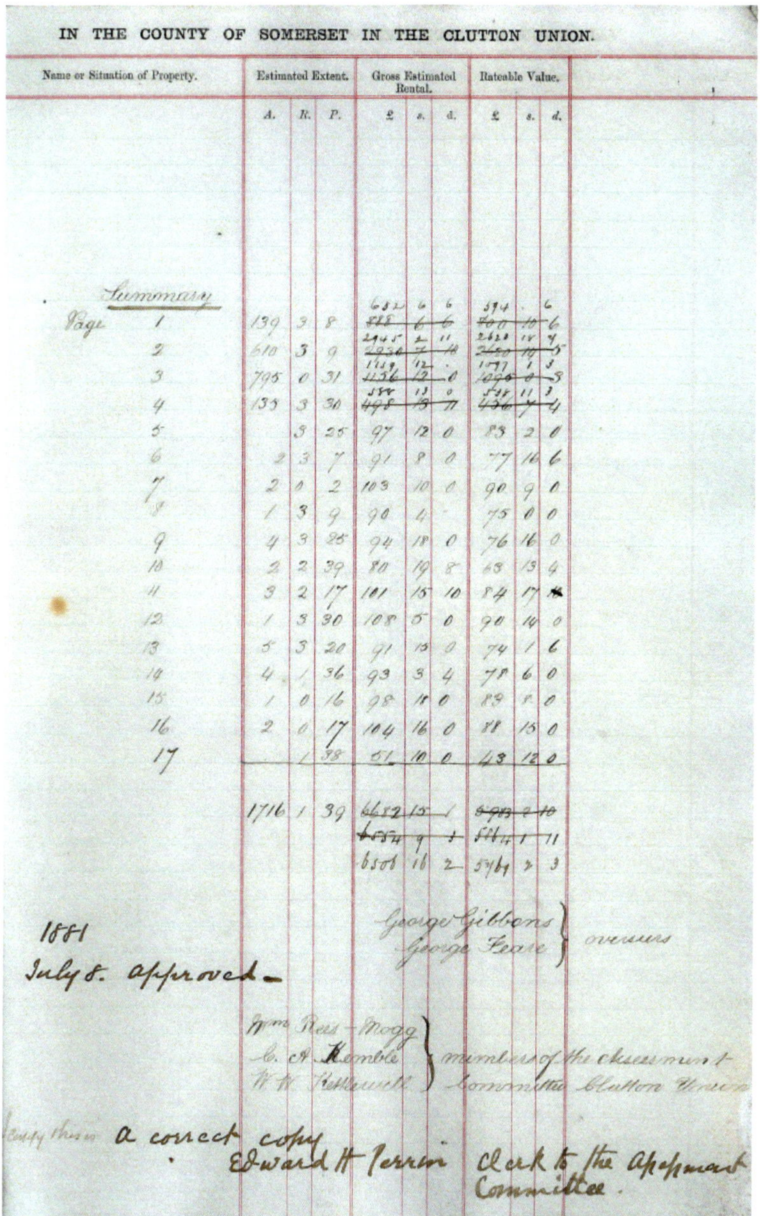

IN THE COUNTY OF SOMERSET IN THE CLUTTON UNION.

Name or Situation of Property.	Estimated Extent. A.	R.	P.	Gross Estimated Rental. £	s.	d.	Rateable Value. £	s.	d.
Summary Page 1	139	3	8	682 ~~888~~	6 ~~6~~	6 ~~6~~	594 ~~700~~	. ~~10~~	6 ~~6~~
2	610	3	9	2945 ~~2930~~	2 ~~7~~	11 ~~10~~	2620 ~~2620~~	18 ~~10~~	4 ~~5~~
3	795	0	31	1259 ~~1156~~	12 ~~12~~	. ~~0~~	1097 ~~1090~~	1 ~~0~~	3 ~~3~~
4	135	3	30	580 ~~498~~	13 ~~3~~	0 ~~11~~	548 ~~436~~	11 ~~7~~	3 ~~4~~
5		3	25	97	12	0	83	2	0
6	2	3	7	91	8	0	77	16	6
7	2	0	2	103	10	0	90	9	0
8	1	3	9	90	4	-	75	0	0
9	4	3	25	94	18	0	76	16	0
10	2	2	39	80	19	8	68	13	4
11	3	2	17	101	15	10	84	17	[illegible]
12	1	3	30	108	5	0	90	10	0
13	5	3	20	91	15	0	74	1	6
14	4	1	36	93	3	4	78	6	0
15	1	0	16	98	18	0	83	8	0
16	2	0	17	104	16	0	88	15	0
17		1	38	51	10	0	43	12	0
	1716	1	39	~~6652~~ ~~6554~~ 6506	~~15~~ ~~9~~ 16	~~1~~ ~~1~~ 2	~~5913~~ ~~5864~~ 5761	~~2~~ ~~1~~ [illegible]	~~10~~ ~~11~~ 3

1881
July 8. approved –

George Gibbons
George Feare } overseers

Wm Rees-Mogg
C. A. Kemble
W. W. Kettlewell } members of the Assessment Committee Clutton Union

I certify this is a correct copy
Edward H Perrin Clerk to the Assessment Committee.

By 1891 the population in Camerton had risen to 1,877.

In 1893 - Anna Jarrett - died a spinster leaving no children, the Camerton estate was left to her sister Emily to run.

Entries of Tenants from the 1900 Poor Rate Book (Meadgate East)

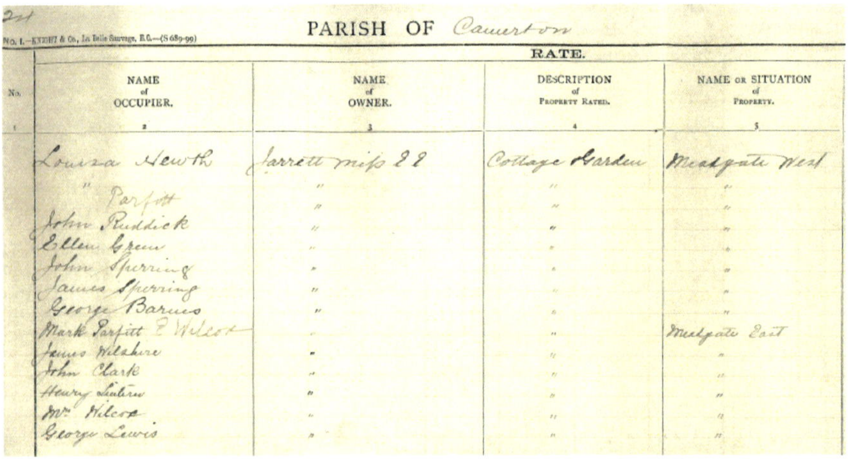

24

No. 1.—KNIGHT & Co., La Belle Sauvage, E.C.—(S 689-99)

PARISH OF Camerton

No. 1	NAME of OCCUPIER. 2	NAME of OWNER. 3	DESCRIPTION of PROPERTY RATED. 4	NAME OR SITUATION of PROPERTY. 5
	Louiza Hewth	Jarrett Miss E E	Cottage Garden	Meadgate West
	" Parfitt	"	"	"
	John Ruddick	"	"	"
	Ellen Green	"	"	"
	John Sperring	"	"	"
	James Sperring	"	"	"
	George Barnes	"	"	"
	Mark Parfitt E Wilcox	"	"	Meadgate East
	James Wilshire	"	"	"
	John Clark	"	"	"
	Henry Linton	"	"	"
	Mrs Wilcox	"	"	"
	George Lewis	"	"	"

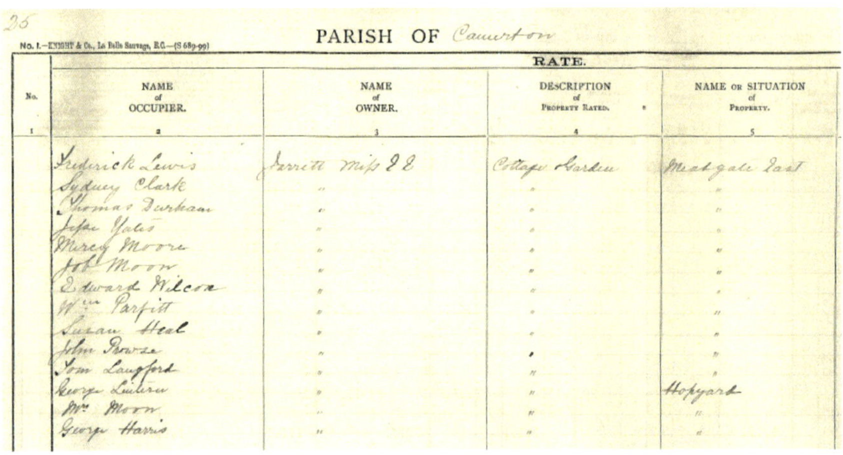

25

No. 1.—KNIGHT & Co., La Belle Sauvage, E.C.—(S 689-99)

PARISH OF Camerton

No. 1	NAME of OCCUPIER. 2	NAME of OWNER. 3	DESCRIPTION of PROPERTY RATED. 4	NAME OR SITUATION of PROPERTY. 5
	Frederick Lewis	Jarrett Miss E E	Cottage Garden	Meadgate East
	Sydney Clark	"	"	"
	Thomas Durham	"	"	"
	Jesse Yates	"	"	"
	Mercy Moore	"	"	"
	Job Moon	"	"	"
	Edward Wilcox	"	"	"
	Wm Parfitt	"	"	"
	Susan Heal	"	"	"
	John Prowse	"	"	"
	Tom Langford	"	"	"
	George Linton	"	"	Hopyard
	Mrs Moon	"	"	"
	George Harris	"	"	"

By 1911 the population had reached a peak at 2,386.

In 1911 – Miss Emily Jarrett died a spinster, also leaving no children. The Camerton estate was in the hands of the Jarrett family for nearly 100 years. It was left for Trustees to manage, a few years later the whole of the estate was purchased by Sir Frank Beauchamp.

Although a lot of land and property was owned by Miss Emily Jarrett, individual private land owners also owned parcels of land, property and cottages; e.g James Daniels, Job Moon etc.

Entries of Tenants from the 1913 Poor Rate Book (Meadgate East)

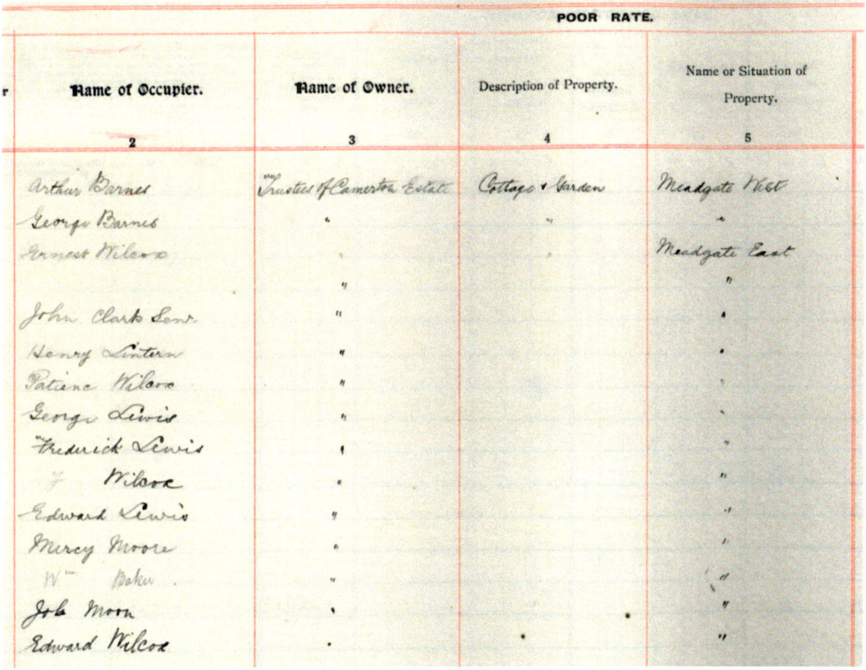

POOR RATE.

Name of Occupier. 2	Name of Owner. 3	Description of Property. 4	Name or Situation of Property. 5
Arthur Barnes	Trustees of Camerton Estate	Cottage & Garden	Meadgate West
George Barnes	"	"	"
Ernest Wilcox	"	"	Meadgate East
	"		"
John Clark Senr	"		"
Henry Lintern	"		"
Patience Wilcox	"		"
George Lewis	"		"
Frederick Lewis	"		"
F Wilcox	"		"
Edward Lewis	"		"
Mercy Moore	"		"
Wm Baker	"		"
Job Moon	"		"
Edward Wilcox	"	"	"

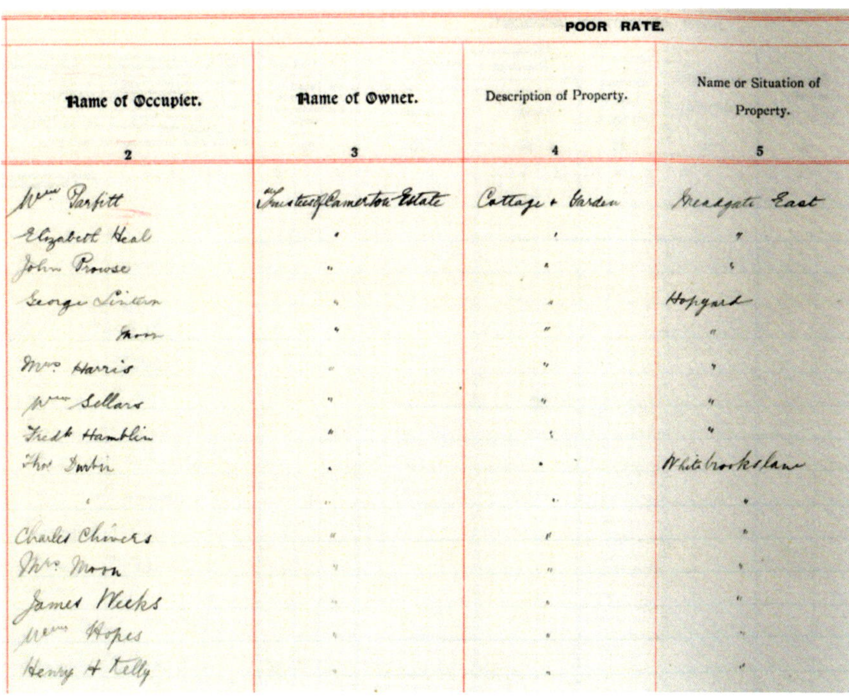

POOR RATE.

Name of Occupier. 2	Name of Owner. 3	Description of Property. 4	Name or Situation of Property. 5
Wm Parfitt	Trustees of Camerton Estate	Cottage & Garden	Meadgate East
Elizabeth Heal	"	"	"
John Prowse	"	"	"
George Lintern	"	"	Hopyard
Moon	"	"	"
Mrs Harris	"	"	"
Wm Sellars	"	"	"
Fredk Hamblin	"	"	"
Thos Durbin	"	"	Whitebrookslane
	"	"	"
Charles Chivers	"	"	"
Mrs Moon	"	"	"
James Weeks	"	"	"
Wm Hopes	"	"	"
Henry H Kelly	"	"	"

On the 14th June 1913 Overseers; James Sellars, Percy Emery, F Miles and F Holvey's names are recorded and their final accounts are signed off by two of His majesty's justices of the peace.

As you pass the old Camerton Inn, you will a see a beautiful old detached cottage on your right, it is a natural white lias stone built cottage; with solar light panels in its roof.

No: 27 Meadgate used to be known as the 'Royal Cottage'

In 1823 there was a peppercorn law agreement for 2,000 years between a tenant William Beling and Mrs Anne Jarrett.

Indenture dated 1823

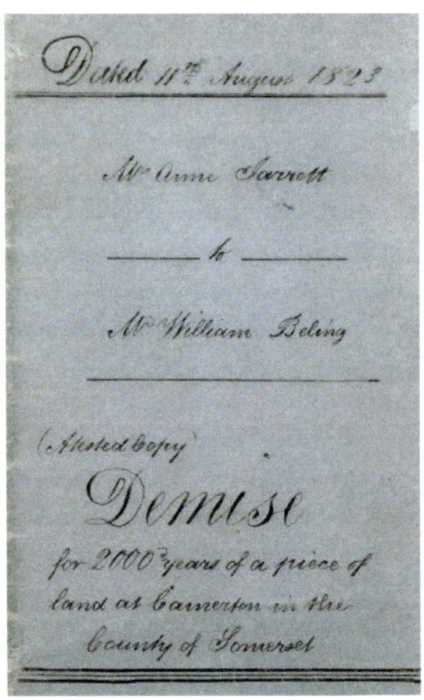

Dated 11th August 1823

Mrs Anne Jarrett

to

Mr William Beling

(Attested Copy)

Demise

for 2000 years of a piece of land at Camerton in the County of Somerset

Witness Signatures

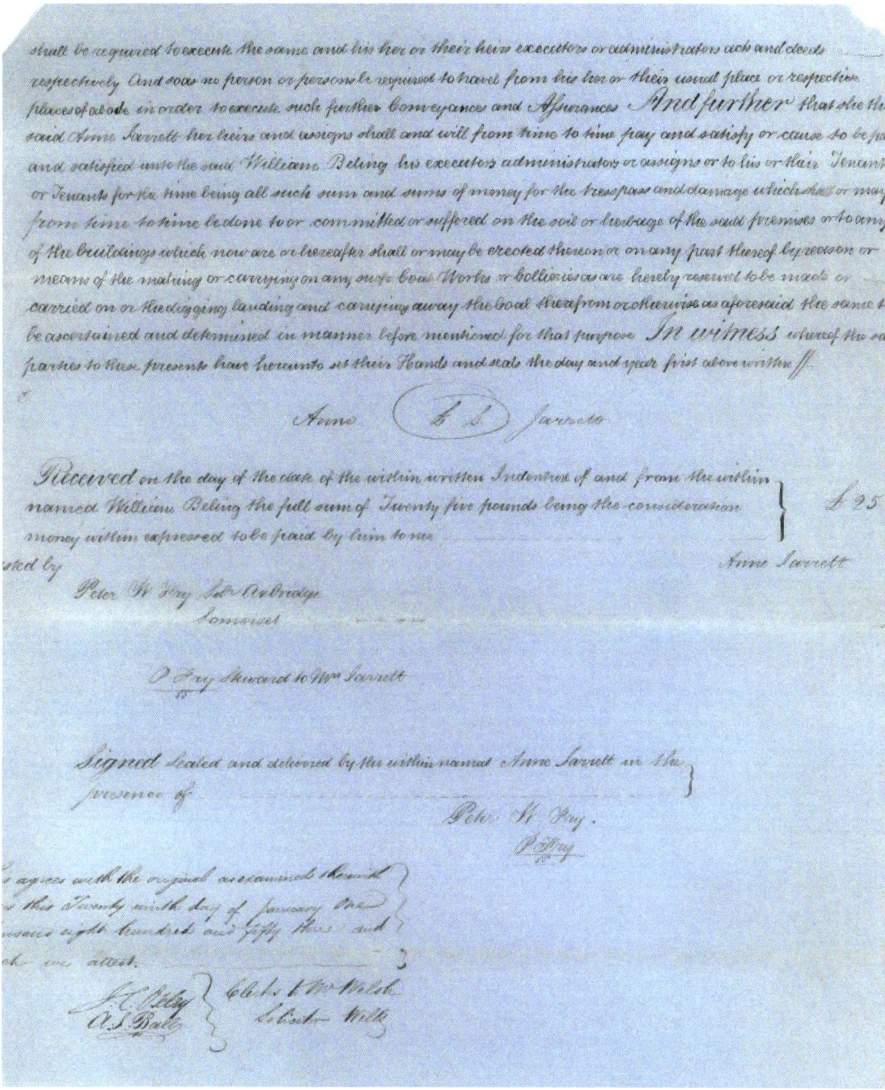
shall be required to execute the same and his her or their heirs executors or administrators each and deeds respectively And so as no person or persons be required to travel from his her or their usual place or respective places of abode in order to execute such further Conveyances and Assurances And further that she the said Anne Sarrett her heirs and assigns shall and will from time to time pay and satisfy or cause to be paid and satisfied unto the said William Beling his executors administrators or assigns or to his or their Tenant or Tenants for the time being all such sum and sums of money for the trespass and damage which shall or may from time to time be done to or committed or suffered on the soil or herbage of the said premises or to any of the buildings which now are or hereafter shall or may be erected thereon or on any part thereof by reason or means of the making or carrying on any such Coal Works or Collieries as are hereby reserved to be made or carried on or the digging landing and carrying away the Coal therefrom or otherwise as aforesaid the same to be ascertained and determined in manner before mentioned for that purpose In witness whereof the said parties to these presents have hereunto set their Hands and seals the day and year first above written

Anne (L.S.) Sarrett

Received on the day of the date of the within written Indenture of and from the within named William Beling the full sum of Twenty five pounds being the consideration money within expressed to be paid by him to me } £25

Anne Sarrett

...sted by
Peter W Fry Solr Axbridge
Somerset

P Fry Steward to Mrs Sarrett

Signed Sealed and delivered by the within named Anne Sarrett in the presence of }

Peter W Fry.
P Fry

...agrees with the original as examined therewith ...this Twenty ninth day of January One ...usand eight hundred and fifty three and ...h we attest.

J C Oxley
A. S. Ball } Clerks to Mr Welsh Solicitor Wells

In the early 1900s the (Royal Cottage) was used by an insurance agent for the Royal Sun Alliance company who used to live there. Apparently above the front door used to hang a metal sun/cross symbol, it would have been the insurance company's emblem. At the end of a week, miners and other workers would collect their hard earned wage, call in to the Royal Cottage and pay their insurance money to the agent.

A local family by the name of Brimble lived in No: 26 Meadgate,
George Brimble fell in love with the girl next door, Edie Lodge who lived at No: 27 Meadgate. George and Edie got married and lived locally, when Edie's mother died, they both moved into Edie's mother's house No: 27 Meadgate.

George Brimble was a well liked man and to this day, local people speak very highly of him; he also served as a paratrooper during the 2nd World war. His neighbours Tony and Win can recall seeing a photograph of George wearing the famous red beret. George and Edie moved out and sold their cottage to Dean and Julie Taylor in 1986.

No: 27 Meadgate was the home to Dr Jenny Scott, Mr C Carey and their family. They moved in to the cottage in February 2004, they worked hard making various alterations; turned the cottage into a beautiful home. Although they loved living there for 11 years they needed a bigger property and sold it in July (2015). It is currently owned by Steven and Megan Shepherd.

In the mid 1900s a Mrs Owen moved from Wales to Camerton and purchased Nos: 26, 25 and 24 Meadgate. Mrs Owen lived in No:24 and let out Nos: 25 and 26. In the late 1960s both cottages stood empty for nearly a decade.

Nos: 26,25, 24 and 23 Meadgate as seen today

Tony Walker, a young builder in the mid 1970s, was travelling through Camerton and noticed two cottages No: 25 and No:26 Meadgate up for sale. He could see the potential in the cottages and managed to purchase them both from Mrs Owen for the sum of £7,000.

With the help of Tony's brothers who were all skilled tradesmen, he set about renovating the cottages; turning them into one dwelling. It cost Tony £2,000 to carry out the work.

In their original deeds to No: 25 it mentioned a peppercorn rent agreement between a previous tenant and the Jarrett family.

Tony, his wife Win and family have lived at No: 25 for 36 years, having retained the one No: 25. Tony and Win felt quite passionate about the peppercorn agreement and thought it should be recorded, they had a special stone plaque made with the word 'Peppercorn' carved on it and placed it above their front door.

Stone Plaque

Although Nos: 26 and 25 are now one house and beautifully rendered, it conceals the beautiful old stone work underneath.

Nos: 26 and 25 Meadgate

No: 26 was constructed from white lias stone and believed to have been built in the early 1820s.

Whilst renovating No: 25 Meadgate, Tony revealed Bath Stone slabs about 6" thick.

Cottages showing Bath stone and White Lias stone

Original Fire Place inside No: 25 Meadgate

South facing - in 1823 No: 26 was built to the right hand side of No: 25 and in the same year No: 24 was built to the left of it.

Tony and Win believe the cottage was built in the early 1700s, a cottage that stood alone that could have been a farm house.

No: 24 Meadgate – the cottage is believed to have been built in 1823.

John Prowse and his family moved from South Wales to Camerton, in the 1891 census it records John Prowse (coal miner) his wife Harriet with their 5 children living at Meadgate.

John and Harriet had a son George, he was born on the 29th August 1886, he left school at the age of 15, followed his father's footsteps by working down the local pit as a coal miner. George enjoyed football and joined the Meadgate football team, not long after he was made Captain of the Camerton reserve team. In 1908 George Prowse was 22 years of age and decided to move to South Wales. In August 1914 the great war began; the minister of war, Lord Kitchener; appealed for volunteers to join the new forces. George was a miner and coal was essential to the war effort therefore George was made exempt from the war.

George did not enlist until 26 February 1915 at the age of 29, at Swansea he joined the Royal Naval Volunteer Reserve (RNVR). He completed his basic training in Dorset in the summer of 1915, he progressed rapidly and by 1916 he was Chief Petty Officer.

In 1914 the First Sea Lord Winston Churchill, learning of a shortage of trained soldiers, offered the trained manpower of the RNVR to fight alongside the British army. George Prowse served in the Drake Battalion.

Photo of George Prowse in a Royal Navy uniform

George Prowse in his Naval Khaki uniform
(Drake Battalion Bn1 Royal Navy Division)

by kind permission of the Imperial War Museum

George Prowse's medal with the Victoria Cross on the left

The blue ribbon is unusual because it is a naval VC and is quite rare.

George Prowse – was a very brave man who led his men in to a lot of action and almost at the end of the war, he was awarded.

London Gazette 30th October 1918

Chief Petty Officer George Prowse

Royal Naval Volunteer Reserve (Landore) Citation No: WZ/24
For most conspicuous bravery and devotion to duty when, during an advance, a portion of his company became disorganised by heavy machine-gun fire from an enemy strong point. Collecting what men were available, he led them with great coolness and bravery against this strong point, capturing it together with twenty three prisoners and five machine-guns.

Later he took a patrol forward in face of much enemy opposition and established it on important high ground. On another occasion he displayed great heroism by attacking single handed, an ammunition limber which was trying to recover ammunition, killing three men who accompanied it and capturing the limber. Two days later he rendered valuable services when covering the advance of his company with a Lewis-gun section, and located later on two machine gun positions in a concrete emplacement, which were holding up the advance of the Battalion on the right.

With complete disregard of personal danger he rushed forward with a small party and attacked and captured these posts, killing six enemy and taking thirteen prisoners and two machine-guns. He was the only survivor of this gallant party, but by this daring and heroic action he enabled the battalion to the right to push forward without further machine gun fire from the village. Through out the whole operations, his magnificent example and leadership were an inspiration to all, and his courage was superb.

George was tragically killed in France on the 27th September 1918, he died of his wounds aged 32. His father, John Prowse was an invalid widower by the time he received official notification of his son's heroism and death in 1918.

Thanks to fellow historian and friend, Ken Taylor; helped the author put together the story of this remarkable man 'George Prowse'. Ken also shared a story that was passed to him by a well known local man, the late Jack Sellers.

John Prowse was employed as a coal miner and later as a banks-man in Camerton pit. He was regarded as a taciturn man and known locally as an enthusiastic supporter of Camerton Football team. Whenever a goal was scored he got very excited and dragged his boot complete with a wooden sole, along the corrugated fencing; making one hell of a racket in approval.

No: 23 Meadgate – believed to have been built in the 1850s.

The late James Hawkins, locally and fondly known as Jim, lived here with his wife Irene. Jim was born in No: 6 New Pit Cottage, which is situated very close to the old mine, he started working down the pit as a young boy, just 14 years of age. Jim became a winding engineman and worked at Camerton colliery for many years.

Pit Winding Engine with Engineman the late Jim Hawkins

The above steam engine was a two cylinder horizontal type built by Leeds Engineering Co. It drove the cages up and down the mine shaft, carrying the miners to and from the pit.

A cage transporting local miners up and down the mine shaft in the early 1920s

Jim moved to various addresses with his wife Irene and family over the years, their last move was to No: 23 Meadgate in 1943. Jim played football for Camerton's Football team.

Camerton's Football Team in the early 1950s

Back Row from left to right: Jim Hawkins, John Fielding, Ian Clark, Brian Jones, Roy Chivers, Gordon Hawkins and Mactravers. Front Row from left to right: Roy Harris, Don Bull, John Hipsley, Donnald Sellars, Jimmy and Brian Stevens.

Jim was treasurer for the Miner's Welfare Institute, he worked alongside many local people, helping to plan the relocation of the old hall. A new purpose built hall was needed, it took over a decade to fundraise for; involving the whole of the community, (please see volume no. 2)

Sadly in 1991, Jim Hawkins and his wife Irene passed away just within 10 days of each other, their son Bryn decided to split the cottage into two parts by building a main inner wall. He moved in to one part with his wife Teresa and kept the No: 23. His sister Janet and husband Mike Collins moved into the second part and named it No: 23a.

No: 23 and No: 23a Meadgate as can been seen today

Bryn Hawkins can remember football being played out on the main road, the men would play whilst waiting for the pub to open. He said it was quite safe to play in the road as you would not have seen a car for hours. How time has changed, you would risk your life now, if you tried to cross the main road; there is so much fast traffic passing by.

Bryn also followed his father's footsteps by working as an engineer at several collieries in Somerset. He made headlines in the local newspaper (The Somerset Guardian):

Article 'They flattened the coal tips' June 2003

They flattened the coal tips

Bryn is currently enjoying retirement but still likes to keep busy, he sings in the Mendip Voice Choir; he is the president of the Purnell Bowls Club; still loves football and is the Chairman of the Midsomerset Football League. Any spare time Bryn has he enjoys giving talks on what it was like to work underground in Somerset mines.

No's: 22, 21 and 20 Meadgate are 3 terraced cottages believed to have been built around 1840.

No: 22 Meadgate used to be known as No: 3 Meadgate, the reason for the change is because the local council changed the numbers to run from Meadgate west starting with No:1 through to Meadgate east ending with No:29.

A local man, Jack Cavil worked at Tunley Farm used to live at No: 3
(Cross reference: Chapter 3 page 126 Jack is the driver of the horse and cart)

In 1920 Sir Frank Beauchamp owned the 3 cottages until he sold them to the Kembery family who kept them until the early 1970s.

No: 3 Meadgate

The late Tom Parfitt (coal miner), his wife Olive (nee Tanner) and their son Alan moved into No: 3 in 1949. Olive recalls seeing hundreds of hessian sacks stacked up in a cupboard; it took her a long time to get rid of them. Tom and Olive expanded their family by having two daughters, Lyn and Pauline whilst living at No: 3. When the new council houses were built along Meadgate west; they moved to No: 5 about 1955, the house was later re-numbered No: 11. Tom Parfitt worked down Camerton pit all his working life, until the pit closed in 1950.

Tom Parfitt (miner)

After having their daughter Pauline there was a 15 year break Olive became pregnant, both Tom and Olive were pleasantly surprised. In 1967 Olive gave birth to a baby boy at home, No: 11 Meadgate, named him Steve; Olive and Tom were over the moon.

Olive recalls, when she was a small girl, her mother and sisters used to send her on errands, usually to the local shop. It meant Olive would have to walk along the main road dodging the traffic! She often had to jump in to the verge to stay clear of some lorries; otherwise she would have been knocked down! Olive did not want her own children to experience the same dangers she did, and would not let them out of her sight for a minute.

Olive decided not to pay her rent in protest, forcing the local council to hear her plea of how unsafe the main road was, just outside the front doors of Meadgate. After a long debate, the local council finally agreed to put a new path down the whole length of Meadgate.

Olive Parfitt thankfully, had plenty of spirit to stand up for something she felt so passionate about and thanks to her; people can walk along Meadgate; on a path and have the peace of mind that they are safe.

No: 22 is currently owned by Tony and Christine Shearing, they purchased the property in 1995. The cottage was in a terrible state it needed of a lot of work doing to it before Tony and Christine could actually move in. The stairs were so steep and narrow, to be able to get their bed up stairs they had to cut it in half! Tony and his wife gradually brought the cottage back to it's original state and it is lovely.

No: 22 Meadgate

No: 21 Meadgate – used to be known as 'Moriah' cottage and believed to have been built in 1840 in later years it was also known as No: 2 Meadgate. Mr & Mrs Curtis used to live in this cottage.

The current owner is Anna Goodship who moved in to the cottage in 2005, she was able to inform the author that the word 'Moriah' was the previous name of the cottage and shown her the carved letters in the front of the garden wall.

No: 21 Meadgate

Carved letters of the word 'Moriah'

No: 20 Meadgate – Used to be known as No: 1 Meadgate, Cecil Ruddick and his wife Betty (nee Tanner) lived in this cottage.

Tom Parfitt and his wife Olive (nee Tanner) moved in to No: 1, Olive's sister, Betty and her husband whilst waiting for a home of their own. They didn't have to wait long, a house became available, just a couple of houses along; No: 3 Meadgate.

Currently Mr & Mrs Evans live at No: 20 Meadgate, they moved in to the property in 2007.

No: 20 Meadgate

No: 19 Meadgate – used to be known as 'Woodlands Cottage', the date this property was built unfortunately is unknown.

Village Store - Local residents can remember Mrs Davies selling sweets and general goods in the mid 1930's, in particular they can remember her kindness and say she was a lovely lady.

An extract from Kelly's Directory 1935

PRIVATE RESIDENTS.

(For T N's see general list of Private Residents at end of book.)

Beauchamp Col. Sir Frank bart. C.B.E., J.P. Woodborough ho

Budgen Lt.-Col. Hugh Vincent, Down Side house

Greenall Mrs. Red Hill house

Randell John B. School house

Thomas Rev. J. Llewellyn M.C., A.K.C., hon. C.F. (rector), Rectory

COMMERCIAL.

Marked thus † farm 150 acres or over.

Arnold Hy. Wm. beer retlr. Tunley

Bath Electric Tramways Ltd. (parcels receiving office) (Mrs. A. Sperring, agt)

Butler Edwd. Jn. beer retlr

†Candy Wm. Alfd. farmer, Tunley farm. T N Timsbury 16

Canvin Frank, engnr. to Camerton Colliery, Meadgate ho

Davies Kate M. (Mrs.), shopkpr. Meadgate

Durham Albt. Camerton inn

Flower Tom, farmer, Bridge farm

Gay Chas. cowkeeper

†Kembery Bros. farmers, Abbey farm

In April 1944 Mrs Olive Davies gave a jar of sweets to the Camerton's working party fund and Mr Frank Canvin won them, she helped raise 30/-.

St Peter's Parish Magazine dated April 1944

tron, was present, and in spite of the hundreds of women there found time for a word with so many of us.

March 25th. The Feast of the Annunciation. Four members present at our own Church for the special Mothers Union Day Festival.

The Camerton Working Party Fund has benefitted by nearly 30/- through the kindness of Mrs. Olive Davis. The bottle of sweets given by her was won by Mr. F. Canvin. Two dances have further increased this fund by £3/8/11.

There are still a few lavender bags available.

The 'Osiris' Repertory Players— gave an excellent performance of "Mr. Pim Passes by." The men's parts were so well done, that it was difficult to believe they were not "men"

Our thanks are extended to Mr. W. Wedlake and Mr. J. Boxall for so ably carrying out all the final arrangements.

The Dances will be resumed, we hope, after Easter.

Most of them have been well attended.

April 9th (Easter Day) and **April 16th (Low Sunday)**—

High Altar Mrs. Stephens
Lady Chapel Mrs. Maconochie

April 23rd (Easter II.) and **April 30th (Easter III.)**—

High Altar Mrs. G. Tucker
Lady Chapel Mrs. Bourton

FREE-WILL OFFERINGS FOR FEBRUARY

88—2/6, 98—1/-, 100—4/-
Church Box 5/9. Total 13/3.

CHURCH OFFERINGS & COLLECTIONS FOR FEBRUARY

Altar Fund £2/4/11.
Church Expenses £2/19/3.

The shop changed hands several times over the years.

The rear of the No: 19 (Village Store) 1960

Miss Bray is fondly remembered by local residents, running the shop as a general village store in the 1980s. Since the shop closed it reverted back to a private dwelling; it has changed hands many times over a period of time.

Currently No: 19 Meadgate is the home to Janet and Richard Tibbs and their son Jack aged 3 and baby daughter Rachel Rose. Richard and Janet moved into the cottage in 2007, Richard is an agricultural engineer and is currently working hard renovating their home. Richard and Janet are enjoying the challenge and love living in the village.

Below is a photo showing No: 19 Meadgate today

Meadgate Garage

In 1948 Mr Skudimore turned the corner piece of ground on the edge of Parkrow lane into a garage. He used an old army hut from the nearby base as a building. Local builder, the late Ken Biggs, helped Mr Skudimore erect the hut; plastered the inside to make it more pleasant.

Mr Reg Coles took the garage over, later knocked down the hut and constructed a new building. Reg had petrol tanks installed in the 1960s, but due to VAT being brought in, he never used the tanks and left them dormant for years.

Trevor Dibble and his partner Neil Sampson purchased Meadgate garage from Reg Coles in the mid 1980s. Trevor and Neil were the first people to sell petrol from Meadgate, they sold Lyon brand petrol. The garage also provided a repair, service and recovery service as well as having a small shop that sold sandwiches, bars of chocolate and sweets.

Meadgate Garage in the 1980s - Petrol only 50p per litre

Meadgate Garage freshly decorated

In 2007 Chris Fogen took on the running of the garage and renamed it 'Camerton Auto Repairs'. It is a well supported garage and so nice that it is still providing a good service to the public after all these years!

Camerton Auto Repairs as seen today

As well as being known as Camerton Auto Repairs it is currently also referred to as No: 18 Meadgate.

Acknowledgements

Julieann would like to thank the following for their contributions, help and support, they have made this book possible.

St Peter's Church
Ken & Ivy Biggs
John Kembery
Ken & Joy Taylor
Elaine Millbank
John & Joy Arnold
Ann & Mike Meloy
Pete & Gay Fear
Ruth & Lee Cundick
Stephen Cleaves
May & Cyril Fear
Kath & Pete Dando
Mike & Janet Holbrook
Pete Redman
Colin & Joyce Pulsford
Clive & Marya Turner
Dave & Nick Offfer
Elenor Biggs
John & Caroline Fry
Penny Fahie (nee Fry)
Bill Blanning
Stephen Jones
Tony & Win Walker
Tony & Christine Shearing
Bryn & Teresa Hawkins
Dr Jenny Scott
Olive Parfitt
Trevor Dibble
Hilary Sellars
Harold Millen
Jay Symes
Richard & Janet Tibbs
Cheryle Ashley
Kath Gregory
Dan & Rhian Fox
Bath Record office
BAINES/OS Maps
Bath Preservation Trust
Tintinhull History group
Ivo & Julian Peters

To anyone who may have been missed, Julieann extends her thanks

Bibliography

Domesday book

The History of Antiquities by J Collinson

Journal of a Somerset Rector
by Howard & Peter Coombs

Greenwood, Morris and Kelly's Directories

The Heart of the Mendips by Francis A Knight

The Sign, Camerton Parish magazine

In the Company of Heroes by Bill Blanning

Many of the above books will be out of print but can be ordered from your local library

Illustrations

Sketches by accomplished artist Dave Gallop

Crown Copyright, reproduced maps by kind permission of Ordnance Survey Open Data
Parochial Returns, schedule III by kind permission of Radstock Museum
Maps, various documents etc by kind permission of the Somerset Archeological and Natural History Society
Photograph of George Prowse by kind permission of the Imperial War Museum, London
Handwritten letter by kind permission of Warwickshire Records office (ref: CR341/327/109)
Illustration of a section of the Bayeux Tapestry by kind permission of Reading Museum
O/S map of Somerset 1817 by kind permission of the British museum (map room)

Disclaimer